GLOBALIZATION AND
LABOR CONDITIONS

GLOBALIZATION AND LABOR CONDITIONS

Working Conditions and Worker Rights
in a Global Economy

ROBERT J. FLANAGAN

OXFORD
UNIVERSITY PRESS

2006

OXFORD
UNIVERSITY PRESS

Oxford University Press, Inc., publishes works that further
Oxford University's objective of excellence
in research, scholarship, and education.

Oxford   New York
Auckland   Cape Town   Dar es Salaam   Hong Kong   Karachi
Kuala Lumpur   Madrid   Melbourne   Mexico City   Nairobi
New Delhi   Shanghai   Taipei   Toronto

With offices in
Argentina   Austria   Brazil   Chile   Czech Republic   France   Greece
Guatemala   Hungary   Italy   Japan   Poland   Portugal   Singapore
South Korea   Switzerland   Thailand   Turkey   Ukraine   Vietnam

Published by Oxford University Press, Inc.
198 Madison Avenue, New York, New York 10016

www.oup.com

Oxford is a registered trademark of Oxford University Press

Library of Congress Cataloging-in-Publication Data
Flanagan, Robert J.
Globalization and labor conditions : working conditions and worker rights in a global economy
/ Robert J. Flanagan.
   p. cm.
Includes bibliographical references and index.
ISBN-13 978-0-19-530600-2
ISBN 0-19-530600-7
1. Labor policy.   2. Labor.   3. Labor laws and legislation, International.
4. Employee rights.   5. Industrial welfare.   6. Foreign trade and employment.
7. Globalization—Economic aspects.   I. Title.
HD7795.F63 2006
331.2—dc22   2005034574

9 8 7 6 5 4 3 2 1

Printed in the United States of America
on acid-free paper

To Susan,
for support, understanding, and inspiration

ACKNOWLEDGMENTS

I am grateful to the Graduate School of Business, Stanford University, for research support and for funding the sabbatical leave during which much of the work on this book was completed. The Tinbergen Institute at the University of Amsterdam, its then-director, Professor Coen Teulings, and its staff most graciously provided a productive environment during that sabbatical leave from Stanford. I am also indebted to several scholars for generously sharing data that they developed in the course of their own research on some of the topics addressed in this book: Romain Wacziarg (Stanford University), Doris Weichselbaumer and Rudolf Winter-Ebner (University of Linz), Frederic Docquier (University of Lille), and Abdeslam Marfouk (Universite Libre de Bruxelles). The book benefited from the research and preparation assistance of Vidya Reddy, Alexei Tchistyi, and Marcelino Clarke. Comments received during presentations at Stanford University, the Tinbergen Institute, the Tjallings Koopmans Institute at Utrecht University, the Institute for Labor Studies at the University of Amsterdam, and the University of Aarhus improved the final product, as did the exceptionally constructive comments of Bill Gould, Joop Hartog, Susan Mendelsohn, John Pencavel, Mel Reder, Ken Swinnerton, Lloyd Ulman, and several anonymous reviewers for Oxford University Press. These reviewers may not share all my conclusions, and as always, I am solely responsible for any remaining shortcomings.

CONTENTS

GLOBALIZATION AND
LABOR CONDITIONS

CHAPTER 1

Introduction

The world has experienced two great waves of globalization driven by the free trade policies of major trading countries and falling transportation costs. The first wave ran from roughly the dawn of the Industrial Revolution in the mid-nineteenth century to the outbreak of World War I, and the second has run since 1947. International trade and international migration grew substantially during the first wave, but world trade increased even more rapidly during the first 25 years of the post–World War II growth wave. For reasons that will interest us, international migration has been a much smaller part of the second wave of globalization.

Both periods of globalization eventually encountered significant suspicion about the consequences of globalization for labor conditions. The fact that the first wave ended abruptly with the onset of World War I sometimes obscures how serious such suspicions can become. Responding to perceived threats to unskilled wages in domestic labor markets, the United States and other destination countries passed significant restrictions on immigration beginning in the late nineteenth century. Cycles of retaliatory tariff increases choked off trade flows between the two world wars. In short, domestic political backlash against world economic integration effectively reversed the globalization of international product and labor markets achieved during the late nineteenth century.

At the same time that many national governments tried to prevent global forces from eroding local labor conditions, fledgling efforts at international governance responded to concerns that countries with superior labor conditions would be at a competitive disadvantage in international markets. Concerns about a worldwide "race to the bottom" in which countries maintaining high labor standards would be at a competitive disadvantage with countries with low standards led to the development in 1919 of the International Labor Organization (ILO), a branch of the League of Nations and later the United Nations. The ILO was authorized to develop and promulgate voluntary international labor standards in tripartite consultations between representatives of labor, management, and national governments. As national governments passed laws that foreclosed international product and labor market competition as mechanisms for equalizing labor conditions around the world during the interwar period, international organizations opted for the regulation of labor standards. The respective roles of international markets and regulations in advancing labor conditions constitute a central concern of this book.

A sequence of post–World War II trade negotiations under the auspices of the General Agreement on Tariffs and Trade (GATT) and its successor, the World Trade Organization (WTO), successfully reversed the interwar disintegration of the world economy by significantly reducing the barriers to international trade erected after 1914. These important negotiations never addressed domestic restrictions on international migration that arose over the same period, however. Migration has therefore been less of a factor in the second wave of globalization, and the prominence of trade and capital flows has changed the emphasis of recent opposition and backlash to globalization. Though some concern for international migration's effects on labor in destination countries remains, modern anti-globalists express far more concern about the effects of trade and capital flows on production conditions in Third World countries and the possibility that a global economy might spread poor labor conditions to more advanced countries.

The Anti-Globalization Indictment

The anti-globalization indictment contains many themes. An overriding concern is that globalization increases the gap between the haves and the have-nots of the world. Baobabconnections.org, a nonprofit organization concerned with globalization, asserted that "the globalization of Market Forces has increased world inequities over and beyond any historical parallel. . . . Inequality worsened both internationally and within countries."[1]

The most specific concern is that globalization exploits labor and degrades working conditions. Another nonprofit dealing with globalization claims:

> Sweatshop workers are routinely forced to work beyond their physical limits. Even as they toil around the clock, workers are barely paid enough to exist. On-the-job injuries occur regularly, and physical abuse and sexual intimidation are not uncommon. And when workers try to stand up for themselves and form a union, they almost

always face repression by factory management—a clear violation of workers' basic human right to freedom of association.[2]

Most complaints about sweatshops add that child labor is common. Some allude to bonded labor, trafficking in human beings, and other forms of forced labor. In short, critics associate globalization with a particularly unsavory package of working conditions and labor rights: low wages, long work hours, unsafe and abusive job conditions, child labor, and suppression of collective representation. The general importance of these labor conditions to workers and society is signaled by the fact that they are the most frequent targets of international and domestic regulatory action.

The critiques are not always clear on whether the forces of globalization may produce a general deterioration of working conditions around the world or increase the inequality of working conditions among countries. Concerns over the former have been supplemented by suggestions that the dynamics of international competition induce all trading countries to degrade their labor conditions in an international race to the bottom. Although many critiques focus on labor conditions in the poorest countries, self-interested opposition to globalization in rich countries stems from fears that (1) cheap imports or immigrants from other countries will lower the relative wages of low-skilled workers, (2) more rapid economic change and shifting patterns of comparative advantage will increase economic insecurity, and (3) international competition will squeeze out social spending.

Others see the activities of large multinational companies as the prime drivers in the alleged deterioration of global working conditions. Addressing the concerns of workers in the United States, an international human rights organization states that "workers here are beginning to understand that jobs here will not be secure and wages will not rise if corporations are free to exploit foreign workers living under dictatorships, unable to organize free trade unions." In contrast, the critics have little to say about the effects of international migration.

Some critics also offer a solution. They argue that effective international regulation of labor standards provides a way to reconcile globalization with superior labor conditions. The second wave of globalization has occurred in an environment of domestic and international regulation of labor standards that was largely missing from the first wave. But both international organizations and multinational corporations come under intensive criticism for their failure to enforce labor rights and standards. In the early years of the twenty-first century, there are proposals to strengthen the enforcement of international standards, even to the extent of urging the WTO to permit trade sanctions against countries that do not enforce international labor standards. Both international and nongovernmental organizations urge multinational companies to adopt codes of conduct that include commitments to superior working conditions.

But is this the way that globalization works? Countering the claims of globalization skeptics is a century-old economic theory that predicts free trade will induce a convergence of labor conditions around the world. Heckscher and Ohlin argued that countries would tend to specialize in the production of commodities requiring inputs that were relatively abundant, and hence cheap, in the country. Each country would then have a comparative advantage in international markets over countries in which that input was relatively scarce, and hence expensive. Countries with abundant land would specialize in land-intensive products; countries with abundant unskilled labor would specialize in products requiring much unskilled labor, and so on. "In short," Ohlin writes, "commodities that embody large quantities of particular scarce factors are imported, and commodities intensive in relatively abundant factors are exported" (1933).

In the Hecksher-Ohlin world, international trade effectively increases the price of a country's relatively abundant inputs and reduces the price of relatively scarce inputs. That is, trade produces an international convergence of factor prices. Clearly, the convergence results from disparate movements in different factor prices. Consider Country A with much land and few workers and Country B with many workers and little land. With no trade, each country must be self-sufficient. Labor will command a high wage in A and a low wage in B; land rents will be low in A and high in B. With international trade, countries will export goods made by their abundant input and import goods made by their scarce factor. Country A will export land-intensive products to Country B and import labor-intensive products from B. Wage rates will rise more rapidly in B (the low-wage country) than in A (the high-wage country). Land rents will rise more rapidly in A (the low-rent country) than in B (the high-rent country). The result is a convergence of labor conditions. That is, free trade produces greater worldwide equality in wages and other working conditions along with distinct patterns of winners and losers within each country.

The same patterns of factor scarcity also explain how international migration produces a convergence of working conditions. If labor commands a high wage in countries where it is scarce relative to land and capital and a low wage in countries where it is plentiful, some workers will move from the latter to the former countries, absent barriers to migration. Wages in low-wage countries rise as workers leave; wages in high-wage countries fall or grow more slowly as immigration swells the labor force. Labor conditions also converge from international migration. A parallel analysis applies to international capital flows. Capital should flow from labor-scarce countries (where the marginal product and hence return to capital is relatively low) to labor-abundant countries (where it is relatively high). The process will raise the marginal product (compensation) of labor in the low-wage, labor-abundant country and lower compensation in the labor-scarce country.

Despite the sound and fury associated with these contending visions of globalization's effects, surprisingly little research has appeared linking labor conditions to the various aspects of globalization. This book seeks to close that gap. Part of its task is to trace the specific effects of the diverse mechanisms of globalization—international trade flows, international migration, and foreign direct investment (particularly the activities of multinational companies)—on labor conditions. The book provides separate treatment of the different mechanisms. Another objective is to contrast the effects that market forces and national and international regulations have on labor conditions.

One semantic note will clarify our discussion of labor conditions. Both the academic and nonacademic literature often use the terms "labor standards" and "labor conditions" interchangeably, leading to significant confusion and imprecision in discussions of international labor policy. In fact, the two terms refer to quite different concepts, and this book emphasizes the difference. *Labor standards* will refer to actual or proposed policy objectives or legal requirements. The key fact about labor standards is that they are established through a *political process*. In contrast, *labor conditions* refer to the actual working conditions—wages, hours, other job attributes—and labor rights that workers experience.

What This Book Is About

This book is concerned with how the three main mechanisms of globalization—trade, international migration, and international capital flows—alter working conditions and labor rights and with the role of national and international labor policies in improving labor conditions around the world. It seeks to establish the facts and test hypotheses that are relevant for informed policy choice in this area.

Here are some of the questions that the book addresses. In chapter 2: Have labor conditions improved or deteriorated over time? Has there been a convergence or divergence of labor conditions around the world? In chapter 3: How does general economic growth influence labor conditions? Why are some labor conditions more responsive to economic growth than others? Why do labor conditions differ among countries at the same level of development? In chapter 4: Does free trade degrade labor conditions in industrialized countries or developing nations? Do poor labor conditions enhance export performance? Is there a race to the bottom in labor conditions? In chapter 5: How does international migration influence labor conditions in sending and receiving countries? Does trade or migration have the more powerful effect on labor conditions? In chapter 6: Do multinational companies exploit foreign workers? Do they degrade local labor conditions? Do countries with poor labor conditions attract more foreign direct investment? Do voluntary codes of conduct improve the labor practices of multinational companies? In chapter 7: Does national and international regulation of labor standards improve labor conditions? Are incentives superior to regulations for producing changes in labor conditions? In chapter 8, I summarize the book's findings on these questions and discuss the implications for producing future advances in labor conditions.

This is perhaps the place to mention some concerns about globalization that the book does *not* address. With its focus on labor conditions, the book does not in general consider how globalization influences environmental quality, the level of social spending, cultural characteristics, or the likelihood of international financial crises. These subjects are all large and interesting and the subject of admirable studies and discussions by other authors (e.g., Bhagwati 2004; Wolf 2004), but they are distant from this book's focus on globalization's effects on labor.

CHAPTER 2

Labor Conditions around the World

In 2000, almost three-quarters of the countries in the world were open to international trade. Because China and India were largely closed economies, slightly less than half of the world's population lived in open countries. Just 40 years earlier, only 16 percent of the countries, with 19 percent of the world's population, were open to international trade (Wacziarg and Welch, 2003). If criticisms of globalization given in the previous chapter are correct, the dramatic advance in international economic integration in the last decades of the twentieth century should have produced sharply deteriorating labor conditions.

This chapter confronts this expectation with the basic facts about labor conditions around the world over the past 40 years. These facts themselves answer several important preliminary questions: Have world labor conditions deteriorated on average during the second wave of globalization? Has the international inequality of working conditions worsened? How have labor conditions changed at the extremes of the distribution? Do international differences in labor conditions tend to converge, as theories of international trade and migration predict? The answers to these questions provide a foundation for examining the specific effects of globalization in later chapters.

Distributions of Income and Well-Being

To place current conditions in historical context, we begin with a review of trends in the world distribution of income. Income is the central measure of the well-being of individuals and families, and for most people wages provide the main source of income. As such, the distribution of this key measure of well-being provides information on the distribution of a key working condition. Wages are not the only concern of labor, however. Unlike capital, land, and other inputs to production, workers can think and care about nonmonetary aspects of their jobs. Health, safety, and basic human rights all matter. One must therefore consider whether trends in income and its distribution adequately summarize the evolution of all labor conditions. Will measures of labor income adequately capture the evolution of inequality and concerns about sweatshop labor?

Most studies of global inequality focus on the income of the overall population. After examining historical trends in income inequality, both *between* countries and *within* countries, one of the most ambitious recent studies of worldwide income inequality finds that income inequality increased more or less continually between 1820 and 1980. Inequality grew most rapidly between 1820 and the beginning of World War I, a period that includes the first wave of globalization. Income inequality continued to grow between the wars, but at a slower rate, which has slowed further since World War II.

The determinants of income distributions are many and complex, and the authors of the study do not try to link changes in the worldwide income distribution to trends in globalization. But they do offer some tantalizing observations. For example, most of the increased inequality from 1820 to World War I, a period that included the first great wave of globalization, reflected growing divergence of incomes *between* countries. Yet within the overall divergence, "a strong convergence was taking place among European countries and their offshoots in America and the Pacific after 1890" (Bourguignon and Morrisson 2002, p. 728). Williamson (2002) makes a similar point about the first wave of globalization, which largely involved increased trade and migration between Europe and the New World. What is striking is that within worldwide divergence, distinctive income *convergence* occurred for the countries influenced by growing flows of international trade and migration. Where the forces of globalization operated, they *countered* the general tendency toward greater inequality between countries. (Chapter 5 describes some dimensions of the convergence in greater detail.) A second important observation is that the increase in global inequality through 1980 was almost entirely the result of increasing inequality *between* countries. Diverging national growth rates—the topic of chapter 3—explain most of the increased world inequality. Changes in inequality of individual incomes *within* countries played a minor role (Bourguignon and Morrisson 2002).

Changes in average income differences between countries also dominated the evolution of world inequality in the last decades of the twentieth century. According to the unweighted measure used in the historical study, cross-country inequality changed little between 1965 and 1982, but it then increased into the 1990s. Roughly speaking, per capita income differences between countries declined within the Organization for Economic Cooperation and Development (OECD) club of mainly North American and

Western European countries but diverged elsewhere. Weighting each country's per capita income by its population transforms the picture of late-twentieth-century inequality trends, however. Now inequality between countries falls more or less continually from the mid-1960s. The entire decline reflects rapid growth (relative to OECD countries) in India and China (Milanovic 2005). Clearly, a key issue in linking globalization to inequality is how free trade and other mechanisms of international exchange influence a country's average income growth rate. (This issue is addressed in the following chapter.) Inequality among persons within a country remains a small part of world inequality—less than 20 percent by most measures. Within-country inequality increased slightly between 1988 and 1998 (Milanovic 2005). Chapters 4 through 6 include discussions of how the forces of globalization may influence within-country inequality.

Turning to the bottom of the income distribution, the *proportion* of the world's population living in poverty has declined historically, although the total number of people in poverty continued to grow with increases in population until the last decades of the twentieth century (Bourguignon and Morrisson 2002). Declining poverty is compatible with increasing inequality when incomes increase more rapidly at the top than the bottom of the income distribution. For measurement purposes, income below a certain threshold, such as $2 per day, constitutes poverty. By the end of the twentieth century, 2.9 billion people—about half the world's population—were poor by this criterion. About half of the world's poor people are in China and India, two countries that play a large role in this book. Ninety percent of the poor reside in 31 poor countries (Cline 2004).

The world poverty rate has continued to fall during postwar globalization. It appears that the number of people in poverty also began to fall by the end of the twentieth century. One study finds that during 1970–1990, the number of people in poverty worldwide declined—that is, the poverty rate fell rapidly enough to offset population increases (Sala-i-Martin 2002). Studies based on household budget data from around the world also find (slower) reductions in the poverty rate at the end of the twentieth century, but they record higher poverty levels throughout the period than studies based on national accounts statistics. These studies differ from earlier studies in measuring poverty based on the distribution of consumption rather than the distribution of income.[1] Whatever the exact count of the poor, economic growth is a powerful force for poverty reduction. To the extent that openness to international trade raises growth, as discussed in the next chapter, poverty falls. In particular, policy changes that facilitate the ability of the poorest countries to export to the richest countries would reduce world poverty (Cline 2004).

Income per capita is a widely accepted measure of average living standards in a country, but economists have long recognized that per capita income provides an incomplete measure of economic welfare. Every introductory economics course summarizes the measure's limitations. The question is whether income per capita is sufficiently correlated with nonincome measures of well-being to serve as an adequate proxy when measuring growth and inequality trends for countries at very different levels of development. Recent research indicates that it is not. After finding that "the evolution of world inequality in life expectancy is quite different from that of GDP [gross domestic product] per capita," the same study discussed above states, "It is worth noting that the evolution of world inequality may not be the same along income and nonincome dimensions of well-being" (Bourguignon and Morrisson, 2002, pp. 741, 728).

Another recent study indicates that the inclusion of worldwide changes in life expectancy in measures of national welfare can alter perceptions of whether economies are becoming more or less alike. Empirical studies of economic growth find no tendency for a worldwide convergence of per capita income. That is, contrary to the predictions of some growth theories, the poorest countries do not in general grow more rapidly than the richest countries. Note, however, that the well-being of a society depends not only on average income per capita, but also on how long the income is earned. Given a choice between two countries with the same per capita income, most people will choose to live in the country with the longer life expectancy. The study finds international convergence in life expectancy at birth between 1965 and 1995 and constructs longevity-adjusted "full income" measures for these countries (Becker, Philipson, and Soares 2005).[2] After adjusting income measures for the fact that the poorest countries experience the largest gains in life expectancy, clear evidence of convergence among countries in well-being per person emerges. Between 1960 and 2000, the annual growth rate of "full" income (incorporating changes in longevity) averages 4.1 percent for the poorest half of the study's sample countries and 2.6 percent for the richest half of the sample.

These analyses of the evolution of life expectancy around the world make the point that different measures of well-being evolve differently over time; a reliance on any single measure, notably per capita income, may produce misleading conclusions. The lesson applies at least as strongly to working conditions, for both monetary and nonmonetary conditions of work influence workers' well-being and job choices. Indeed, since the days of Adam Smith, economists have recognized that total compensation includes both monetary pay and the implicit value of nonmonetary working conditions. Workers and employers trade between the monetary and nonmonetary working conditions in ways that are discussed more fully throughout the book. For now it is sufficient to recognize that in well-functioning labor markets, employers must pay relatively high wages to induce workers to accept inferior nonmonetary conditions and conversely. Wage inequalities across firms, industries, and even countries may signal much narrower inequalities in "compensation" levels, depending on nonmonetary working conditions.

The list of labor conditions that could be examined is potentially limitless, ranging from conditions that face all of society, such as health status or life expectancy, to conditions that are a direct consequence of the employment relationship. Two objectives inform the choice of labor conditions analyzed in this book. The first is a desire to examine how globalization affects the monetary and nonmonetary working conditions associated with "sweatshop" labor. Specifically, do free trade, international migration, and the growth of multinational companies produce lower wages, longer hours of work, and unsafe or unhealthy working conditions? The second objective is to assess the effects of globalization on broader aspects of the condition of labor in society. Here, modern discussions of worker rights influence the focus. Many international and nongovernmental organizations now emphasize four "core" rights of labor: (1) freedom of association (including the right to organize and bargain collectively at the workplace); (2) nondiscrimination in employment and pay; (3) limitations on child labor (minimum age of employment and prohibition of the worst forms of child labor); and (4) the abolition of forced labor. In public policy discussions, these four areas are often referred to as "core labor standards," and they become an important part of the discussion of international regulation of labor standards in chapter 7. Chapters 3 through 6 will examine how economic growth and the forces of globalization have influenced the development of these rights in recent times.

Labor Conditions: Contexts, Concepts, and Measurement

The measurement of key economic concepts combines science, art, and statistical convention. The tradeoffs and choices involved in developing a picture of labor conditions around the world need to be understood, because economic measurements rarely match theoretical economic concepts exactly. International comparisons of countries at very different levels of development magnify the problems. This section summarizes the choices made in matching concepts and measurement in this book. (Appendix A provides a more detailed account of measurement issues along with a guide to the sources of the variables.)

Pay

Wages and fringe benefits play a dual role in economic life. As the key monetary return from work, pay provides both an indication of a worker's welfare and a key incentive motivating worker behavior. At the same time, pay constitutes an important cost—often *the* important cost—of doing business. Labor cost differences provide incentives that motivate behavior by profit-seeking companies. To understanding the significance of pay patterns or proposed pay policies, one must evaluate how changes in pay affect interests on each side of the labor market. Comparable data on pay are widely available for industrialized countries but scarce for developing nations. This book uses data on annual pay per worker in the manufacturing sector (World Bank 2001a), a measure that includes the cost of fringe benefits required by national legislation. The data are five-year averages for 1980–84 and 1995–99.

Hours of Work

The view that global competition leads to excessive hours of work, particularly in export sectors, implies that employer preferences alone determine work hours. In fact, international differences in work hours also reflect the work-leisure choices of employees in response to the wage offers that they receive, their nonwage income, and public policies or collective bargaining requirements defining "normal" workweeks, overtime pay, holidays, vacations, and sick leave.[3] Employer preferences also play a role, but they are not necessarily determinative, and they too may be influenced by public policy. When workers face a choice of employers, competition among employers will limit their power to insist on work schedules that deviate from worker preferences. Employers offering preferred work hours will obtain labor for a lower wage than those that insist on less attractive schedules— another example of the tradeoff between monetary and nonmonetary working conditions that emerges in competitive labor markets. Public policies often influence employer preferences about how labor input should be balanced between the number of employees and hours per employee. Policies that raise the fixed cost of employment encourage employers to employ fewer workers for longer hours, for example.

Reliable information on hours of work is sparse in general, sparser in export industries specifically. Countries variously report "hours worked" or "hours paid for" (a concept that includes many hours spent away from work on vacations, holidays, and other forms of leave) depending on whether data are gathered from households, companies, or social insurance programs. This book addresses such national differences in statistical practice in two ways. First, the study looks for evidence of onerous work schedules in three different measures of long work hours. The proportion of employees who usually work more than 40 hours a week provides the most reliable measure. Weekly hours of work in manufacturing provides a measure that is likely to include most export activities, but is subject to national differences in definition and measurement. The broadest measure, annual work hours for all employees, is probably the least comparable measure across countries. (Appendix A reports details of the measurement issues and statistical adjustments.)

Workplace Health and Safety

In addition to low wages and long hours, the image of global sweatshops includes working conditions that threaten the health or safety of workers.

Risky workplace environments vary significantly by industry. Mining activities, commercial fishing, and logging are among the highest risk activities. Women rarely work in these industries, which helps to account for the fact that overall injury rates are generally lower for women than men. Ideal comparisons of on-the-job risk among countries would remove the effects of different industrial compositions and demographic structures, but such measures are rare.

This book uses two indicators to assess workplace health and safety, each with particular strengths and weaknesses. Industrial accident rates provide the most direct indicators of job safety risks. Measures of fatal and nonfatal on-the-job injuries exist for several countries and are helpful as far as they go. They also suffer from significant limitations. They rarely capture the effects of occupational diseases, and the actual definition and measurement of an injury rate varies widely among countries—far more than for indicators of other working conditions.

The study adjusts reported country data on *fatal* work injuries to a common measure—the number of fatal industrial accidents per 100,000 employees—and reduces distortions introduced by different national industrial structures by reporting data for the manufacturing sector only. (Data limitations prevent the use of gender-specific accident rates.) For most years, data on fatal accidents exist for only about three dozen countries, reported irregularly during 1970–2000. *Nonfatal* industrial accidents are a more common workplace hazard, but reliable data on nonfatal accidents do not exist prior to the 1990s and then only for about two dozen countries. The limitation of the nonfatal accident data rule out their use in this book, but the larger sample for fatal accidents includes countries representing a reasonably wide range of economic development. Per capita GDP for the countries reporting data on fatal accidents ranges from $606 (Tanzania) to $21,335 (United States) in 1980 and from $870 (Togo) to $33,293 (United States) in 2000.

An alternative measure of workplace health and safety is life expectancy at birth. This measure has the advantage of capturing all factors that shorten life, including all workplace influences on health and safety. The measure is also available for a large sample of countries for most of the postwar period (World Bank 2001a). Of course, life expectancy is determined by many factors other than workplace health and safety, including the overall state of a country's health care system, so the measure is less focused on workplace injuries. Still, this measure has much to recommend it for a study of globalization's effects on the condition of labor because the overall condition of labor is much broader than labor conditions at the workplace. Rather than sacrifice information by making an arbitrary choice of measure, this book uses both measures and checks whether results are robust to each of the measures.

Data on pay, hours of work, job safety, and other working conditions emerge from official national statistical systems and tend to be available on an ongoing basis. With the exception of measurements of child labor, however, these same statistical systems do not provide measures of labor rights. It has been left to social scientists to devise and implement measures of freedom of association, nondiscrimination, and forced labor. One consequence of this division of labor is that although indicators of labor rights now exist for a substantial cross-section of countries, many are not available for multiple years.

Freedom of Association

Critiques of globalization often assert that global competition leads countries to suppress workers' rights, including freedom of association and collective action. International support for these rights is found in the United Nation's Universal Declaration of Human Rights, passed by a unanimous vote of the UN General Assembly in 1948, and more recently in the 1998 International Labor Organization's Declaration of Fundamental Principles and Rights at Work. Article 20(1) of the UN document provides that "everyone has the right to . . . freedom of association," and Article 23(4) states that "everyone has the right to form and join trade unions for the protection of his interests." The ILO Declaration includes freedom of association (including recognition of collective bargaining rights) as one of four core labor rights.

Measuring freedom of association rights at the workplace presents a challenge because the de jure rights that national laws provide may be different from the de facto rights that a country actually honors and enforces. This study uses two indices of freedom of association, each of which evaluates both de jure and de facto rights. In other respects the indices have different strengths and weaknesses. The first index does not exclusively target rights at the workplace, but is available from 1972. The second index targets workplace rights, but is available only for the mid-1990s.

A broad measure of civil liberties developed by Freedom House provides the first measure of freedom of association rights. This index ranges from 1 to 7, with a score of 1 indicating the strongest liberties.[4] In determining the value of the civil liberties index for each year, Freedom House uses press reports, publications by nongovernmental organizations, academic analyses, and country visits to evaluate the presence of freedom of choice of employment, equality of opportunity, gender equality, free trade unions, and effective collective bargaining. To the extent that workplace and nonworkplace liberties are positively correlated, it provides a widely available index of broad trends in workplace liberties. It may be helpful to know that in 2000, the Netherlands, the United States, and the Scandinavian countries all received a score of 1, indicating the strongest civil liberties, and France, Italy, and Spain received scores of 2. Countries with the weakest civil liberties rating (7) included Afghanistan, Iraq, Saudi Arabia, and Syria. China, Iran, and Rwanda were among the countries receiving a slightly better score (6).

A more workplace-oriented index of freedom of association and collective bargaining rights (FACB hereafter) reflects an evaluation of 37 potential limitations on these rights (Kucera 2002). Each country's raw index number reflects (a) the number of rights criteria that are restricted in the country and (b) the subjective importance attached to each criterion.[5] After rescaling, index numbers range from 0 to 10, and as in the Freedom House index, low scores signal superior rights. Austria, Ireland, and Portugal provided the strongest freedom of association and collective bargaining rights in the mid-1990s, and China, Colombia, Iran, Laos, Rwanda, Saudi Arabia, Somalia, Syria, the United Arab Emirates, and Vietnam provided the weakest rights. Though the Freedom House measures of civil liberties and FACB overlap, the workplace focus of the latter produces a different list of countries at the extremes. The case of the United States illustrates why a nation's position may differ in the two rankings. All U.S. workers have a constitutional right of freedom of assembly. Statutes must provide collective bargaining rights, however, and federal law provides such rights only to some workers. (The National Labor Relations Act does not cover employees in agriculture and the public sectors, for example; they must seek collective bargaining rights from state laws.) Moreover, under U.S. law, the right to strike does not necessarily include the right to return to your job at the end of a strike. Contrary to practice in many other countries, U.S. employers have a legal right to hire permanent replacements for strikers, as long as employers have not induced the strike by committing unfair labor practices. Such qualifications to collective bargaining rights lower the U.S. position on the FACB index, notwithstanding its high ranking in the general index of civil liberties.

The actual formation of labor unions and conduct of collective bargaining provide less reliable indicators of workplace freedom of association. Less reliable because freedom of association usually implies a right to form or *not* to form or join labor unions. Recent history shows the ambiguities inherent in measuring freedom of association by the extent of union membership. Prior to the 1990s, Soviet bloc countries persistently recorded near 100 percent unionization rates, but these countries never were highly regarded for their civil liberties. At the other extreme, low unionization rates may simply indicate that workers are not convinced that they will benefit from collective representation, although low membership may also signal union suppression activities by employers or governments. As a practical matter, only a small sample of countries provides data on the extent of union membership. Reasonably comparable international data on union membership as a percent of "formal sector employment for wages and salaries, including agriculture" are available only from 1985 (Visser, 2003). For the 41 countries with data in the mid-1990s, the correlation between unionization and each of the indices of freedom of association rights was about −.4.[6] (The sign reflects the inverse scaling of the two freedom of association indices.) Although freedom of association rights and unionization are related, they are clearly somewhat different phenomena.

Nondiscrimination in Employment

Of the four core labor rights targeted by international organizations, nondiscrimination in employment is the most controversial to measure. One must first clarify the scope of discrimination. Discrimination may arise in many ways in any society, but not all varieties of discrimination are relevant to the focus of this book. The distinction between market and premarket discrimination illustrates this point. Premarket discrimination limits the access of some groups to schooling, training, and other services that influence the skills and abilities that individuals bring to the labor market. Market discrimination occurs when groups with the same skills and abilities receive different employment opportunities and compensation. This book focuses on the relationship between mechanisms of globalization and market discrimination.

The many criteria for discrimination present another difficulty: What single measure could adequately capture employment discrimination by gender, race, color, religion, national origin, age, sexual orientation, political opinion, social origin, and disability and other health conditions (e.g., HIV/AIDS)? Moreover, some types of discrimination are not found in all countries. Finding a common denominator for all countries presents a challenge.

Even when there is agreement on the type of discrimination, it is difficult to devise a convincing single measure of discrimination or its opposite, equal employment opportunity. Discrimination can occur at virtually any point in an employment relationship—hiring, training, promotion, pay, termination—and no single measure adequately summarizes the dominance of discriminatory tastes over merit in all aspects of the relationship. The fact that not all group differences in wage and employment outcomes signal discrimination presents a final difficulty. In well-functioning labor markets, differences in personal qualifications and in other working conditions will produce differences in hiring, pay, and other personnel actions. Much research on labor market discrimination over the past three decades has addressed the problem of parsing the effects of worker qualifications from discrimination in personnel outcomes. Since not all qualifications can necessarily be observed or measured, some imprecision in purported measurements of discrimination always remains after adjustment for the effects of observable qualifications on outcomes. The need for a measure that is available on a reasonably comparable basis for many countries magnifies these difficulties.

This book uses a measure of the pay differences between men and women as the indicator of discrimination. Pay gaps offer the advantage of summarizing the ultimate effect of a variety of discriminatory personnel practices on two groups. Discrimination in job assignment and promotion, two of the most important sources of higher wages in an organization, will ultimately show up as pay differences, as will the payment of unequal wages for equal work. The focus on gender provides a benchmark for discrimination that is available for many countries in the world.

The measure is the percentage difference between male and female wages that remains *after* adjustments for gender differences in observable nondiscriminatory influences on wages. This "net" gender wage difference is the amount of the overall male-female wage gap that cannot be accounted for by gender differences in schooling, experience, training, and other performance-related variables that may be available to a researcher. The data come from a meta-analysis of 263 published papers measuring gender pay differentials in various years from the 1960s through the 1990s in 63 countries from all regions of the world (Weichselbaumer and Winter-Ebner 2003). Since many papers provide estimates for different populations or time periods, the meta-analysis uses 788 separate estimates of the gender differential. With so many authors approaching the measurement of gender pay differences with different data sets, different econometric techniques, different control variables, and so on, it is necessary to put the studies on a common footing in order to develop comparable estimates of the net gender differential for different countries. A meta-analysis tries to establish a common footing by studying how estimates in different studies vary with features of their research design, including characteristics of the data sets, control variables, and econometric techniques.

The study by Weichselbaumer and Winter-Ebner shows the importance of the distinction between "difference" and "discrimination." After controlling for the characteristics of the studies and country, the wage *difference* between men and women falls from 65 percent to 30 percent between the 1960s and the 1990s, but the decline is almost entirely ascribable to relative improvements in female education and training. In contrast, the net gender wage *differential*, often interpreted as a measure of discrimination against women, fell from 26 percent to 21 percent over the period.[7] It is important for the present study that the meta-analysis also generated estimates of net gender wage differentials for each of the countries, after controlling for year and characteristics of the study. These estimated country effects constitute the measures of discrimination used in this book.[8] Only one observation per country is available—dated here as 1985, about the middle of the period covered by the studies in the meta-analysis.

Child Labor

In 1960, 76.4 million children between the ages of 10 and 14 were economically active. Even the most industrialized nations reported some work by children in this age group until the mid-1970s. Child labor continued to increase for two decades, peaking at more than 98.5 million around 1980. By 2000, the numbers had fallen to 67.4 million, despite population growth. As a proportion of the 10–14 year old population, child labor fell during the 40-year period, from 25.4 percent in 1960 to 11 percent in 2000.

Virtually all but about 4.5 million child workers are in less developed African and Asian countries. African nations, which accounted for 15 percent of child labor in 1960, now account for 37 percent. Though the number of children working in Africa has increased continuously over the past 40 years, the growth has not kept up with population growth, and the child labor force participation rate declined from 36 percent to 25 percent between 1960 and 2000. Asian countries accounted for more than three-quarters of child workers through 1980. A rapid decline in reported child labor after 1980 reduced the Asian share to about 56 percent by 2000. By 2000, the labor force participation rate of children for Asian countries (10 percent) was well below the African rate (25.9 percent).

Popular images of children working long hours for low wages in restricted factory settings support an association of child labor with child abuse. Such Dickensonian images may be accurate in some cases, but they are not typical. In modern times, less than 3 percent of children's work occurs for pay in industrial settings (Bhalotra 2003, Edmonds 2003a). Most child labor consists of unpaid work in agricultural or household settings. Typical tasks include collecting wood and water, tending to animals, preparing foods and meals, and caring for family members. Interestingly, the typical employer is the child's parent, a relative, or other foster parent. Proxy parents are particularly common in Africa, where the AIDS epidemic orphaned as many as 34 million children by 2001. In short, "a focus on wage work alone omits almost all of the activities performed by children" (Edmonds 2003a, p. 12). As we shall see, most child labor seems to reflect family poverty that forces parents to place their children in employment. Recognizing the many ambiguities of modern child labor, the policy focus of international organizations has increasingly been on eliminating the "worst forms of child labor," including participation in armed conflict, forced labor (see below), prostitution, and drug trafficking.

Given the nature and location of the work, no count of child labor will be complete, but some estimates are more convincing than others. The most direct approach counts the proportion of children in a particular age group who are economically active—working for pay in the market sector. This study adopts this approach by using ILO data on the labor force participation rate for workers 10 to 14 years old.[9] It may seem that school enrollment rates can provide an indirect indication of working children, but surveys of child labor in developing countries show that child labor is not the inverse of school enrollment (Bhalotra 2003; Edmonds 2003). Some working children also attend school; not all children who do not attend school are working.

Forced Labor

At first glance the concept of forced labor seems obvious and offensive. Images of slavery and prison labor come to mind. The international community almost uniformly condemns the practice; the constitutions and criminal codes of most countries prohibit forced labor. Many readers may believe that forced labor conditions are extremely rare and limited to a few of the least developed and least democratic countries. In fact, forced labor conditions are more varied, more subtle, and more widely distributed than most people realize. In the words of the International Labor Office (ILO 2005, p. 1): "Forced labor is present in some form on all continents, in almost all countries, and in every kind of economy." Despite widespread condemnation, few prosecutions of forced labor occur anywhere in the world, allegedly because of difficulties in defining forced labor clearly enough to guide enforcement and prosecution activities (p. 2).

A recent study delineated eight current forms of forced labor from qualitative human rights reports (Busse and Braun 2003a). Slavery and abductions, often involving children, are said to be common in Liberia, Mauritania, and the Sudan. The practice of bonded labor, in which individuals work for unspecified, indeterminate periods of time to repay debts, occurs frequently in Bangladesh, India, Nepal, and Pakistan. China and Myanmar have been accused of using prison labor to complete large public projects. Coercive employment recruitment policies, also frequently involving children, are reported in Benin, Cote d'Ivoire, and Togo. Instances of international trafficking in humans appear to be increasingly common. In terms of numbers of people, these are probably the most important contemporary forms of forced labor. But human rights reports also note instances of compulsory participation in public projects (in Cambodia, Vietnam, Kenya, and Sierra Leone), work imposed by the military (in Guatemala and Myanmar), and domestic workers in forced labor (Haiti). Modern examples of trafficking and forced domestic labor continue to emerge in the most advanced economies (including the United Kingdom and the United States), which can be destination countries for some forms of forced labor (Anti-Slavery International/ ICFTU 2001). In a 2004 study, Free the Slaves, a nongovernmental organization, and the Human Rights Center at the University of California at Berkeley collected data suggesting that "forced labor operations have existed in at least ninety U.S. cities over the past five years" (Human Rights Center 2004, p. 10).

Prison factories offer an instructive borderline case. The United States has run factories employing prison labor since 1934. A federal agency, UNICOR, runs Federal Prison Industries, described at its website as "Factories with Fences." The company's mission statement is simple and to the point: "It is the mission of Federal Prison Industries, Inc. to employ and provide skills training to the greatest practicable number of inmates confined within the Federal Bureau of Prisons . . . [and] to produce market-price quality goods for sale to the Federal Government."[10] In 2004, Federal Prison Industries ran 100 factories employing 20,274 federal inmates—about 19 percent of the eligible population. At a time when the federal minimum wage rate was $5.15 per hour, the inmates received 23 cents to $1.15 per hour. Six percent of the revenues of Federal Prison Industries went for inmate pay, while 19 percent went for (noninmate) staff salaries.[11] The UNICOR website also notes that under the Inmate Financial Responsibilities Program, "all inmates who have court recognized financial obligations must use at least 50 percent of their FPI earnings to pay their just debts."[12] Since inmates apparently volunteer for employment, this is not technically regarded as "forced" prison labor.

Some forms of forced labor begin as seemingly legitimate employment contracts, as when workers in one country voluntarily sign an agreement to be transported surreptitiously to another (usually higher income) country and employed in a legitimate job under specified employment conditions. Those who sign the contracts receive two services: circumvention of national immigration barriers and employment in the destination country. If the contract is honored, the issue of forced labor does not arise. Forced labor emerges with the breach of such contracts, as when workers are held in approximate captivity with reduced remuneration and no exit from the contract. The illegal immigration status of trafficked workers facilitates compulsion and bondage.

National statistical systems provide no reliable estimates of the extent of forced labor. Given its criminal status in most countries, those who practice slavery are reluctant to report it, and most governments are embarrassed to acknowledge its presence. Official national estimates are prone to understatement, and estimates by some nongovernmental organizations eager to publicize and dramatize the problem may err in the other direction. In the face of these difficulties, two quite different estimates of the extent of forced labor have emerged in recent years.

One study estimates that there were 27 million slaves worldwide in the late 1990s, of which 15 million to 20 million were bonded laborers in Bangladesh, India, Nepal, and Pakistan (Bales 2004a, 2000). Bales has also published tentative country-by-country estimates of slavery with many caveats (2004b). Bales begins by defining slavery as "a social and economic relationship in which a person is controlled through violence or its threat, paid nothing, and economically exploited" (2004b, 326–27). His estimates result from weighing qualitative and quantitative information from a variety of sources, including the reports of national governments and their agencies, ILO reports and particularly the sessions that precede them, reports and analyses by nongovernmental organizations such as Anti-Slavery International and Human Rights Watch, and press reports. In weighing the evidence, he considers the possible biases of different sources, including the effects of "political filters" applied in publications by many official sources. Finally, he asked country-level experts to critique his "very rough if informed" estimates, before publishing a low and a high estimate for each country. The estimate of 27 million slaves worldwide emerged from this process. The SLAVERY variable used in analyses of forced labor in this book is the midpoint of his published range for each country.[13]

More recently, the ILO published a much lower estimate of 12.3 million victims of forced labor worldwide based on reports between 1995 and 2004 (ILO 2005). Private agents extract about 80 percent of forced labor (e.g., in bonded labor or trafficking arrangements), while state or military authorities compel the remaining 20 percent. For the ILO, forced labor occurs when work is performed involuntarily and is compelled by menace or the credible threat of a penalty for nonperformance. The estimates were developed by "doubly sampling" validated claims of forced labor cases, and the ILO stresses that there are many reasons to interpret these figures as minimum estimates.[14]

Counting the varieties of forced labor found in a country, as indicated in qualitative reports by the U.S. Department of State and human rights organizations, provides an alternative approximation of the extent of forced labor in a country. Busse and Braun (2003a) use this approach, and this book also uses their published data (available only for the late 1990s). There are separate indicator variables for the four most important types of forced labor (slavery and abduction, coercive recruiting, bonded labor, and prison labor) and for all eight varieties. In contrast to the slavery variable, the majority of countries receive a value of zero "varieties of forced labor," notwithstanding evidence of human trafficking in most countries. Clearly, these data provide only rough approximations of the problem.

Have World Labor Conditions Deteriorated?

As the number of countries following open trade policies increased over the last third of the twentieth century, the volume of trade and foreign direct investment flows rose accordingly. We now examine the evolution of working conditions and labor rights during this period of increasing international economic integration.

The contrast between anecdotes of sweatshop labor and the actual development of labor conditions around the world is striking. All measures of working conditions and labor rights for which comparisons are possible improved during the last decades of the twentieth century (table 2.1).[15] Fatal job injury rates, child labor force participation, and hours of work (whether measured by annual hours, average weekly hours, or the percent of employees working more than 40 hours per week) all declined. Wages, life expectancy, and civil liberties (including freedom of association) increased.[16] The meta-analysis of studies of gender wage differences reported a very small improvement in male-female pay differentials, our indicator of discrimination over time (Weichselbaumer and Winter-Ebner 2003). No data on trends in forced labor are available. If globalization has a negative impact on working conditions, a proposition to be examined carefully in subsequent chapters, its influence must have been overwhelmed by other factors during the late twentieth century.

For most working conditions and labor rights, both the worst-case and best-case countries improved during the late twentieth century. Work hours, life expectancy and child labor all improved at the extremes of the distribution. In 1980, for example, Korea had the highest weekly hours of work in

Table 2.1

Changes in Labor Conditions, Late Twentieth Century

	Year	Mean	Min	Max	Coefficient of variation	Number of countries
Pay (annual)	1980	4174	104	19103	1.41	66
	1995	7521	94	38415	1.50	66
Long work hours	1990	62.6	18.4	88.1	0.26	26
	2000	59.6	15.8	84.6	0.28	26
Annual work hours	1990	1821	1432	2514	0.11	30
	2000	1760	1368	2474	0.11	30
Weekly work hours	1980	42.7	33.7	53.1	0.10	27
	2000	41.9	32.9	49.5	0.12	27
Fatal accident rate	1980	8.7	1.8	61.8	1.02	19
	2000	5.5	0.7	65.2	1.11	19
Life expectancy	1970	57.0	34.3	74.5	0.16	109
	2000	68.0	37.3	81.1	0.12	109
Child labor partici- pation rate	1970	25.1	0.02	75.1	0.60	115
	2000	9.7	0	51.1	0.96	115
Civil liberties index	1972	4.5	1	7	0.49	109
	2000	4.0	1	7	0.42	109
FACB index	1995	6.65	0	10	0.45	117
Gender differential	1960–90	−0.09	−0.351	0.277	0.91	58
Forced labor	~2000	0.81	0	2	0.98	110
Slavery (millions)	~2000	3.4	0.00005	22	2.2	97

Notes: All observations weighted by average labor force. For weekly hours and fatal accidents, 2000 data are latest of 1998, 1999, or 2000. Weekly hours pertain to manufacturing only. Long work hours variable is the percent of employees working longer than 40 hours per week.

For sources and full definitions, see Appendix A.

manufacturing (53.1). By 2000, average weekly hours in Korean manufacturing declined to 49.3. In 1980 and 1990, the shortest weekly hours schedules are found in Sweden and Belgium, respectively, countries long engaged in international competition. Not all of the countries experienced declining weekly work hours, however. Work hours increased in half a dozen industrialized countries, raising weekly hours in those countries to a range between 38.5 hours (in Australia) to 43.7 hours (in Japan).[17] Such work schedules hardly constitute sweatshop conditions. The two countries with the longest workweek at the end of the century, Singapore (49.8 hours) and Thailand

(50.1 hours), had experienced increases (of 1.1 and 2.4 hours per week, respectively) over the last 30 years of the twentieth century. These two countries are the most notable exceptions to the general pattern of declining weekly hours.

Most industrialized countries eliminated child labor before the end of the twentieth century, and the high child labor force participation rates in African and Asian countries have also been declining. In fact, no country reported an increase in the child labor force participation rate over the last 30 years of the twentieth century. In Burkina Faso, which had the highest rate (75.1 percent) in 1970, the rate declined to 43.5 percent in 2000. Child labor force participation declined more slowly in Mali, which had a rate of 62.5 percent in 1970, leaving it with the highest rate (51.1 percent) in the sample in 2000. These rates remain extraordinarily high by the standards of developed countries, but their decline has been significant.

Over the 28 years from 1972, civil liberties gained around the world. Globalization did not spread in a general environment of declining liberties. A few African and Middle Eastern countries constitute most of the worst cases, but even at the bottom of the league there has been improvement since 1972, when the series started.[18] Only Iraq and Syria remained on the worst-case list throughout the period.

Fatal accident rates improved on average in the small sample of countries providing data throughout the period. Once again, the identity of the worst cases changed over the period. Austria had the highest rate of fatal industrial accidents (29 per 100,000 employees) in manufacturing in 1970, but by 2000 the Austrian rate had declined to 4.2. Hong Kong, with a rate of only 6 in 1970, increased to 14.6, however, the highest among the countries in the sample, in 2000.[19] In both 1970 and 2000, life expectancy was lowest in Sierra Leone, but there was nonetheless some modest improvement. Fourteen other African countries reported the only declines in life expectancy experienced in the world between 1970 and 2000, but this likely is an effect of the HIV/AIDS epidemic rather than deteriorating workplace safety.

Within the general pattern of improving labor conditions, was there a general tendency for the international dispersion of working conditions to narrow in the late twentieth century? Changes in the coefficient of variation, a measure of the dispersion in national working conditions relative to the world average, indicate a mixed picture in the late twentieth century (table 2.1). For life expectancy and civil liberties, there has been convergence; national differences have become smaller relative to the (improving) average. For pay, fatal industrial injury rates, child labor, and all three measures of work hours, there has been divergence; national differences have become larger relative to the (improving) average.

To summarize, a first look at the data for the late twentieth century shows a general trend of improvements in working conditions and advances in labor rights, both on average and at the extremes of the distribution of countries. There are also a few exceptions to this rule—countries in which one or another of the labor conditions deteriorated. Individual exceptions can be important, but they are not typical. Much the same may be said about the anecdotes of sweatshop labor conditions advanced by globalization skeptics: The anecdotes may be accurate, but in the face of the data reviewed above, they cannot be said to be typical.

Trade Policy and Labor Conditions

Globalization skeptics may find the general improvement in working conditions and labor rights during the late twentieth century unconvincing. After all, the evidence mixes labor conditions for countries whose open trade policies make them full participants in international economic integration with countries whose closed trade policies limit their exposure to globalization. Perhaps labor conditions in the latter countries dominate the data in table 2.1, and open economies really offer poor labor conditions. Comparisons of labor conditions in countries that participate in global competition with those in closed economies help sort this out, but first we must consider how to distinguish between open and closed economies.

MEASURING OPENNESS. Efforts to study the effects of globalization encounter many potential measures of openness, ranging from estimates of a country's trade volume to indicators of its trade policy. Attempts to measure trade policy in turn confront the difficulty of capturing the large variety of interventions that inhibit international exchange, including tariffs, quotas, licenses, and exchange controls. Which measures best capture how openness may influence domestic labor conditions?

Measures of trade volumes offer one view of openness. A country's overall trade share, exports plus imports as a percentage of GDP, signals competitive pressures on both exporters and import-competing industries. Separate export or import shares may provide more nuanced information on how free trade influences labor conditions in these two sectors. Yet measures of trade volumes fail to address directly the complaint that international organizations negotiate openness *policies* without considering the effects of those policies on labor conditions. Trade shares reflect both policy *and* nonpolicy influences on a country's international competitiveness. To evaluate some arguments, one must isolate the effects of trade policy.

A country's gains from free trade policy flow from a superior allocation of scarce resources. (Chapter 4 provides details.) From this perspective, an ideal measure of openness would indicate a country's losses resulting from departures from free trade. No one has yet designed such an ideal measure, unfortunately. Alternatively, one can focus on departures from free trade policy, including tariffs, quotas, and other quantitative restrictions on trade, but efforts to provide simple measures of these departures encounter significant practical difficulties. The desire for a representative average tariff rate for each country obscures the difficulty of actually constructing one.[20] Few countries have measures of quantitative restrictions on trade.

Gaps between trade policy and implementation also undermine the ability to signal distortions with a single measure of trade protection. General tariff cuts may appear to reduce simple average tariffs, but customs officials who reclassify goods from low- to high-tariff categories in an effort to maintain tariff revenues may undermine the practical effect of the policy change. Single policy indicators, such as a tariff rate, provide incomplete measures of a country's overall degree of protection from international competitive pressures in a world in which countries may shift from tariffs to direct quantitative restrictions on trade to exchange-rate controls.[21]

Two research strategies have addressed the limitations of single indicators of trade policy to measure the distortions associated with protectionist policies. A simple binary indicator developed by Sachs and Warner (1995) circumvents some of the limitations of specific policy measures by requiring that a country pass several tests to be considered "open."[22] As revised and updated by Wacziarg and Welch (2003), the variable is available for many countries over most of the postwar period. The strong point of the Sachs-Warner indicator of openness is that it captures a range of alternative policies that countries may use to close their countries to international competition. The main weakness is that the indicator does not capture the degree of openness: an economy is either open or closed. For assessing general claims that openness degrades labor conditions, however, the stark, binary feature of the indicator is appealing. By this indicator, "open" countries have eschewed a wide range of protectionist policies.[23]

A second research strategy examines how sensitive links between openness and growth are to the choice of openness measure. Edwards (1998) analyzes *nine* indices of trade policy—including measures of trade volumes, individual protection policies, and broad trade distortions (among them the Sachs-Warner index)—on a cross-section of 93 countries and concludes that total factor productivity grows more rapidly in open economies. The conclusion is supported by most of the measures of openness, and it survives tests for influences other than open trade policies.

This book adopts a mixture of these two approaches. In the many cases in which the effects of a country's trade policies are of interest, the study focuses on labor conditions in open and closed economies as defined by the revised Sachs-Warner indicator. In broader assessments of the effect of globalization, the study examines the effects of both trade volumes and this openness indicator.

FREE TRADE AND LABOR CONDITIONS. We now can study how working conditions and labor rights differed between open and closed economies at the end of the twentieth century. For this purpose, "open" countries had open trade policies for at least two-thirds of the 1970–2000 period, while "closed" countries had closed policies for at least two-thirds of that period. Figures 2.1 and 2.2 provide comparisons of working conditions and labor rights, respectively, in open and closed countries by these definitions. (For each labor condition, the value for open economies is set equal to 100 in the figures so that values for closed economies can easily be interpreted as a percentage of the values for open economies.) Countries with open international trade policies generally had superior working conditions during the last decades of the twentieth century. Average pay was six to eight times higher, reflecting, as we shall see, the higher labor productivity of open economies. (Not shown in the figures is the fact that pay in the worst-case open economies was roughly 8 to 10 times higher than the pay in the worst-case closed economies.) Fatal industrial accident rates are lower. Life expectancy (not shown in figure 2.1 but available for a much larger sample of countries) is longer in open economies. The three measures of hours of work, each available for only a small number of countries, do not show a consistent relationship with openness. Countries with open trade policies have shorter average workweeks in manufacturing, but annual hours worked in all industries and the percentage of employees working more than 40 hours per week is slightly higher in open economies.

Open economies have a superior record on the labor rights that are the focus of international public policy discussions (fig. 2.2). (Recall that lower values signify superior outcomes for each of the measures of labor rights.) The average labor force participation rate of 10- to 14-year-old children in closed economies was more than five times the rate in open economies by

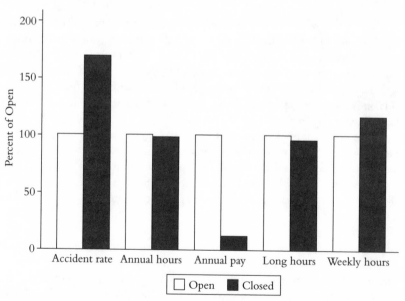

Figure 2.1. Working Conditions in Open and Closed Economies

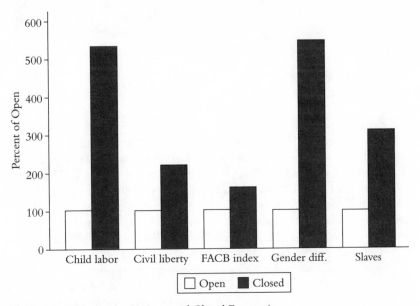

Figure 2.2. Labor Rights in Open and Closed Economies

2000. Though the child participation rate declined during the late twentieth century in all countries, by 2000 the rate in the worst-case open country approximated the average for closed economies. Both the broad measure of civil liberties, which includes workplace rights and equality, and the workplace-oriented measure of freedom of association and collective bargaining rights (the FACB index) show stronger labor rights in open economies. The civil liberties measure also shows improvement over time in both the average and worst cases. The gender wage differential and the estimated number of people in slavery are also lower in open economies. Overall, limitations on key labor rights appear more likely in economies that raise barriers to free trade. Labor conditions improved in both open and closed economies in the last decades of the twentieth century. Measured by percentage changes, open economies show more rapid improvement in wages, workplace safety, and civil liberties. In other areas, improvements were similar in both open and closed countries.

One should not read causality into these data. They describe differences in labor conditions between countries with open and closed trade policies. Though these differences do not correspond to common claims about the effects of globalization on labor conditions, neither do they prove that participation in international competition improves labor conditions. "Open" and "closed" countries may differ on many other dimensions that influence labor conditions. But the stark contrast between critiques of globalization and the data in figures 2.1 and 2.2 should caution against uncritical acceptance of race-to-the-bottom arguments and related policy proposals. The data raise the possibility that freer trade may improve rather than degrade labor conditions. Subsequent chapters examine questions of causality raised by these data.

Where Do People Work?

The material reviewed in this chapter describes *how* labor conditions vary around the world. The rest of this book explores *why* conditions vary as they do and the role that globalization plays. *Where* people work constitutes one important influence, for societies differ in the occupations and industries in which employment is available. This section describes the variety of employment situations around the world as a caution against assuming that employment conditions in industrialized countries provide a natural model for many countries in which the poorest labor conditions are observed.

The evolution of productive activities from agriculture to manufacturing and finally to private and public services constitutes one of the oldest regularities of economic development. The distributions of jobs and working conditions change accordingly. Two economic forces guide this evolution. The first is the nature of income elasticities of demand. As incomes advance, populations move beyond purely subsistence expenditures for food, shelter, and basic health care to manufactured conveniences and finally to services. The second factor is economies of scale and technical advances that enable huge increases in productivity in agriculture and manufacturing. The combination of comparatively low income elasticities of demand for food with historically rapid productivity growth in agriculture gradually reduces the demand for agricultural workers. Later in the development process, a similar scenario emerges in manufacturing. In short, employment structures in advanced countries provide a poor guide to the nature of employment opportunities in the rest of the world.

Discussions of working conditions and labor rights around the world must recognize that agriculture still provides most of the jobs in low-income countries and about 40 percent of the work in middle-income countries (table 2.2, panel A). In contrast, more than two-thirds of the jobs in high-income countries are in services, which provide only one in five jobs in low-income countries. Working conditions in the manufacturing sector become salient when the sector gains importance in early stages of the development process. Yet manufacturing no longer provides a majority of jobs in countries at any income level. Much the same story emerges when the data are organized by region (table 2.2, panel B).[24]

How does globalization fit into these figures? Most countries do not record the level of employment in export activities, so we cannot report the proportion of employment in the "international sector" by country. Instead, we report on the importance of exports and imports in production: how much of a country's production is for export and what fraction of income

Table 2.2
Distribution of Employment (Percent)

	A. By income level		
	1980	1990	2000
Agriculture			
High-income countries	9	6	4
Middle-income countries	52	43	40
Low-income countries	n.a.	67	n.a.
Industry			
High-income	34	30	27
Middle-income	22	22	n.a.
Low-income	n.a.	14	n.a.
Services			
High-income	58	64	69
Middle-income	20	23	n.a.
Low-income	n.a.	19	n.a.

	B. By region, 1990		
	Agriculture	Industry	Services
Region			
East Asian Pacific	54	18	14
European Monetary Union	8	32	60
Latin America & Caribbean	19	25	53
Middle East & North Africa	27	25	48
South Asia	67	14	18
World	43	21	29

Note: n.a. not available

Source: World Bank, *World Development Indicators* online database.

goes to the consumption of imports (table 2.3). The data tell two simple stories. First, over the last third of the twentieth century, globalization, as measured by the relative importance of international trade, has expanded for countries at all income levels. Second, although the data in table 2.2 remind us that national industrial structures are quite different, the average importance of trade and its growth are quite similar for countries at all levels of development.

Table 2.3
Trade as a Percent of GDP

	1960	1970	1980	1990	2000
Exports					
High-income countries	12	14	20	19	24
Middle-income countries	n.a.	12	17	21	30
Low-income countries	10	9	17	17	26
Imports					
High	12	14	21	19	24
Middle	n.a.	11	17	19	28
Low	11	11	18	19	25

Note: n.a. not available

Source: World Bank, *World Development Indicators* online database.

Employment in the Informal Sector

One key fact enhances understanding of labor conditions outside of agriculture in most of the world: most nonagricultural employment is in the informal sector. The leading authority on informal employment around the world reports that "informal employment comprises one half to three-quarters of non-agricultural employment in developing countries: specifically, 48 per cent of non-agricultural employment in North Africa; 51 per cent in Latin America; 65 per cent in Asia; and 72 per cent in sub-Saharan Africa. If South Africa is excluded, the share of informal employment in non-agricultural employment rises to 78 per cent in sub-Saharan Africa. If data were available for additional countries in Southern Asia, the regional average for Asia would likely be much higher" (ILO 2002, p. 7).[25]

Workers in the informal sector include employees of shops and workshops, casual day laborers in some hotels and restaurants, street vendors, and home workers making garments or embroidery. Informal jobs can exist in both developed and developing countries, where they share two key characteristics: they lack secure individual or collective employment contracts, and they do not include the social benefits, including health and social security benefits, that formal employment arrangements offer. Varieties of self-employment—including petty trading, service repairs, and some street vending—account for most informal work. "In all developing regions, self-employment comprises a greater share of informal employment (outside of agriculture) than wage employment: . . . self-employment represents 70 per cent of informal employment in sub-Saharan Africa, 62 per cent in North Africa, 60 per cent in Latin America, and 59 per cent in Asia" (ILO 2002,

p. 7).[26] All of these activities operate outside a country's social benefits system and beyond the reach of labor regulations.

As will become apparent in chapter 7, costly regulations may reduce employment in the formal sector as employers opt to subcontract work to the informal sector, which operates beyond the reach of such regulations. The size of the informal sector also reflects cyclical influences on employment in the formal sector. One careful review of evidence for several Latin American countries concludes that formal-sector employment moves procyclically while employment in the informal sector moves countercyclically (Galli and Kucera 2003). The informal sector can serve as a buffer over business cycles as workers lose jobs in the formal sector during recessions.

The persistence and importance of the informal sectors into the twenty-first century challenges an early influential theory of the development process. Nobel laureate W. Arthur Lewis (1955) predicted a gradual loss of agricultural and informal jobs as workers transferred to a growing industrialized sector in developing countries. Fifty years later, there is little sign of the demise of informal sectors, however. Opportunities in the industrialized sector have developed slowly, relative to the growth of the labor force, reflecting in part both a country's labor regulations and its globalization policies.

The large informal sector presents distinct challenges to those who seek improved labor conditions around the world, for informal work is by definition beyond the reach of national labor regulations and tax systems. Observing trends in informal employment, representatives of labor organizations ask: Does the growth of the informal sector amount to a "replacement of decent employment with insecure internal casual and contract work"? (ILO 2004a, p. 27). Improvements in working conditions in low- and middle-income countries come from adopting policies that shrink the size of the informal sector by increasing opportunities in the formal sector. Policies that raise the relative attractiveness of informal work are recipes for deteriorating labor conditions. Subsequent chapters will explore the role of globalization and domestic policy actions in expanding and diminishing the size of the informal sector.

One cautionary note: The importance of the informal economy in many countries signals limitations in some of the data used in this book. Economic activities that occur beyond the reach of taxing and regulatory authorities also elude most official statistical agencies. Official data that are collected at the workplace, such as some measures of wages, job safety, and work hours, almost certainly underrepresent conditions in the informal sector. Data collected from households, official documents, and other sources outside the workplace, including data on life expectancy and *all* the labor rights variables used in this study, are not subject to this caution.

Summary and Looking Ahead

A significant reduction in world poverty and widespread improvement in the condition of labor accompanied the remarkable expansion in globalization during the second half of the twentieth century. Real compensation increased; work hours, gender discrimination, and child labor declined; work became safer; and civil liberties, including several that pertain to the workplace, improved. Labor conditions also generally improved in countries at both extremes of the international distribution. Though improvements in labor conditions during this period of increased economic integration were not reserved for the richest countries, changes in the overall international dispersion of labor conditions were mixed: for some conditions, the differences between countries decreased; for others, the differences increased; and for some, there was no change in the international dispersion.

The data also indicate that countries that insulate themselves from international economic integration do not have superior working conditions and stronger labor rights. Instead, both on average and in extreme cases, labor conditions in countries with open trade policies are superior to those in countries with closed trade policies. This initial look at the data provides more support for the predictions of international trade theories than for the notion that countries with free trade policies have the worst labor conditions. In short, the evidence on labor conditions around the world does not match the anecdotes emphasized by globalization skeptics. The anecdotes may be correct, but they are not typical. Subsequent chapters trace the relationships between globalization and labor conditions hinted at by the data reviewed in this chapter. This task requires a careful appraisal of how labor conditions advance in the absence of globalization—including the effects of economic growth and institutions—before evaluating the effects of globalization. Chapter 3 begins that appraisal.

CHAPTER 3

Economic Development and Labor Conditions

Although significant advances in working conditions and labor rights during an era of increasing international economic integration undermines concerns that globalization degrades labor conditions, one cannot rule out the possibility that nonglobal influences largely account for labor's gains in the late twentieth century. Indeed, the influence of other factors can be inferred from improvements in labor conditions during historical periods in which global exchange was quite limited. These influences need to be spelled out, for understanding how labor conditions might evolve in a world without trade will help us to assess the role of trade and other globalization mechanisms in later chapters.

This chapter shows that one of the strongest influences on labor conditions is economic development itself, measured as increases in real per capita income. In any particular year, countries with higher per capita income generally have superior labor conditions. Over a period of time, the countries that grow most rapidly enjoy the greatest improvements in labor conditions. It should come as no surprise that wages improve with economic growth, since growth is an important cure for poverty, and wages are the largest part of income for most people. Less obvious are the often subtle effects that higher incomes have on nonmonetary working conditions and on labor rights. Just as consumers change spending patterns as their income increases, workers change their preferred mix of labor conditions. Examining the role of economic growth helps us understand why labor conditions change over time within a country and why changes in labor conditions in the last half of the twentieth century were largely in the direction of improvement.

While we will see how economic development produces significant advances in labor conditions, we will also see that labor conditions vary widely among countries at a given level of development. Some countries have much better labor conditions and others have much worse conditions than one would predict from their level of development. The second part of the chapter begins an exploration of distinctive national factors that account for this variance. Of course, we are most interested in the influence of globalization in explaining this variance, but we accord international trade, international migration, and the activities of multinational corporations separate treatment in subsequent chapters.

Economic Growth and Labor Conditions

How and why would labor rights and working conditions change in a country that did not participate in international markets—one with no trade, no international migration, and no foreign capital? Brief reflection suggests that change would likely come through economic growth and the domestic regulation of labor markets by governments or by other collective institutions. Growth is a likely influence because advances in per capita GDP are the most common approach to reporting improvements in economic well-being, and such improvements ought to reach the workplace. Regulation is a factor because it is the common approach to altering market outcomes or to pursuing outcomes not provided by markets.

The suspicion that economic growth improves the condition of labor leaves many questions unanswered. How does growth improve labor conditions? Does growth stimulate across-the-board improvements in labor conditions? If not, which working conditions or labor rights are bypassed? Many of the same questions can be raised regarding labor regulations, but we postpone that discussion till chapter 7. This chapter focuses on how growth and domestic institutions influence labor conditions.

Compensation

Productivity provides the link between growth and compensation. Countries grow by increasing their productive inputs and by increasing the efficiency with which the inputs are used. Though countries can grow rapidly for periods of time by increasing labor and capital inputs (as happened in the Soviet bloc countries during the early postwar period and more recently in some Southeast Asian countries), long-run growth of per capita output rests on a country's productivity growth. Over long periods of time, countries with the most rapid productivity advances grow most rapidly. At the same time, elementary economic theory predicts that labor productivity ultimately determines the real compensation of workers. Every textbook demonstrates that self-interested, profit-seeking employers will pay more productive workers higher wages. Countries with the most rapid productivity advances also have the most rapid real wage growth. Moreover, economic theory predicts that the vast international differences in pay that concern many globalization skeptics rest on international differences in labor productivity. The proposition that differences in productivity drive differences in pay—among individuals, among industries, and among countries—is so fundamentally important to but relentlessly underappreciated in debates over how globalization influences labor conditions that it merits careful documentation.

Even at the end of the twentieth century, differences in worker pay among countries remained huge. Between 1995 and 1999, annual compensation per manufacturing production worker ranged from a low of $94 in Kenya to $38,415 in Norway, including the cost of social benefits required by legislation. Since compensation is the mirror image of labor costs, such differences in pay fuel claims that international competition sets off a global race to the bottom in labor conditions. How can countries whose labor costs are large multiples of labor costs in other countries continue to sell products in international markets? Labor productivity provides the answer: value added per worker in high-wage countries is also a large multiple of productivity in low-wage countries. Figure 3.1 illustrates the tight cross-country correlation between manufacturing workers' wages and productivity in the late 1990s. (Each point in the figure describes the labor cost and productivity combination observed in a different country.) Formal statistical analyses confirm that cross-country variations in manufacturing labor productivity and price levels account for more than 90 percent of the cross-country variation in

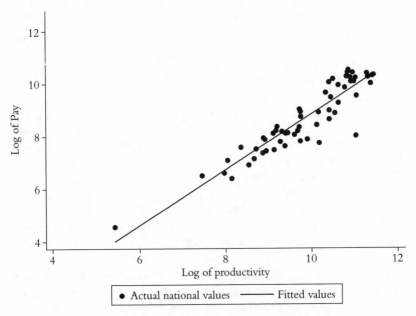

Figure 3.1. Pay and Productivity in Manufacturing, 1995–99

manufacturing labor compensation. (See the appendix to chapter 3.) Workers in low-wage countries do not drive workers in high-wage countries from the market because productivity differences ensure similar labor costs per unit of output in all countries. Pay per unit of output, not pay per worker, determines the product prices that govern a country's competitiveness in international product markets.

Globalization raises particular concerns with the pay received by low-wage workers. The fact that productivity drives pay in overall manufacturing does not directly address the question of whether the lowest paid manufacturing workers gain from economic growth. Are workers in apparel, footwear, and other low-wage industries trapped in subsistence employment, absent domestic or international labor standards? Alternatively, does economic development improve their pay along with compensation in the rest of the manufacturing sector?

The number of countries with substantial apparel or footwear production is much smaller than the number with a manufacturing sector—an illustration of the specialization predicted by international trade theories. Nonetheless, pay varies widely even among the shorter list of countries with apparel or footwear production. In 1995, the lowest paid apparel workers in the world worked in Kenya and received a small fraction of the pay of the highest paid apparel workers (in Denmark). These two countries also had, respectively, the lowest and highest labor productivity worldwide in the industry. As with pay differences for all of manufacturing, productivity differences largely explain international pay differences in low-wage industries (fig. 3.2). In the underlying regression analyses, international differences in labor productivity explain more than 90 percent of the international real pay differences in these low-wage industries. No country that produces apparel or footwear strays far from the average relationship illustrated in figure 3.2.

Clearly, cross-country differences in real employee compensation are closely related to productivity differences.[1] Can the same be said of within-country pay variations over time? "Panel" data—cross-country data for multiple years—permit analysis of intracountry variations between pay and productivity over time. In relying only on variations in the data over time, "fixed-effects" estimates from panel data ignore the information provided by cross-country variation in the data. Sometimes, using less information provides more reliable results. Some part of cross-country variations in data may reflect international differences in statistical practice or data quality, for example. The influence of variables that cannot be observed on observable variables, such as pay and productivity, may bias the results of cross-country analyses, in some instances. (The appendix to this chapter provides examples.) The fixed-effects statistical technique removes the influence of country-specific measurement error and unobservable variables that are constant over time from the statistical analysis. This adjustment can sharpen the results and reduce biases that might influence cross-country estimates. (For these reasons, the results of fixed effects analyses will also be useful in later chapters.)

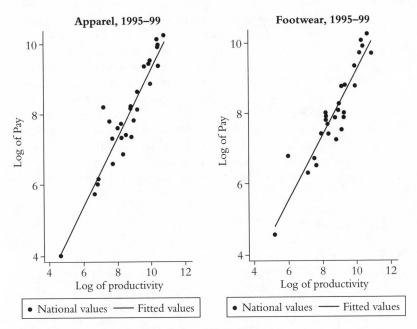

Figure 3.2. Pay and Productivity in Low-Wage Industries

Fixed-effects estimates using averages of data for the early 1980s and late 1990s confirm the statistically significant relationships between productivity, price levels, and compensation observed in the cross-country data for total manufacturing and the apparel industry. (Data limitations preclude panel analysis of the footwear industry.) Changes in labor productivity in the industries over time within a country drive changes in pay. Whether one looks across countries or over time within a country, one observes a strong link between productivity and pay for total manufacturing and for specific low-wage industries at the heart of the debate over the effect of globalization on labor conditions. Countries with high labor costs can continue to compete successfully in many activities as long as high productivity supports the high labor costs.

One cannot make sense of pay differentials around the world or the growth of real compensation within countries without understanding the underlying productivity differentials and growth. This finding provides a key insight into why working conditions vary around the world. Actions to increase worker productivity will increase the scope for improvements in pay and other (costly) working conditions. Working conditions around the world will vary with (1) investments in education, skills, and health that workers make in themselves to improve their productivity; (2) investments that firms make in the training of workers and the health and safety of the work environment; and (3) investments that governments make in workers to raise their productivity. Government support is particularly important in areas such as education, where there are important external benefits to the investment that are likely to be ignored by workers and firms in making private investment decisions and where private capital markets may not provide financing.

The tight relationship between pay and productivity also signals a fundamental flaw in many race-to-the-bottom arguments. The low pay associated with poor labor conditions reflects the low productivity associated with those conditions. Low pay signals low skills, poor health, malnutrition, fatigue, and other conditions undermining the effort and efficiency of workers. As a result, countries with low labor standards and poor labor conditions may not offer lower labor costs per unit of output, the cost variable that determines the success of exporters.

Nonwage Working Conditions

Nonmonetary working conditions and labor rights also improved notably in the late twentieth century. Economic growth again plays an important role in the advance, but for reasons different from those offered in the case of pay.

HOURS OF WORK. The relationship between economic development and hours of work is subtler and less certain than the link between development and pay. If per capita income growth simply provided lump-sum real income transfers to the population, the effect on preferred hours would be trivially predictable. Individuals would use the income to buy more leisure (and more of other desirable goods and services) and would work less. But lump-sum income transfers are not the mechanisms through which economic growth improves living standards of most people. Instead, productivity growth provides the basis for higher real wages, as demonstrated in the previous section, but the wages must be earned through work. How does the fact that economic development permits workers to earn more per hour of work influence the number of hours that they are willing to work?

Economic theory predicts a schizophrenic response. On the one hand, the higher incomes produced by higher wages lead workers to consume more of desirable goods and services, including leisure or nonmarket time. (In the language of economics, leisure is considered a "normal good" because its consumption increases with income.) Increased leisure means less work time. But with higher wages, each hour of leisure now "costs" more, in the sense that workers sacrifice more income than previously for each hour away from the job. With leisure now relatively expensive, workers may tend to "purchase" less of it; that is, they will tend to work longer. Hence the schizophrenia: the "income" effect of economic development tends to reduce work hours, while the "substitution" effect tends to increase them.

What actually happens to hours of work with economic development depends on which of these two effects turns out to be stronger, an issue that economic theory cannot resolve. To add to the ambiguity, there is no theoretical reason why the balance between the two effects should be the same in each country; ultimately the outcome depends on the distinctive preferences of each country's workers. How increased per capita income influences average work hours in a country is an empirical question, although an understanding of income and substitution effects aids in interpreting differences in the response of work hours to changes in per capita GDP.

The evolution of work hours in a society will also reflect employer preferences. Employers who try to maintain longer workdays or workweeks than workers prefer have to pay higher wages to attract and retain a workforce than do employers who offer more preferred work schedules. An employer's interest in maintaining relatively long workweeks, even at the cost of paying a higher wage, rises with the fixed costs of hiring workers. An interest in obtaining labor input from fewer employees working longer hours is increased by fixed costs arising from search and training costs, social charges levied per worker rather than per work hour, and restrictions on firing. Interest in longer work hours per worker will also grow to the extent that regulations raising the fixed costs of employment increase with economic development.

JOB SAFETY. How markets provide job safety is one of the oldest stories in labor economics, reaching back at least to the writings of Adam Smith 250 years ago. How the level of job safety in labor markets changes over time has only recently emerged from research studies. The combination of venerable analysis and modern evidence shows how job safety evolves and how the mechanisms of globalization may influence the evolution.

The previous chapter briefly introduced the broad definition of labor compensation used in economics since the writings of Adam Smith. The key notion is that in competitive labor markets, wages adjust to compensate workers for the nonmonetary advantages and disadvantages of different jobs. Job choices in labor markets where some jobs offer risk of on-the-job injury or death provide an important application of this idea. Risk-averse workers will accept risky jobs only if they are paid a higher wage than they can receive on safe jobs. The "compensating" wage differential emerging from workers' voluntary job choices between safe and risky jobs indicates how an average worker values workplace risks.[2]

These wage premiums also provide incentives for employers to invest in workplace safety, for risk-averse workers will accept lower wages in safer workplaces. Profit-maximizing employers invest in workplace safety as long as the benefits of lower wages exceed the cost of additional safety investments. Competitive labor markets transform workers' preferences for workplace safety into improved safety through the mechanism of compensating wage differentials—at least for health and safety threats that workers recognize. Employer altruism is neither expected nor required to increase workplace safety. A market mechanism that transmits workers' preferences for safety, reflected in compensating wage differentials for risk, to self-interested employers is all that is needed.

Over time, market incentives to provide workplace safety depend on how workers' attitudes toward workplace safety change as their income increases and how the cost of providing safety changes with economic growth. If workers experience diminishing returns to safety as their income increases, they will be willing to pay less for safe workplace environments. Compensating wage differentials for risk and the implied value of a statistical life will decline. If workers instead demand more safety as their income increases, compensating wage differentials for risk and the implied value of a statistical life will rise. Effectively, workers are willing to "pay" more for safety by accepting lower wages in safer workplaces. Rising incomes usually reflect rising wages—increases in the value of a worker's time. With a rising value of time, one would expect the individual costs of workplace accidents to increase, implying that workers' demand for safety should also increase.

Two types of research provide evidence that the demand for safety does increase with income. A historical study of U.S. male workers, ages 18 to 45, between 1940 and 1980 finds that workplace injury rates declined as compensating wage differentials for risk increased. That is, the demand for safety among U.S. workers must have been increasing in the last half of the twentieth century so that the tradeoff between wages and job safety was much steeper in 1980 than in 1940. Moreover, the compensating wage differences for risk were greatest early in a worker's career when most job choices are made. This study estimates an income elasticity of the value of a statistical life of 1.5 to 1.7 for this period in the United States, an estimate that is in line with elasticity estimates of 1.5 to 2.5 for Taiwan, a less developed country (Costa and Kahn 2002; Hammit, Liu, and Liu 2000). In both countries, the time-series evidence reveals that long-term economic growth raises demands for workplace safety and increases wage costs incurred by companies with unsafe conditions.

A long and growing empirical literature estimates tradeoffs between wages and workplace risks among countries at different stages of development. Such cross-country studies of the value of a statistical life can also provide insight into how workers' demands for workplace safety change with increases in real income. The task is not as simple as it may seem, for the studies vary in the measurement of risk and wages, the sample industries and labor force groups, and statistical methodologies. One careful review of four previous meta-analyses of wage-risk studies around the world finds a significant income elasticity of the value of a statistical life equal to .5 to .6 (Viscusi and Aldy, 2003). That is, the cross-country evidence indicates that the demand for workplace safety increases with income, although the effect of income on that demand is smaller among countries than it is over time within a country. In short, workers' job choice behavior indicates that they prefer an increasing fraction of the proceeds of economic growth and development to be spent on greater job safety. Higher per capita income also permits better diets, health care, and other activities contributing to safer workplace behavior and longer life expectancy.

Labor Rights

CHILD LABOR. Higher incomes expand the range of market and nonmarket choices faced by families. With higher incomes, families who view work by their children as undesirable can cover their basic food, housing, and health needs and still have money left over to "purchase" reduced labor force participation by children. With subsistence needs covered, families can afford to let children remain in school longer and engage in other activities that build, or at least do not depreciate, human capital. By raising future human capital, this reallocation of children's time provides a foundation for future wage income growth.[3]

More generally, one would expect the effects of income in reducing child labor to be strongest where the incentives to attend school are greatest—where the costs of obtaining schooling are lowest and the market returns to schooling are highest. Costs of schooling include the time and effort required to attend school—a factor that is sensitive to the location and quality of educational facilities—and the income forgone by attending school rather than working. National education policies have a crucial influence on the costs of schooling investments. Economic growth reduces the subsistence imperative that leads some families to place their children in employment. Market returns to schooling depend on the structure of market wages, with higher absolute wage differentials producing higher rates of return to schooling. This dimension of inequality has a useful function in encouraging schooling investments. Empirically, returns to schooling are inversely related to level of development. Studies have documented relatively high returns to schooling in relatively poor countries (Psacharopoulos 1985; Psacharopoulos and Patrinos 2002). Absent concerns over immediate survival, the incentives for school attendance appear to be high for well-functioning education systems.

The few available studies of household behavior in developing countries often confirm that child labor is a consequence of low incomes. For example, a study of Vietnamese households surveyed in 1993 and 1998 reports that in 1993 the proportion of working children ranged from 1.5 percent for 6-year-olds to 69.4 percent for 15-year-olds. The vast majority of the work was in agriculture, and less than 8 percent of child labor occurred outside the home. Over the next five years, child labor force participation rates dropped across the board and ranged from 1.1 (age 6) to 49.3 (age 15) percent in 1998. The study finds that changes in a family's resources (measured by expenditures rather than income) explain 60 percent of the large reduction in child labor between the two years. The relation between income and child labor is actually nonlinear near the subsistence level of income, so that changes in resources explain 80 percent of the decline in child labor in households that emerged from poverty between 1993 and 1998. The income effects are strongest for children working in agriculture and in work outside the household. Changes in income also predict most of the increase in school attendance among the poorest households (Edmonds 2003b).[4]

This study is revealing but may not be typical of the relationships between family income and child labor. In fact, other analyses of household data have found mixed evidence of this relationship. A cross-country analysis discussed later in this chapter will provide a broader view of the robustness of this relationship.

FORCED LABOR. Qualitative accounts clarify that forced labor thrives when there is a large supply of people with very limited education and few economic opportunities (Bales 2004). Economic deprivation leads people to accept unenforceable labor contracts and degrading labor conditions as a matter of survival. Once enslaved, escape may be discouraged both by coercion and the fact that superior alternatives are not available.

These considerations suggest an inverse relationship between per capita GDP and the main varieties of forced labor in the world. The higher incomes that accompany economic development relieve the conditions that lead to bonded labor, trafficking in human labor, and outright slavery. To the extent that economic development provides more choices in labor markets, it reduces the odds that large numbers of workers will have to accept alternatives that commonly produce forced labor.

Economic reasoning does not yield clear predictions on the relationship between economic development and two other labor rights: freedom of association and nondiscrimination. Much appears to rest on whether increased market competition accompanies development. Competition increases alternatives and economic choice in markets. Freedom of association and other civil liberties may be enhanced by exposing workers to a wider range of economic choices, as when centrally planned economies embrace capitalism. Similarly, economic theory predicts that greater competition undermines market discrimination as minorities have more opportunities to identify and work for the least prejudiced employers (Becker 1957). Nevertheless, the links between development and competition are not clearly established.

The Role of Economic Development

There are clearly a variety of reasons why a country's level of development may influence the quality of its working conditions and labor rights, but how important is the influence in practice? This section examines the links between level of development and labor conditions in the last decades of the twentieth century using data from a large panel of countries at all stages of development and representing a variety of political systems. Panel data permit analysis of how differences in labor conditions among countries are related to differences in national per capita income and of how labor conditions within a country change as per capita income changes over time. Income elasticities—the effect of a 1 percent change in per capita income on a labor condition—summarize the responsiveness of labor conditions to differences or changes in per capita income.

The study of differences among countries also provides an opportunity to examine the effects of national institutions and social structures on labor conditions. Institutional structures vary substantially among countries and are known to be important determinants of economic growth (Acemoglu, Johnson, and Robinson 2004), but they generally change slowly if at all. Their effects are most likely to be detected across countries, not over time. Against this benefit is a potential cost: cross-country estimates of income elasticities will be biased *if* real per capita income is correlated with *unobserved* country-specific influences on labor conditions. Labor regulations may be enforced more aggressively in high-income countries, for example, influencing both labor conditions and (via effects on the cost of doing business) per capita income.

Estimates of how labor conditions vary with per capita income within countries over time have two virtues. As explained in the discussion of pay and productivity earlier in this chapter, such fixed-effects estimates eliminate the influence of unobserved country-specific factors that might bias cross-country estimates of the effect of per capita income on labor conditions. More substantively, these estimates describe the effect of economic growth—changes in the level of development over time—on labor conditions. Of course, there is no free lunch: the fixed-effect technique that avoids potential biases in cross-country estimates also eliminates the ability to estimate how institutions and other *observable*, country-specific factors that do not change over time influence the variance in labor conditions observed among countries at a given level of development.[5] Here, the two approaches are wed to detect bias in the sensitivity estimates.

Like the earlier findings for pay, the estimated income elasticities for nonmonetary working conditions and labor rights convey a simple message: countries with higher per capita income have superior labor conditions (table 3.1). High-income countries have shorter work hours (whether measured by weekly hours or annual hours),[6] safer jobs, longer life expectancy, more freedom of association (whether measured by the civil liberties index or the FACB index), less child labor, and less forced labor (whether measured by the number of varieties of forced labor present or the estimated number of slaves). (Recall once again that lower values of each measure of labor rights signal superior conditions.) Only the gender wage differential is insensitive to the level of development. The cross-country estimates indicate that per capita income accounts for between 14 percent (for child labor) and 77 percent (for life expectancy) of the cross-country variation in working conditions and labor rights.

The highest income elasticities are found for the measures of child labor and forced labor. (Because there is only one observation on forced labor and gender wage differentials, no fixed-effect panel estimates are possible.) The

Table 3.1
Income Elasticities of Labor Conditions

Working conditions		Labor rights	
Long hours	−0.005	Child labor	−5.42**
Annual hours	−.05**	Civil liberties	−0.21**
Weekly hours	−.033**	Freedom of association[a]	−0.34**
Fatal accidents	−0.47**	Forced labor[a]	−29.01**
Life expectancy	0.14**	Slavery[a]	−1.47**
		Gender differential[a]	−0.006

** Statistically significant at 5 percent level or better.
[a] Cross-section estimates. All other estimates are fixed effects.

Source: Table A3.2

lowest income elasticities are observed for measures of work hours, a result that no doubt reflects the schizophrenic response of workers to the wage increases embedded in aggregate income increases.

The finding that virtually all working conditions and labor rights improve with advances in per capita income is compatible with a policy implication of great simplicity and power: Policies that stimulate economic growth improve labor conditions. The menu of such policies is quite broad but, in comparison with some proposed regulatory interventions, may seem quite indirect. The past 20 years have seen the development of a large literature on growth empirics as economists study the correlates of international differences in the growth rate of per capita income. The research has provoked extensive debates over the relative role of physical and human capital investment, institutions, and geographical luck. The studies differ in their conclusions regarding some determinants of growth, and the literature is not easily summarized. One recent study employs novel techniques to determine which growth determinants retain statistical significance over a variety of statistical specifications (Sala-I-Martin, Doppelhofer, and Miller 2004). This study finds that primary school enrollment, the relative price of investment goods, life expectancy, malaria prevalence, and religious characteristics are all robust determinants of cross-country differences in growth rates. This research implies that countries with relatively high rates of school enrollment, relatively low prices of investment goods, and good health conditions and policies (signaled by long life expectancy and low malaria prevalence) will have higher growth and hence superior working conditions and labor rights. Countries in which government intervention into the economy (measured by the share of government consumption in GDP) is relative low also have superior growth and labor conditions.

The fact that growth-enhancing policies are associated with better labor conditions signals a possible link between globalization and labor conditions. To the extent that free trade or other mechanisms of globalization alter a country's growth rate, labor conditions change accordingly. Links between trade and growth constitute an important part of the discussion in chapter 4, but a finding from the Sala-I-Martin et al. study provides a clue to the tenor of that discussion: growth rates increase with the length of time that a country has followed an open trade policy. Chapter 4 explores the implication that free trade improves labor conditions in much greater detail.

Outliers

As important as economic growth is for advancing working conditions and labor rights, considerable international variation in labor conditions remains at any level of development. Cross-country differences in per capita income account for less than half of the international variation in the measures of working conditions and labor rights, with the exception of life expectancy. Clearly, eliminating international differences in the level of development would still leave notable cross-country variations in most labor conditions.

Which countries are outliers? The answer varies by labor condition. For better and worse, table 3.2 identifies the international outliers: countries that offer superior and inferior working conditions and labor rights relative to other countries at the same level of development.[7] The qualification is important. Readers who are surprised to see that Syria has the highest pay in the table or that Bangladesh has the second lowest fatal accident rate should recall that these results are conditional on each country's level of development. Similarly, if one is surprised that certain countries with notably good or bad labor conditions do not appear on the list, it simply means that those countries' labor conditions do not depart markedly from the norm for their level of development (or that data on the labor conditions were not available for the country). (In interpreting table 3.2, bear in mind that *lower* values denote superior values for weekly hours, fatal accidents, civil liberties, and the FACB index.) For child labor force participation and forced labor, most advanced countries are "outliers" in the sense that they report none or very little of either phenomenon, while areas of Africa and Asia discussed earlier are outliers in the other direction. Clearly, factors other than a country's level of development influence its labor conditions. The rest of this chapter examines the role of prominent national social and institutional characteristics that may shape a country's working conditions and labor rights.

Institutions and Social Conditions

Economic growth requires "good institutions": institutions that reduce the cost of economic commerce (Acemoglu et al. 2004). Good institutions may promote ownership by clarifying property rights, supporting the enforcement of contracts, and limiting opportunities for corruption. Clear property rights encourage investment and exchange. Commenting on the

Table 3.2
Outlier Countries, 1995

Pay					Weekly hours of work				
+			−		+			−	
Syria	2.83	Bolivia	−3.65		Jordan	4.24	Austria	−3.27	
New Zealand	2.61	Argentina	−2.38		Egypt	3.72	Belgium	−2.98	
Iran	2.38	Zambia	−2.35		Singapore	2.44	Jamaica	−2.13	
Israel	2.08	Kenya	−2.29		Korea	2.06	Norway	−1.64	
		Thailand	−2.27		Thailand	1.66	Australia	−1.64	

Fatal industrial accidents					Life expectancy				
+			−		+			−	
Panama	2.33	U.K.	−2.12		Jamaica	1.54	Sierra Leone	−5.88	
Togo	1.83	Bangladesh	−1.59		Costa Rica	1.40	Rwanda	−4.88	
Korea	1.83	Sweden	−1.51		Sri Lanka	1.29	Guinea	−4.27	
					Nicaragua	1.24	Botswana	−4.20	
					China	1.04	Gabon	−4.15	

Civil liberties					Collective bargaining rights (FACB)				
+			−		+			−	
Singapore	2.64	Dominica	−3.06		Columbia	1.34	Burkina Faso	−2.58	
Iran	1.72	Benin	−3.01		Iran	1.30	Guinea-Bis	−2.57	
Malaysia	1.50	Malawi	−2.90		Syria	1.19	Madagascar	−2.55	
Syria	1.43	Mali	−2.68		Turkey	1.14	The Gambia	−2.38	
		Australia	−2.66						

Note: Numbers are the ratio of actual minus predicted labor conditions (given a country's per capita income) to the mean squared error of log linear regressions reported in table A3.3.

Source: Computed from table A3.3.

role of property rights in sub-Saharan Africa, Robert Guest observes that "not even Africans want to invest in Africa: an estimated 40% of the continent's privately held wealth is stashed offshore." One reason, he says, is:

> Less than 10% of the continent's land is formally owned, and barely one African in ten lives in a house with title deeds. Farmers and urbanites, unlike nomads, usually have a clear idea what their homes and maize-plots are worth. . . . Sound property rights have great advantages. . . . [P]eople . . . are more inclined to make long-term investments, such as . . . buying a new plough. Property rights promote flexibility, too. They allow peasants who want to move to the city to look for work to sell their land, or to rent it out without fear of being unable to get it back later. (2004, pp. 4, 6, 7)

In short, property rights influence working conditions indirectly by raising output and income.

Secure property rights may also have a direct influence on the workplace.

Improvements in workplace health and safety, labor productivity, and other working conditions also require investments at the place of work. Property rights influence the willingness of employers to invest in working conditions and the willingness of lenders to finance the investments. Lenders require collateral, and property itself may serve as collateral in societies with well-defined property rights. Where property rights are uncertain, investments requiring external financing are less likely to occur. Much the same may be said about the consequences of corruption and weak enforcement of contracts.

Clearly, fundamental economic institutions may have both direct and indirect (via per capita income) effects on labor conditions. Measures of the rule of law and risk of expropriation in each country enable an appraisal of the strength of the direct effect (International Country Risk Guide). Poor institutions appear to cluster; the simple cross-country correlation coefficients between indices for the rule-of-law index and the risk of expropriation of private assets are around .8. Turning to extreme cases, Iraq had the worst (lowest) rating for risk of expropriation in 1990, followed by the Democratic Republic of the Congo (formerly Zaire), which also had the lowest ratings for rule of law in 1990. The highest ratings were in several industrialized OECD countries.

Political Institutions

Can political institutions also help to explain the worldwide distribution of working conditions and labor rights? Political institutions vary in many interesting ways that might be linked to labor conditions. Here we concentrate on the influence of democracy—specifically whether countries with democratic political institutions have superior labor conditions. But most of the world's richest countries are democracies. Per capita income may determine both a country's degree of democracy *and* its labor conditions. A recent study rules this possibility out, however, finding that the level of per capita income does not enhance democratic political institutions (Acemoglu et al. 2005). Instead, the two forces operate independently of each other, leaving scope for a separate and supplementary influence of political institutions on a country's labor conditions. Another study concludes that democracy is good for workers' pay. After controlling for labor productivity and other factors, this study of international wage differences concludes: "There is a robust and statistically significant association between the extent of democratic rights in a country and the level of wages received by workers in manufactures. . . . Our findings indicate that democratic institutions tend to shift the functional distribution of income in manufacturing from profits to wages" (Rodrik 1999, pp. 708, 725–26). The author proposes that wages are determined by bargaining between workers and employers and that democratic institutions produce increased worker political participation that raises their relative bargaining power.

Democracy is likely to influence labor conditions in complex ways. Indeed, it is easier to see how political institutions may be more important for labor rights than for working conditions, assuming that markets are free to function under a variety of political regimes. When markets function, the market mechanisms outlined earlier in the chapter continue to establish many working conditions. Workers' preferences regarding job safety or desirable work hours should influence the wage structure and hence the incentives facing employers to provide safer work environments or more favorable work schedules. (This reasoning rules out countries with extensive central planning of wage structures and worker allocation. The number of countries with such arrangements decreased dramatically in the late twentieth century.) On the other hand, the degree of democracy in a country may have a large effect on freedom of association and other labor rights.

Social Divisions

Ethnic and religious divisions that breed conflicts within countries and distort resource allocation may also influence labor conditions, both indirectly through their effect on per capita income and directly. Ethnic fragmentation often results from accidents of colonization, as the following excerpt from a World Bank report explains:

> In Sub-Saharan Africa nation-states were fashioned out of arbitrary divisions of territory by colonial powers—divisions often based on convenient geographic markers such as lines of latitude and longitude, with no consideration of the social units of local populations. With disparate groups and few supra-ethnic institutions to mediate among them, the creation of nation and state has been fraught with problems. Colonial rulers and local politicians have often manipulated ethnic tensions for private gain, sometimes leading to gruesome civil wars. Inflaming ethnic tensions and civil unrest is a frequent strategy for gaining and keeping power in these circumstances, since it justifies expanding brutal military forces while undermining the capacity of opposition groups demanding reform. . . . Ethnic cleavages can affect development outcomes in many ways. They can influence the internal organization of government and the allocation of public spending, leading to unequal distribution of public goods and services. They can encourage rent seeking, reducing the efficiency of public spending. (2001b, p. 127)

Twenty of the twenty-one most ethnically diverse countries are in Sub-Saharan Africa (Alesina et al. 2003, p. 160), a feature of the data that makes it difficult to disentangle the effects of ethnic diversity from purely geographical influences.

Religious diversity also can arise from colonial history; countries with the greatest religious diversity include South Africa, Malawi, and Ghana. In contrast to ethnic diversity, however, high-income countries with historically low barriers to immigration also have considerable religious diversity. Examples include Australia, New Zealand, and the United States. As a result, religious diversity is relatively high at both ends of the development scale. Countries with the least religious diversity include Yemen, Somalia, Morocco, Turkey, and Algeria.

Ethnic and religious diversity can affect working conditions and labor rights in several ways. One World Bank report states: "Ethnicity can become a basis for competition for political power and for access to material resources. Unless institutions of the state and civil society offer forums for mediating intergroup rivalries and forging cross-cutting ties among diverse ethnic groups, these ethnic cleavages can lead to conflicts, tearing a society and economy apart, leaving everyone vulnerable to poverty" (2001b, p. 126). When filtered through the political process, ethnic and religious divisions can produce poor working conditions and significant limitations on labor rights. The governments of highly fractionalized societies may be reluctant to provide labor and employment rights that would apply equally to all members of society. Even where rights are provided, they may not be enforced. In other instances, the geographic isolation of some ethnic groups may limit their access to schooling, health services, and jobs. Finally, ethnic conflicts raise mortality and diminish time horizons. Individuals with lower life expectancy, like those who lack property rights, are less likely to pursue human capital (and other) investments whose current costs can be justified only by benefits (including higher wages and better working conditions) that occur far in the future (Lorentzen, McMillan, and Wacziarg 2004).

Many studies of economic development find that social divisions reduce economic growth, implying that they would also retard the improvement of labor conditions. The role of social divisions on growth has been particularly crucial in Africa.[8] We shall be interested in whether social divisions in a country influence labor conditions beyond their indirect influence through growth. The analysis of social divisions uses measures of ethnic and religious "fractionalization" developed by Alesina et al. (2003).[9] Ethnicity is measured in different ways in different parts of the world. This measure is constructed from information on the diversity of languages spoken and, where available, from information on the distribution of racial groups in the population. The measure of religious divisions is computed from information on the shares of different religious groups in a country's population.

How are a country's economic and political institutions and social diversity related to the quality of its working conditions and labor rights? Do they help to explain the international variation in labor conditions not captured by level of development? Supplementing the earlier analysis of the role that the level of development plays in determining labor conditions with measures of economic and political institutions and of social diversity helps to address these questions.[10] Table 3.3 summarizes the relationships between labor conditions and these variables found in an analysis of country panel

Table 3.3
Labor Conditions, Institutions, and Social Divisions, 1980–95

Influence of	Weekly hours	Fatal accidents	Life expect.	Civil liberties	Child labor	Forced labor	Gender differential
Per capita income	−		+	−	−	−	
Rule of law				−	−	−	
Expropriation			+		+	+	+
Democracy	−	−		−	−	−	
Ethnic diversity		+	−		+	−	
Religious diversity	−			−	−		

Note: Each entry describes the sign of a statistically significant relationship between the labor condition denoted in the column and the measure of institutions or social diversity indicated by the row. No entry appears for relationships that are not statistically significant. The appendix to this chapter describes the underlying regression analysis.

Source: Table A3.4

data for 1980, 1985, and 1990. For *statistically significant results*, entries in the table describe whether the association between a particular labor condition and a particular institution is positive or negative. With the effect of other variables held constant, the fatal job accident rate is lower in democratic countries with high religious diversity, but higher in countries with relatively high ethnic diversity, for example. (No entry appears for associations that are not statistically significant. The exact quantitative values for all entries appear in appendix table 3.4.)

Several conclusions emerge from the analysis. Even with the inclusion of variables capturing economic and political institutions and social diversity, per capita income continues to be associated with superior working conditions. Institutional characteristics and social divisions do not trump economic development as an influence on labor conditions, except in the case of fatal on-the-job accidents, where the development effect is no longer statistically significant. (Life expectancy, for which many more countries report data, still increases with the level of development, however.)

Institutions and social divisions also have a direct influence on labor conditions. For a given level of development, the most consistent force for superior labor conditions is the presence of democratic political institutions. Countries with more democratic institutions tend to have lower hours of work, fewer fatal accidents, stronger civil liberties, less child labor, and less forced labor. The rule of law is more likely to be associated with stronger labor rights than with improved working conditions. Broadly speaking, countries with superior institutions have superior labor conditions.

Conditional on level of economic development, social diversity in a country has a mixed influence on labor conditions. For some conditions— work hours and gender discrimination—ethnic and religious diversity do not seem to matter at all. For others, they pull in opposite directions. For a given level of development, higher ethnic diversity is associated with a higher fatal job accident rate and more child labor, while countries with greater religious diversity tend to have safer workplaces and less child labor. Countries with high religious diversity also tend to have stronger civil liberties. (Recall that high religious diversity is found in both high-income and low-income countries.) Curiously, greater ethnic diversity is associated with *less* forced labor and has no significant relationship with civil liberties.

A society's institutions and social divisions appear to have an important influence on its labor conditions. The relationship is strongest in the case of weekly hours and gender wage differences, where differences in the level of development account for little of the international variance. But international differences in institutions and social divisions help us understand some of the variation in most labor conditions that remains at each level of development.

Conclusion and Looking Ahead

The previous chapter documented the widespread improvement in working conditions and labor rights in the last third of the twentieth century without explaining why the broad improvement occurred. This chapter began the study of why labor conditions change by reminding us that trade, migration, and capital flows between countries are not the only potentially important influences on working conditions and labor rights. Putting globalization aside, the foremost influence on labor conditions is level of development. At any given time, international differences in per capita income are associated with significant differences in virtually all labor conditions. Over time, economic growth improves most working conditions and labor rights. During the last third of the twentieth century, economic growth improved working conditions and labor rights in most countries. Negative growth of real per capita GDP between 1970 and 2000 is found only in Jamaica, Nicaragua, Peru, Venezuela, and a dozen (mainly sub-Saharan) African countries. To an important extent, the inequality in incomes, nonmonetary working conditions, and labor rights observed around the world result from differences in the level of economic development and national economic growth rates. Improving economic growth in the poorest countries encourages improvements in their labor conditions.

Recognizing the powerful role of level of development opens a broad policy menu for advancing labor conditions. Any country, no matter what its stance toward economic integration, can improve national labor conditions by implementing policies and building national institutions that raise its economic growth rate. Factors that raise economic growth in closed economies include higher rates of technical progress, investments in physical and human capital, and establishment of institutions that clarify property rights and enforce contracts. Looking forward, the connection between growth and labor conditions has an important implication for globalization: any effect that international trade or other globalization mechanisms have on per capita income will influence working conditions and most labor rights. If trade and other globalization mechanisms raise growth—an issue addressed in the next chapter—then by the evidence in this chapter, increasing trade also improves a country's labor conditions. The connection between growth and labor conditions is symmetrical. Policies and institutions that slow or reduce economic growth retard improvements in labor conditions. Actual declines in real per capita GDP, as in the few countries mentioned above, eventually reduce the quality of labor conditions.

As important as economic development and growth are for the level and improvement of working conditions and labor rights, substantial national differences in labor conditions remain at each level of per capita income. This chapter made a start at demystifying the remaining variance by demonstrating the importance of economic and political institutions and social divisions for the worldwide distribution of labor conditions. Though an important strain of the economic growth literature stresses an *indirect* relationship of institutions (through their influence on per capita income), many national institutional and social characteristics also have a *direct* relationship with labor conditions. Countries with comparatively democratic political institutions and low ethnic conflict tend to have superior labor conditions, for example.

To some extent, these findings signal the limits of public policies in equalizing labor conditions around the world. Though the institutional and social characteristics of countries may not be frozen over time, they generally change very slowly if at all. Much less is known about changing institutions than about changing a country's per capita GDP, for example. Legislative action may change the status of property rights in a country, but how do countries develop democratic political processes that produce such actions? The ethnic or religious mix of a country's population and the antagonisms that the mix may produce seem well insulated from simple policy actions. To an important extent, countries may have to live with the labor conditions that flow from their institutional and social characteristics.

The rest of the book investigates other likely explanations for the dispersed labor conditions around the world. The next three chapters turn to the main focus of the book and consider the role of globalization on working conditions and labor rights. One of the many questions raised by this chapter is whether globalization alters the institutions and social divisions that appear to influence labor conditions. The final chapters then explore how domestic and international labor market regulations influence national differences in labor conditions.

CHAPTER 4

Trade and Labor Conditions

Previous chapters established several important facts about the evolution of most labor conditions in the last third of the twentieth century, a period of rapidly increasing international economic integration. During that period:

- World poverty declined, and labor conditions improved.
- The quality of labor conditions was higher in countries with open trade policies. Countries with closed trade policies had the poorest labor conditions.
- Economic growth is a powerful influence on improving working conditions and labor rights.
- Labor conditions varied widely among countries at any given level of development, reflecting in part differences in national economic and political institutions and social diversity.

With this chapter, we begin a closer analysis of the links between labor conditions and globalization. This chapter explores the relationship between international trade and labor conditions; subsequent chapters address the role of international labor migration, the employment practices of multinational corporations, and domestic and international policy issues.

Does free trade degrade labor conditions? Merely raising the question puzzles most professional economists, since theories of international trade generally conclude that freer trade should improve working conditions on average and produce a convergence of working conditions among countries engaged in trade. Trade theories also acknowledge different short-run effects on exporting and import-competing industries within a country with open trade policies. Some globalization skeptics instead subscribe to the view that global competition degrades labor conditions around the world. Understanding how international trade influences labor conditions in exporting and import-competing industries is important, since most opposition to free trade stems from concerns about its potential distributional consequences. This chapter therefore begins by discussing the predictions of international trade theories. These theories offer more direct implications for working conditions than for labor rights. Nevertheless, the chapter also explains how free trade may influence freedom of association, labor market discrimination, forced labor, and child labor. There are sound reasons for expecting most labor rights to be stronger in open than closed economies.

Trade theories predict that free trade raises a country's per capita income. In so doing, trade will have at least an *indirect* influence on labor conditions, because higher per capita income is associated with superior working conditions and labor rights (chapter 3). After reviewing the evidence that trade stimulates growth (rather than the other way around), we turn to the question of whether free trade also has a *direct* effect on labor conditions. The chapter assesses evidence on labor conditions in export firms and export processing zones and on the effects that import penetration has on labor conditions. Using cross-country and panel data for the late twentieth century, the chapter then presents an analysis of the net effect of trade flows and free trade policies on working conditions and labor rights. The various analyses find no evidence that trade degrades labor conditions. Indeed, when trade has any statistically significant direct effect on labor conditions, its effect is positive. The chapter also evaluates the argument that poor labor conditions contribute to superior export performance. In one way or another, proposals for international regulation of labor standards rest on the proposition that under free trade, countries will systematically degrade labor conditions to improve their export sales and attract foreign direct investment. The evidence presented and reviewed in this chapter does not support that proposition.

Free Trade and Working Conditions

The predictions of international trade theories offer interesting contrasts with the view that international competition increases poverty, degrades working conditions, and raises worldwide inequality. According to trade theories, opening a country to international trade may have the following effects:

1. *Reallocation of resources* to their most efficient use (principle of comparative advantage). Under free trade, production and trade patterns will reflect different national factor endowments. National wealth increases when countries export products made from inputs that are relatively abundant (and hence relatively cheap) domestically and import products made from inputs that are relatively scarce (and hence relatively expensive) domestically. Inputs

may be natural or human resources. Oil-rich Nigeria will become wealthier by exporting some of the oil with which it is endowed and importing computers, which it lacks the skills to produce as efficiently as, say, Japan. Oil-poor Japan will become wealthier by exporting some of the computers that its skilled workers make to purchase Nigerian oil. Each country would be less wealthy if it insisted on self-sufficiency and tried to produce both products.

International trade is a leading application of the adage Never make what you can buy more cheaply. Trade permits all countries to become wealthier by concentrating their resources in the production of goods and services in which their relative productivity is greatest in international markets. This concentration maximizes the "currency" that a country may use to purchase goods and services that other countries produce comparatively efficiently. Without trade, some domestic resources would have to remain in less productive activities to satisfy domestic consumption needs. With trade, countries can import consumption goods that are produced more cheaply (i.e., more efficiently) abroad. Trade effectively cuts the dependence between a country's structure of production and its consumption needs, and in so doing permits labor and other resources to move into activities where their productivity, and hence monetary and/or nonmonetary compensation, will be relatively high.

To what extent do the predicted resource reallocations occur? Recent studies find little evidence of expected reallocation of labor between the very broadly defined industries used by national and international statistical agencies (Wacziarg and Wallack 2004). Instead, the initial reallocation of labor following trade liberalizations mainly occurs as workers move from less productive to more productive firms within an industry (Goldberg and Pavcnik 2004). What is crucial for the improvement of working conditions is the fact that the largest aggregate productivity increases occur in the industries that liberalize the most (Goldberg and Pavcnik 2003). Trade liberalizations increase the scope for improved compensation, broadly defined.

Trade-induced *interindustry* reallocation of labor and capital takes some time to achieve. The practical breadth of industry choice for current workers is typically circumscribed by earlier education and training decisions. Thus we should not be surprised that the earliest responses to trade liberalizations occur within "industries." If liberalizations also create opportunities in other industries, the labor response to the new opportunities requires new education and training investments that take longer to achieve. Indeed, much of the reallocation of the labor force across major industrial sectors occurs through the decisions of new labor force cohorts, which make education and training choices that take advantage of the new opportunities.

2. *Greater economies of scale.* When production is subject to economies of scale, even countries with similar factor proportions can benefit from trading with one another. International markets permit countries to expand production beyond domestic needs and enjoy greater economies of scale. Domestic

resources shift toward the industries that are capturing the greatest scale economies. Production is concentrated in particular industries to capture greater scale economies, not because of patterns of relative factor abundance. Although production is concentrated in a limited number of industries, trade again permits consumers to import the variety of products and services that they desire for consumption. After all, the purpose of exporting is to buy imports. Unlike comparative advantage, the economy of scale motivation for trade provides a rationale for intraindustry trade, an empirically important component of trade flows between countries at roughly the same level of development. It does not predict the exact pattern of a country's trade, however. Like comparative advantage, the scale economies theory predicts that resources are used more productively in a free-trade environment than under autarky, and greater efficiency permits higher compensation.

3. *Increased competition* from foreign producers. Competition from imports reduces the monopsony power of domestic companies. Product prices in import industries fall—a gain for all consumers—but so do the rents available to workers. If increased presence of multinational companies accompanies more open trade policies, openness may also reduce the monopoly power of domestic employers, a development that would tend to improve worker compensation and/or nonmonetary working conditions. Increased competition may also influence some labor rights, a topic that will be discussed later in this chapter.

4. *Transfers of technology*, knowledge, and learning. Such transfers should raise productivity and hence worker compensation.

In short, free trade should increase national productivity. Productivity improvements in turn provide the basis for sustained increases in per capita income: more rapid economic growth. Advances in per capita income improve virtually all working conditions and labor rights, as we saw in chapter 3. If free trade in fact raises per capita income, open trade policies provide a method for improving labor conditions.

With such positive prospective benefits for labor, why is free trade so controversial? Why do globalization skeptics and their political allies try to slow down a process that would achieve these benefits? The changing patterns of production that accompany free trade produce redistributions of income and impose transitional costs on resources that must move from activities in which a country is relatively inefficient to activities in which it is relatively efficient. These repercussions are similar to those that accompany technological innovations and changes in consumer tastes, but their source is easier to identify. Those who believe they will be harmed by free trade seek to mitigate that harm through the political process. In this respect, debates over globalization reflect an ongoing tension between the efficiency objectives underlying economic policy recommendations and the distributional concerns motivating much political action. Liberalizing trade influences both domestic and international inequality.

For specific industries, the effects of liberalizing trade can be quite large.

European and American industries protected by significant tariffs and other barriers to trade have large wage premiums—"rents" in excess of wages predicted on the basis of industry skill levels. In a study of European countries, wages were about one-third higher in industries protected by tariff barriers and about 12 percent higher in industries protected by other barriers. In contrast, the average wage in sectors facing import competition is about 84 percent of the average wage in manufacturing (Nicolletti et al. 2001; OECD 1999b). A study of the United States emphasized the interaction between industrial concentration and trade barriers. Concentrated industries, particularly in the durable-goods sector, earn significant rents and employ disproportionately large numbers of low-skill workers. For many years, the rents in some industries reflected the combined effects of the lack of domestic competition and the limits on foreign competition through trade barriers. Partially as a result of collective bargaining, workers shared in the rents earned in these industries. Declining trade barriers increased the penetration of more efficient foreign companies into the U.S. market, reducing employment and relative wages in the domestic firms. Import competition clearly erodes the rents available from trade protection (Borjas and Ramey, 1995), encourages labor and other resources to move to companies and industries in which a country's comparatively high productivity supports relatively high wages, and lowers prices to consumers.[1]

Domestic Inequality

International trade theory predicts that countries export goods made with abundant (cheap) domestic inputs and import goods made with scarce (expensive) domestic inputs. When the removal of trade barriers raises the demand for exports, the rewards to the country's abundant factor increase. At the same time, the demand for (and rewards to) a country's scarce input decline as cheaper imported goods supplement some domestic production (Stolper and Samuelson 1941). In industrialized countries, where capital and skilled labor are plentiful relative to unskilled labor, free trade should increase exports of capital- and skill-intensive products and raise imports of products made by unskilled labor. These developments raise the return to capital and relative wage of skilled labor but reduce the relative wage of unskilled labor. Liberalized trade should initially increase domestic wage inequality in rich countries. In labor-intensive, developing countries, the opposite pattern of exports and imports should emerge. Labor, particularly low-skilled labor, should gain at the expense of scarce capital. For these countries, liberalized trade should initially reduce domestic wage inequality. Clearly, the initial impact of free trade on domestic inequality differs at each end of the trading relationship. In each case, however, the changing pattern of relative wages encourages human capital investments that suit the country's comparative advantage.

Contrary to some critiques of globalization, this analysis implies that in the short run, globalization threatens working conditions of some unskilled workers in the richer countries rather than the employment conditions of workers in the world's poorest countries. (No doubt this contributes to the suspicion in many developing countries of efforts to limit the scope of globalization.) Just how significant is the threat to conditions in advanced countries? During the 1980s and 1990s, a period of increasingly free trade, wage inequality increased in several industrialized countries. With the relative wage of unskilled workers falling (the returns to skill increasing), several economic studies sought to isolate the influence of freer trade on increases in national inequality. Reviews of the large literature that grew around this issue generally conclude that trade and immigration accounted for a small to moderate amount of the increase in the ratio of skilled to unskilled wages (Cline 1997). Technical changes that increased the demand for high-skilled labor provided an empirically more important, albeit less visible, explanation for growing inequality during that period. Yet political reaction to growing inequality tended to assign the dominant influence to trade.

International Inequality

Free trade should also influence differences among countries in the returns to labor and other inputs. But is free trade a force for increasing worldwide inequality in these returns, as some skeptics would have it? By raising returns to a country's relatively abundant input to production, a worldwide reduction in protection should raise the return to unskilled labor in less developed countries and reduce the relative returns to unskilled labor in industrialized countries. By the same argument, a worldwide reduction in protection should raise the return to skilled labor in developed countries and reduce returns to skill in developing countries. (Consistent with the limited supply of skilled labor in most poor countries, rates of return to schooling in developing countries typically exceed those in industrialized countries [Psacharopoulos and Patrinos, 2002]. Reducing trade barriers therefore should also produce a convergence in returns to skill.)

Free trade should produce a *convergence* of returns to labor around the world, but the process will be better received in developing countries than industrialized countries. Moreover, free trade reduces international differences in pay and other factor returns, even when there are barriers to international labor or capital mobility. According to Samuelson's famous "factor price equalization theorem," trade will equalize pay and other factor returns for countries sharing the same technology (1948). In traditional trade theory, free trade is a force for equality, not inequality, among countries.

Outsourcing

Standard trade theories neglect the role of outsourcing, the use of inputs produced in other countries in combination with domestic inputs to produce finished goods. In fact, an increasing portion of trade among countries consists of intermediate goods. By 1995, for example, foreign companies produced all of the parts for laptop computers sold by U.S. companies Dell, Apple, Gateway, and Acer, and 95 percent of the parts used in Hewlett-Packard laptops (Dean and Tam 2005). Since companies in industrialized countries face a higher relative wage for unskilled labor at home than they do abroad, they outsource activities that use considerable unskilled labor to less-industrialized foreign countries, while retaining high-skill activities at home. Stories of offshore performance of routine assembly and other repetitive tasks have become quite common. Outsourcing therefore reduces the demand for unskilled workers in industrialized countries, as does skill-biased technological change.

Though trade in final goods may have had little effect on growing wage inequality in developed countries in the 1990s, trade in intermediate goods could explain why the demand for unskilled workers has declined *within* industries. The most complete empirical assessment of the importance of the outsourcing phenomenon concludes that increased trade in intermediate goods can explain up to half of the decline in returns to unskilled labor in some advanced countries (Feenstra and Hanson 2001). At the end of the twentieth century, changes in the outsourcing component of trade may have influenced domestic inequality trends more than did traditional trade in finished goods. The growing importance of outsourcing in the late twentieth century reinforces the role of trade as a mechanism of international equality. Outsourcing reduces the demand (and relative wage) of unskilled labor in industrialized countries and raises the demand (and relative wage) of unskilled labor in less developed countries. The implication that free trade is a force for international wage convergence remains.

The convergence is not always visible in studies of labor markets in developing countries, however. In some of those countries, freer trade seems to be associated with a *declining* relative wage for unskilled labor, contrary to the predictions of the traditional and outsourcing views of the effects of trade. Efforts to explain this phenomenon generally rely on the effects of the technology transfer that is believed to occur with some foreign trade. Suppose that trade and foreign direct investment transfer technologies developed in industrialized countries to developing countries. Such technologies are designed to work with the skilled labor that is abundant in rich countries, and when transferred to developing countries the technologies raise the relative demand for skilled labor. Contrary to the predictions of traditional and outsourcing theories, the returns to skilled labor in developing countries increase and the relative wage of unskilled labor declines. The technology transfer that accompanies increased trade with industrialized countries thus may raise inequality within developing countries and may increase international wage inequality as well (Arbache, Dickerson, and Green 2004). Though it is not yet clear that this is a general phenomenon, evidence supporting this "skill-enhancing trade" hypothesis has been found for Brazil and Mexico.

Free Trade and Labor Rights

The additional output and productivity associated with free trade provide the basis for improving wages and nonmonetary working conditions. But how is free trade likely to affect the four labor rights stressed by international and nongovernmental organizations: elimination of the worst forms of child labor, nondiscrimination, freedom of association, and abolition of forced labor? Some globalization skeptics claim that trade expands through the exploitation of children and woman and the suppression of freedom of association at the workplace. Much less is said about links between globalization and forced labor.

Child Labor

Earlier chapters demonstrated the strong link between child labor and poverty. Cross-country differences in child labor are inversely correlated with differences in national income, and *changes* in child labor force participation within a country are inversely correlated with changes in national income over time (chapter 3). One way in which free trade can influence child labor is therefore through its effect on per capita income. We have just seen that leading trade theories predict that free trade *raises* income, which should *reduce* child labor force participation. For trade to increase the use of child labor, as some skeptics argue, it must also produce countervailing effects that are sufficiently large to overwhelm the important income effects.

There is a potential countervailing effect of free trade. For a given level of family income, the key determinant of child labor is the relative return to current work versus schooling, which can be summarized in the rate of return to schooling. High rates of return to schooling raise the attractiveness of school attendance over work; low rates of return to schooling can reverse the incentives. A key question is: How does liberalizing trade influence the rate of return to schooling—the tradeoff between schooling and work?

Child labor usually signals a comparatively unskilled labor force. The comparative advantage of countries with extensive child labor is likely to be products made with considerable unskilled labor. In this setting, lower trade barriers increase the demand for products made with unskilled labor, raising the price for unskilled work. By raising unskilled wages, trade could reduce the rate of return to schooling in countries producing unskilled-labor-intensive exports, thereby reducing the relative attractiveness of schooling to children and their families. If present, this effect would tend to increase child labor force participation rates, and, if strong enough, this effect could reverse the income effect of trade. That is, the tendency for the higher incomes associated with more trade to reduce child labor could be swamped by the effect of a lower return to schooling on the allocation of children's time. Two factors may mitigate this effect. First, direct or indirect tax revenues from trade may permit governments to reduce the costs of attending school by increasing the number and quality of public schools. Second, in countries where the "skill-enhancing trade" hypothesis applies, technology transfers raise returns to schooling, thereby increasing incentives for children to remain in school. The empirical work reported below sorts out the net effect of trade on child labor.

Discrimination

Does globalization expand through the exploitation of women and other minorities? Does increased global competition increase the likelihood of such discrimination? The main economic theory of discrimination does not consider globalization per se, but it predicts that increased competition to hire labor should erode discrimination, largely by providing labor force minorities additional employment opportunities with employers who have less discriminatory tastes (Becker 1957).

To the extent that globalization increases the number of export firms and/or multinational companies competing for labor in local labor markets, employer discrimination should decrease. By providing opportunities beyond agriculture and the informal sector, globalization provides an opportunity to increase the status and security that comes with higher income. One effect is that it increases the choices available to women, reflected in part in decisions to postpone the age of marriage (Wolf 2004). Only those unfamiliar with the devastating health and social consequences of exceedingly young marriage and child-bearing ages for women in some poor countries would doubt this benefit of trade (Thurow 2005; LaFraniere 2005).

Freedom of Association

The basic freedom of association in labor markets permits workers to form and join collective employee organizations and to engage in collective bargaining with employers. These rights are now enshrined in the UN Universal Declaration of Human Rights and more recently in the 1998 ILO Declaration of Fundamental Principles and Rights at Work. Whether free trade threatens freedom of association *rights* is a matter of conjecture. Globalization skeptics sometimes allege that governments may limit freedom of association rights in an effort to improve national export performance, reasoning that freedom of association rights may raise labor costs. Later in this chapter we determine whether there is empirical support for this allegation.

Linking freedom of association rights to labor costs highlights the uneasy distinction between rights and outcomes in labor markets. Representatives of international organizations sometimes argue that "rights are costless," but few workers would be attracted to freedom of association rights that could not be used to alter working conditions. If free trade leads governments to diminish rights, it is because trade alters the outcomes associated with those rights—the results of collective bargaining. The underlying issue is how free trade influences the relative bargaining power of labor and management.

Trade has several effects. Where an expansion in the number of export firms or an increased presence of multinational companies reduces employer monopsony power, liberalized trade increases workers' relative bargaining power. But competition from imports also reduces domestic union bargaining power by offering consumers products and services produced abroad and by providing employers with the opportunity to outsource certain tasks to other countries when domestic labor costs per unit of output exceed the costs of producing elsewhere. (When high union wages are supported by high productivity, the outsourcing motive disappears.) Lower sales may lead employers to resist the formation of unions more strongly and to alter collective bargaining arrangements that are believed to produce higher labor costs. For example, foreign competition reduces the willingness of employers to remain in industry-wide bargaining arrangements that may be unresponsive to the competitive needs of individual companies. In short, the net effect of trade on bargaining power varies from one situation to another. The question of how trade influences freedom of association rights must be settled empirically.

Forced Labor

With one ironic exception, most of the varieties of forced labor discussed in chapter 2 do not appear to be tied to trends in globalization. The important exception is trafficking in human beings. The irony is that much trafficking occurs to *circumvent immigration restrictions* in advanced countries, an issue discussed further in chapter 5. Barriers to globalization, not globalization itself, have produced one of the worst instances of forced labor. Though free trade has no apparent direct effect on forced labor, it can have an indirect effect to the extent that trade raises per capita income. We have seen in chapter 3 that countries with more per capita income have less forced labor. To judge the importance of the indirect effect of free trade on working conditions and labor rights, we now turn to the question of whether free trade raises per capita income.

Impact of Trade on Growth

Economic growth permits countries to buy more of everything, including superior labor conditions. Whether free trade raises or lowers economic growth therefore means a lot for the evolution of labor conditions in a country. If free trade raises per capita GDP by increasing economies of scale or producing the mutual gains promised by comparative advantage theory, open trade policies should improve average labor conditions at both ends of a trading relationship. The "new growth theory" stresses that free trade will also improve growth and labor conditions if more open countries are better able to acquire and use technology produced in industrialized countries. To degrade average labor conditions, open trade policies must diminish a country's output and income. Which scenario fits the facts?

Determining whether free trade retards or stimulates a country's economic growth requires analytical care. Correlations between growth and measures of a country's openness to international competition indicate that open countries grow more rapidly. These correlations encourage the interpretation that openness to international competition raises a country's output and income and improves labor conditions. After all, the case for free trade rests on increasing national productivity by raising the efficiency with which a country's resources are used. But wealthier countries are more likely to adopt open trade policies, a scenario in which openness influences neither growth nor labor conditions. The correlations support two interpretations of causality. Understanding links between trade, growth, and labor conditions requires sorting out the causality.

Even if causality runs from openness to growth, it may be difficult to determine the exact contribution of open policies. Countries with open trade policies also have other policies or institutions that improve growth. Countries with high growth rates tend to have well-established institutions that promote economic exchange: superior protection of property rights, less corruption, and greater political stability. Convincing analyses of the links between openness to international competition and growth must also disentangle the effects of free trade from institutional quality.

Does Openness Stimulate Growth?

After considering these methodological issues, a careful review of the large literature on openness and growth concludes:

> The cross-country variation in the level of GDP per capita and total factor productivity depends on openness, even when openness . . . is instrumented with plausibly exogenous variables. . . . Another conclusion is that openness is often highly correlated with institutional quality, . . . defined broadly in terms of the importance of rule of law, the effectiveness of the government, and so on. (Berg and Krueger 2003, p. 20)

Studies of the relationship between openness and growth over time are most likely to disentangle the effects of openness from institutional quality and geography, because although the latter factors vary widely among countries, they change slowly or rarely in a particular country. These factors are unlikely to pollute statistical estimates of free trade policies in panel studies of changes over time. Moreover, causality issues can be addressed by lagging the openness variable. The same review concludes: "The basic result is that changes in trade volumes are highly correlated with changes in growth with a point estimate suggesting that an increase in the trade share of GDP from 20 to 40 percent over the decade would raise real GDP per capita by 10 percent" (p. 25). Econometric and case study evidence supports two conclusions. First, although "opening to trade does not guarantee faster growth," the authors note "one striking conclusion from the last 20 years of experience": "there are no examples of recent take-off countries that have not opened to an important extent as part of the reform process" (p. 26). Second, there is no systematic relation between openness and the income of the poorest people beyond the effect of openness on growth. A more recent empirical study, which addresses many of the criticisms lodged against cross-section analyses of the connection between openness and growth, also concludes that "trade-centered reforms do have significant effects on economic growth" (Wacziarg and Welch 2003, p. 28).[2]

In short, a professional consensus that open trade policies on average raise per capita income has emerged from a cottage industry of empirical research on links between trade and growth. The data confirm the central prediction of international trade theories reviewed earlier in this chapter. Given the evidence presented in chapter 3, this "income effect" of trade improves virtually all working conditions and labor rights. The remaining question raised by globalization skeptics is whether trade also has countervailing effects that not only diminish labor conditions but also diminish them enough to overwhelm the income effect.

Labor Conditions in the Export Sector

Does the growth associated with trade liberalization improve or degrade labor conditions relative to growth from domestic sources? Answering this question requires consideration of how export and import growth influence domestic labor conditions. Reducing trade barriers should increase imports of goods and services that are produced more efficiently abroad and increase exports of goods and services that are produced more efficiently at home. We have reviewed how a shift of labor from low-productivity, import-competing domestic industries to high-productivity export industries should improve wages and working conditions. The question of how trade expansion alters conditions *within* the export and import-competing sectors requires more investigation, however.

The claim that free trade degrades labor conditions is hardest to understand when open trade policies increase foreign demand for a country's exports and for the services of workers to produce those exports. What then happens to wages and other working conditions depends entirely on labor supply conditions, which themselves are determined by the labor market alternatives available to workers. Much the same may be said of the additional demand for labor from foreign direct investment in a country.

For economies with substantial unemployment or underemployment, the availability of new jobs in the export sector will be enough to attract additional workers. Improvements in working conditions will not be necessary. Such "perfectly elastic" supply conditions in which companies can hire as many workers as they wish at the existing wage are likely to be the norm in countries with huge reserves of underemployed rural agricultural labor or very high urban unemployment rates.[3] Increased export demand is unlikely to improve working conditions in such countries until the reserves of labor are employed. But the additional job opportunities provided by increased export demand will raise total wage income and should not degrade further the working conditions established in the face of significant unemployment. In many countries the floor under working conditions may be a "social minimum" set by public policies.

For economies that are approximately fully employed, firms that produce exports will have to meet increased export demand by attracting workers away from other jobs. To do so, export firms will have to offer wages and working conditions that are superior to what workers already earn in agriculture, in the informal sector, or at other companies in the formal sector. Employers in the latter sectors may raise wages and improve other working conditions in an effort to retain workers in the face of job offers from export firms. Either way, working conditions will improve.

No country illustrates these mechanisms as clearly as modern China, a country long regarded as a bastion of cheap labor. By 2005, a *New York Times* report would note that China, "which has powered its stunning economic rise with a cheap and supposedly bottomless pool of migrant labor, is experiencing shortages of about two million workers in Guangdong and Fujian, the two provinces at the heart of China's export-driven economy." By 2004, two decades of strict family planning policies that limited families to one child was showing up as reduced labor flows from rural to urban manufacturing areas. At the same time, export demand for Chinese products continued to grow. As a result, "young migrant workers coveted by factories are gaining bargaining power and many are choosing to leave the low pay and often miserable conditions in Guangdong. In nondemocratic China, it is the equivalent of 'voting with their feet.' " The stronger labor market conditions serve two functions. Working conditions improve for Chinese workers who now have more job vacancies to choose from and can leave employers offering inferior conditions. Such employers must improve wages and other working conditions in order to recruit workers. In addition, some of the benefits of a tighter Chinese labor market spread to other low-wage countries, such as Vietnam, Cambodia, and India as some companies try to escape higher labor costs in China. Some Chinese manufacturers "could face a fate familiar to many manufacturers in the United States—they would have to move to a country with cheaper workers." The additional demand raises employment and eventually wages in other low-wage countries (Yardley and Barboza 2005).

Conceptually, export producers could force wages down in only two cases. The first seems rather special and unlikely: increased export production would force pay down if it increased monopsony power—that is, if it reduced workers' choice of employers by increasing employer concentration. But it is hard to see how increased export production would increase employer concentration. In countries with elastic labor supply, the social minimum or work in agriculture or informal sectors limit monopsony power. More important, the Internet enables workers in even the poorest countries to stay more informed about employment alternatives than ever before. Workers who might have known only of local employment options in the past can now easily compare their current job conditions to job opportunities available in other cities and regions. The second case is more plausible: some governments may suspend labor regulations and union organizing rights for export producers or in export processing zones (EPZs). Other countries may not enforce labor regulations that apply to exporters. Some examples of such government actions are quite visible (Harvard Business School 1999, 2000). Whether these actions are the norm in the EPZs will be discussed below. For now, we note that EPZs typically account for a small fraction of national employment, and the ability of exporters to profit from lax rules depends on working conditions available outside EPZs.

Globalization skeptics assume that would-be exporters respond to competitive pressures by cutting labor costs—a response that degrades labor conditions. As we have seen, however, labor supply limits what exporters can do, and supply is determined by the alternatives available to workers. Conditions in export firms may not be attractive from the perspective of industrialized countries, but they are unlikely to be worse than conditions elsewhere in the country. The cure is to provide workers with more, not fewer, alternatives.

Comparisons of wages in export and nonexport firms now exist for both developing countries (Chile, Colombia, Estonia, Korea, Mexico, Taiwan, and sub-Saharan Africa) and some industrialized countries (Germany, Spain, Sweden, and the United States). These studies invariably find that exporters pay higher wages than nonexporters. Moreover, the "export wage premia" are considerably *larger* in less developed countries than in industrialized countries. At one extreme, a study of more than 4,000 manufacturing plants in one German region finds an export wage premium of about 2.6 percent, largely reflecting a premium for white-collar workers (Bernard and Wagner 1997). These are the smallest margins found in any of the early studies. Studies of U.S. manufacturing plants find somewhat higher wage premiums, generally in the mid-single digits. Both production and nonproduction workers receive higher wages from exporters (Bernard and Jensen 1995, 1999, 2001). For the European Union, the average wage in export sectors is 109 percent of the average wage in manufacturing (OECD 1999b).

The export wage premiums in most developing countries seem very large in contrast. Studies of manufacturing plants report export wage premiums of 10–12 percent in Korea, 7–9 percent in Mexico, 15–17 percent in

Taiwan and as high as 40 percent in sub-Saharan Africa (Hahn 2004; Zhou 2003; Aw and Batra 1999; Tsou, Liu and Hammit 2002; van Biesebroeck 2003). The facts simply do not support claims that international competition leads exporters to reduce wages below national norms. Particularly for the poorest countries, the opposite is the case.

Yet profit-seeking exporters are unlikely to pay higher wages out of the goodness of their souls. For producers facing stiff international competition, higher productivity must support the wage premiums. Note that the fact that exporters pay higher wages and are more productive than nonexporters is a key implication of the main theories of international trade. Following this thought, one may question whether export wage premiums exist at all for a given skill of worker. Most of the estimates reported above control for differences in some characteristics of firms (such as size and industry) that might influence wages, but data limitations usually preclude controls for worker skills. As a result, the possibility remains that exporters pay more because they hire workers with more education, training, and experience than the employees of nonexporting firms. If worker characteristics *fully* explain the export wage premium, workers of a given skill level would not receive a higher wage from exporters (nor would they receive a lower wage).

The one study to date that was able to include controls for worker characteristics in fact finds that the export premium in German manufacturing firms disappears (Schank, Schnabel, and Wagner 2004). As it happens, Germany had the smallest export wage premium (2.6 percent) of all the countries noted above before adjusting for worker characteristics. Though the effect of adjusting for workforce characteristics cannot be known until studies of other countries are done, two points seem salient. First, it seems unlikely that the very large export premiums found in less developed countries—particularly in the poorest—reflect only differences in the education, training, and experience of the labor force; differences in capital, technology, incentives, and organization design are more likely explanations. Second, even if it turned out that export wage premiums largely reflected the tendency of exporters to use more skilled workers than nonexporters, there is still no evidence that free trade produces a degradation of wages in the export sector. Exporters face either an upward sloping or perfectly elastic supply of labor. In countries at all levels of development, workers have alternatives that prevent exporters from imposing inferior working conditions on them. Since all workers can in principle offer their services to export firms, the existence of an export sector should prevent (further) degradation of working conditions in the nonexport sector.

The finding that exporters are relatively productive does not explain whether only a country's most productive firms choose to enter export markets—part of the natural selection that occurs with free trade—or whether firms that choose to export become more productive from competing in international markets. To the extent that exporters respond to international competition by increasing internal efficiency or learn new production and marketing techniques or organizational tools from interacting with foreign customers and responding to their business needs, exporting may transmit new knowledge that raises productivity. There is evidence that company performance benefits from global exposure. A study of several thousand British enterprises between 1994 and 2000 finds that "globally engaged" firms have relatively high productivity. (In this study, globally engaged firms include both exporters and multinational companies.) These firms employ more research and development personnel, generate more patents, and develop more process and product innovations than firms oriented toward domestic markets. The authors of the study conclude that such firms "have access to a larger stock of ideas through sources including their upstream and downstream contacts with suppliers and customers, and, for multinationals, their intra-firm worldwide pool of information" (Criscuolo, Haskel, and Slaughter 2005, p. 33). When there is "learning through exporting," export experience raises a country's average productivity and hence broadens the scope of real compensation improvements. This effect intensifies if there are knowledge spillovers from export to nonexport firms.

If the "selection" mechanism, in which high-productivity firms choose to become exporters, explains the correlation between export status and wages, participation in international markets simply changes some firms from nonexporters to exporters, but has no effect on a country's productivity, wages, and working conditions. Notice, however, that neither the empirical finding that exporters are more productive nor the competing interpretations of this finding support the view that expanding exports worsen labor conditions.

Panel studies of firms that shift from nonexport to export status produce mixed results regarding the relative importance of the two interpretations. Some studies find that virtually all of the correlation is explained by the fact that high-productivity firms tend to become exporters, as predicted by the theory of comparative advantage (Clerides, Lach, and Tybout 1998). Other studies find that both selection and learning-by-exporting effects are present in the productivity data (van Biesebroeck 2003). In both cases, the effects emerge from studies of manufacturing firms in relatively undeveloped countries (Columbia, Mexico, Morocco, and several countries in sub-Saharan Africa). None of the studies finds evidence that export participation lowers wages, and some find evidence of a significant positive influence on wages. One interesting finding of the studies is that exporters whose costs increase drop out of export markets and revert to nonexport production. That is, international markets discipline upward wage pressures unless they are supported by productivity increases. Conversely, the productivity gains associated with employment shifts to high-productivity sectors and subsequent "learning-by-exporting," where it occurs, provide the scope for real compensation increases that would not have been possible without participation in global markets.

Whether improvements in labor conditions are limited to changes in industrial composition resulting from trade liberalization is difficult to ascertain. Further improvements within any sector would rest on economies of scale from export activities and productivity spillovers from export industries to the rest of the economy. Absent an infinitely elastic supply of labor, improved wages and working conditions will spill over to the nontradable sector as it competes to retain labor and other resources attracted to the export sector.

Labor Conditions in Export Processing Zones

Export processing zones, an important element of export-led growth strategies in many countries, are also a frequent source of concern regarding the effects of globalization on the condition of labor. These are simply industrial zones with special incentives set up to attract foreign investors with complex global supply chains. Foreign investors import materials (duty-free) into the zone, where the materials undergo processing before being reexported (duty-free). Host countries provide infrastructure, cheap labor (relative to foreign investors' home country labor markets), tax holidays, and market access. Some countries also relax national labor regulations within EPZs. Although EPZs have existed for centuries, they have boomed since the 1970s. By 2002, some 5,000 EPZs, located in 116 (mainly developing) countries, employed about 42 million workers. China alone accounted for about 30 million of these workers (table 4.1). Host countries apparently hope that the costs of establishing and maintaining an EPZ pays off through job creation and spillovers of skills and technology to domestic markets.

An evaluation of free trade's effects on labor cannot ignore the quality of working conditions and labor rights in EPZs. The central question is whether EPZs offer labor conditions that are better than what workers can expect in alternative jobs outside the EPZ. According to the International Labor Organization (ILO), the United Nations agency charged with improving labor conditions around the world, EPZs provide much of the formal employment in zone-operating countries, offer more modern and substantial infrastructure than is found outside the zone, and, contrary to many jobs in developing countries, frequently provide labor contracts and/or social benefits. Moreover, "zones have created an important avenue for young women to enter the formal economy of better wages than in agriculture and domestic service. Women make up the majority of workers in the vast majority of zones" (ILO 2003a).

Take-home pay in the zones often exceeds minimum wages and pay in comparable firms outside the zone. Even with very elastic labor supplies, Adam Smith's proposition that wages must compensate for undesirable non-wage working conditions applies: when zone employment acquires a poor reputation, zone employers must pay a premium to induce workers to work

Table 4.1
Employment in Export Processing Zones, 2002

Region	Number of zones	Employment in zones (000s)
Asia	749	36,824
Central America and Mexico	3,300	2,242
Middle East	37	691
North Africa	23	441
Sub-Saharan Africa	64	431
North America	713	330
South America	39	311
Transition economies	90	246
Caribbean	87	226
Europe	55	51
Other	17	141
TOTAL	5,174	41,934

Source: ILO data and estimates reported at http://www-ilo-mirror.cornell.edu/public/english/dialogue/sector/themes/epz/stats.htm.

for them. Moreover, zone enterprises are often large multinationals, which offer higher compensation than local employers (see chapter 6). Finally, zone enterprises often use individual incentive pay systems. These systems attract workers with high rates of output who earn higher pay than workers on time rates (ILO 1999, 2003a).

On the other hand, the ILO reports that:

> there tends to be a very high turnover of zone workers, with the average career of a worker seldom longer than five years. The intensive nature of production, cultural factors, use of fixed-term contracts, a lack of human resource development policies and under-developed labor relations practices in some zone enterprises contribute to the turnover. ˉ . . . Legal restrictions on trade union rights in a few EPZ-operating countries, the lack of enforcement of labor legislation and the absence of workers' organizations representation were among the factors noted as undermining the ability of zones to upgrade skills, improve working conditions, and [raise] productivity. (2003a, p. 7)

In summary, the ILO evaluation presents a mixed picture of employment in EPZs. The zones attract workers by offering more employment opportunities and higher pay than workers find in jobs outside the EPZs. But other working conditions and labor rights can be weaker, raising labor turnover and encouraging relatively short careers in the zones.

The Overall Impact of Free Trade on Labor Conditions

Discussions of globalization and labor conditions produce two conflicting predictions on how greater openness will influence working conditions and labor rights. Prevailing economic theories of the effects of international trade predict that freer trade will improve working conditions and some labor rights in the long run. These same theories also identify short-run gainers and losers from liberalized trade in both rich and poor countries. In contrast, those who view globalization as the stimulus for a race to the bottom in labor conditions expect global competition to degrade labor conditions. In this section we appeal to data from a large sample of countries at various stages of development for a resolution of the conflict over how a country's openness to international trade influences its labor conditions.

The econometric analyses reported in the appendix to this chapter discriminate between these contending hypotheses. The analyses build on the relationship between labor conditions and the level of development (real per capita income) and national economic, political, and social institutions analyzed in chapter 3 by adding measures of a country's openness to international trade. The central question is whether openness has anything to add to—or subtract from—working conditions given a country's level of development and institutions. As in previous chapters, openness is measured in two ways: the importance of trade in national production (exports plus imports divided by GDP) and the multi-hurdle measure of open trade policy first discussed in chapter 2.

If openness influences labor conditions only indirectly, by raising per capita income, the openness measures will not play a significant role in the analysis; the per capita income variable will already capture the indirect effect. If openness has direct effects on labor conditions that are independent of per capita income, however, those effects will show up as statistically significant relationships between the measures of openness and labor conditions. The economic theory of international trade predicts that free trade improves working conditions indirectly, by reallocating workers to jobs where they produce higher per capita income. We have discussed how free trade might also have direct positive effects on some labor rights. In contrast, the race-to-the-bottom hypothesis holds that free trade directly degrades working conditions and labor rights.

The econometric analysis addresses questions of causality and potential biases raised by the analyses. We are mainly interested in the effect of liberalized trade on labor conditions, since free trade may raise the demand for labor and improve labor conditions. As the race-to-the-bottom hypothesis reminds us, however, low wages and poor working conditions may stimulate trade. Does trade influence labor conditions, or do labor conditions influence the volume of trade and a country's willingness to sign trade agreements? The econometric analysis applies a technique (instrumental variables) that was designed to help sort out such issues of causality. A subtler problem arises when an influence on labor conditions that cannot be observed is correlated with openness. For example, the domestic regulation of labor conditions by labor unions or by national governments may depend on the country's openness to international competition. In a cross-country study, we cannot control for influences that we cannot observe. As discussed in earlier chapters, the analysis of panel data (cross-sections of country data for multiple years) permits the elimination of unobservable country-specific influences. The fixed-effect strategy is to estimate the relationship between openness and labor conditions using only the variation over time within each country—effectively ignoring the cross-country relationship, which may be biased.

The analysis, which is conducted a number of ways to address these questions of causality and potential bias, yields three conclusions. First, there is no reliable statistical evidence that countries with relatively large trade flows or open trade policies have poorer working conditions or inferior labor rights, with the exception of gender discrimination (see below). Nor do countries that adopt more liberalized trade policies subsequently suffer deteriorating labor conditions. Anecdotes implying that trade degrades labor conditions may be true, but they are not typical. Second, free trade improves working conditions—pay, hours of work, and job safety—mainly by raising per capita income, as predicted by theories of international trade. Once this indirect effect is captured, openness has no statistically significant relationship with pay or any of the measures of work hours. The analysis does reveal a direct relationship between open trade policies and job safety, however. Lower fatal accident rates and longer life expectancy are found in countries that have or change to free trade policies.

In contrast, free trade has direct effects on most labor rights. Countries with open international trade policies have superior labor rights. The evidence for trade volumes is more mixed, but where there is a significant relationship between the share of trade in GDP and a labor right, higher trade volumes are associated with greater rights. To summarize, the analyses find no evidence consistent with the hypothesis that openness to international trade is a recipe for inferior working conditions and labor rights; openness indirectly improves working conditions by setting in motion forces that raise per capita income; openness both directly and indirectly improves most labor rights. In the rest of this section, these results are compared with findings from microdata analyses and case studies.

Child Labor

At a given level of development and institutional structure, countries that embrace free trade have less child labor than countries that do not. Over time, the adoption of free trade policies is associated with declines in child labor in a country. This evidence (reported more fully in the appendix to this chapter) undermines the hypothesis that trade may move children from school to work. Either trade does not reduce the return to schooling or does not reduce it by enough to influence the work-school choices that children and their families face. This finding no doubt rests on the fact that most adults in poor countries are unskilled. As trade raises unskilled relative wages in these countries, it raises the incomes of unskilled parents, permitting them to "afford" more schooling (less work) for their children. (As we have seen, most children work in agriculture or informal employment rather than the export sector. Widely disseminated images of children stitching soccer balls in Pakistan or making carpets in Nepal do not describe the typical work of children in less developed countries.)

The policy implication of these findings is powerful: using trade sanctions to induce countries to reduce child labor is counterproductive. Free trade reduces child labor; restrictions on trade will increase it by reducing the income that permits families to move their children from work to school. (We will return to this theme in chapter 7 in the discussion of using trade sanctions more generally to enforce labor standards.)

Policies that expand rather than reduce the choices available to families provide a more effective approach to reducing child labor. At least two types of policies expand families' options in ways that reduce child labor—particularly in the poorest countries. One approach relaxes the credit constraints that prevent families in some countries from borrowing to meet their needs in the face of unanticipated income variability. Without effective credit markets, parents in many poorer countries may put their children to work during periods of low income. If they could instead borrow against future income, there would be less child labor. Studies of labor markets in Peru and Tanzania, for example, find a strong link between child labor and income volatility. Families respond to unexpected income losses—crop failures from fire or insect swarms, for example—in part by increasing the amount of work done by their children. Fluctuations in school attendance constitute a form of self-insurance against income volatility. This response is mitigated, however, in families with assets that they can use as collateral in borrowing money to offset income loss (Beegle, Dehejia, and Gatti 2003; Jacoby 1994). Child labor is also negatively related to broader measures of credit, such as the ratio of private credit issue by deposit-money banks to GDP. This measure is negatively correlated with credit constraints and with child labor. The correlation is "several orders of magnitude higher in poor countries than in rich countries" (Dehejia and Gatti 2002, p. 12).

A second productive policy approach subsidizes families who keep their children in school, effectively replacing some of the resources that a child might have earned at work with cash or in-kind subsidy payments contingent on regular school attendance. The Bangladesh Food for Education Program, the Pakistan School Nutrition Program, and similar programs in other developing countries provide food (usually rice) to families for each child who enrolls and attends primary school for 85 percent of the school days each month. The family may consume or sell the food. Other countries provide cash subsidies for school enrollment. Since 1995, for example, the Bolsa Escola program in Brazil has paid a monthly cash grant approximately equal to the minimum wage to families below the poverty line if their children meet a 90 percent attendance requirement. Mexico's Progresa/Oportunidades program has a similar structure, although the payments, which are given directly to the mother, increase with the age of the child, reflecting the increasing probability of employment with age.

Evaluations of these programs confirm that they can dramatically raise school enrollment and attendance and reduce dropout rates. There is some evidence that parents move their children into school even in response to subsidies that replace less than half of their children's earnings (Ravallon and Wodon 1999). The programs also reduce child labor, but not on an hour-for-hour basis. Some children continue working part time while attending school. Some of the additional schooling time comes from nonwork activities in the home. One cannot rule out the possibility that some nonwork activities build human capital, but on balance the programs produce an environment in which children acquire more schooling and enter the labor force with a permanently higher earning capacity.

Targeted enrollment subsidies reduce the opportunity costs faced by impoverished families of placing children in school rather than in a job. Contrary to trade sanctions, they expand the opportunities available to children by lowering a key cost of attending school. National governments can also take many measures to reduce the direct costs and raise the benefits of attending school in countries with significant child labor. Investments in infrastructure that reduce distances that children must travel to school, increased teaching training, and reduced pupil-teacher ratios all raise the attractiveness of school relative to work, although they do not by themselves address the opportunity cost issue.

Discrimination

Both the ordinary least squares and instrumental variables estimates find significantly larger male-female wage differences in countries with open trade policies, after controlling for the effects of per capita income and institutions. (As with child labor, there is no significant relationship with trade volumes.) The finding is not consistent with the prediction of discrimination theory that increasing numbers of employers will reduce labor market discrimination. This is also a labor condition for which there is no indirect effect of trade, for it was the only labor condition that was not influenced by per capita income (chapter 3). With only one observation on the gender wage gap for each country, it is not possible to explore this issue further by studying how gender wage differences change as countries change from closed to open trade policies.

The few disaggregated studies of the effects of trade on employment discrimination produce mixed results and do not help interpret the association of larger gender wage gaps with openness. A study of the relationship between imports and the female-to-male wage ratio in the manufacturing sector of the United States finds evidence that international trade reduces the ability of firms to discriminate against women (Black and Brainerd 2004). Economic theory predicts that discrimination is likely to be greatest in concentrated industries where product market competition is weakest. Increased competition from international trade should increase competition and alter gender wage differences most in concentrated industries. Consistent with this prediction, female relative wages increased most rapidly in concentrated U.S. manufacturing industries as imports increased between 1976 and 1993. Yet, a study of Taiwan and South Korea finds that free trade actually increases wage discrimination against women (Berik, Rodgers, and Zveglich 2003). Understanding of how globalization influences discriminatory practices against women and other labor force minorities remains limited and clearly merits more research attention.

Freedom of Association

Countries with more open trade policies have superior civil liberties, and according to the fixed-effects evidence, which reflects changes over time within countries, civil liberties improve more rapidly in countries that adopt open trade policies. The mechanisms behind these results are not well understood. It may be that exposure to greater economic choice and a greater range of ideas raises the demand for greater political choice. The results imply that lowering trade barriers to repressive regimes is less a reward for bad behavior than a stimulus for political change. Beyond the dollar and cents value of trade are its effects on systemic changes in institutions and political systems. The use of trade sanctions against countries with poor civil liberties records may be counterproductive.

The Freedom House index of civil liberties captures the broad availability of freedom of association rights in a society. At the workplace, the right to form and join or refrain from joining unions is a key application of freedom of association rights. In addition to their workplace activities, labor unions can be a force for increased national political freedom. As one international review of unions noted, "unions in Zimbabwe, Namibia, South Africa, Botswana and Niger, to name the most prominent examples, were in the forefront of the struggle for democracy [in those countries]" (Visser 2003, p. 391). Similar comments could be made about the role of unions in accelerating political transitions in some former Soviet bloc countries. Unions also negotiate benefits for their members, and in this role they can be a source of upward cost pressures on employers. These considerations influence the extent to which workers *choose* to form and remain in labor unions, in an effort to obtain collectively what they cannot obtain individually. They also influence the extent to which employers and/or governments may chose to resist union organization and collective bargaining.

Union membership as a percent of employment (the union density rate) plainly declined in most industrialized countries and many developing countries in the last decades of the twentieth century. The density rate for all of Europe fell from 1978 (Visser 2003, p. 404). For countries with plant- or company-level representation through works councils, union membership data may understate the diminished collective representation of workers. Between 1981 and 1994, for example, the share of employees in plants with works councils in total employment fell from 50.6 to 39.5 percent in Germany, leading one scholar to conclude that "the decline in works council coverage has been more profound than the erosion of collective bargaining" (Hassel, 1999, p. 487). Visser (2003) discusses the variety of economic, social and political factors influencing changes in unionization in many developing countries.

Though local factors may alter the experience in individual countries, the very broad decline in union representation in private industry raises the stature of explanations that are common to many countries. For industrialized countries, the postwar expansion of international trade is an obvious candidate. Increased foreign competition stimulated employer opposition to unions, particularly in countries with decentralized bargaining arrangements, such as the United States. But globalization is not the only candidate. Economic growth produces common changes in the industrial structure of employment, for example. Diverging employment trends in union and non-union firms have produced a "natural attrition" of union membership that has not been countered by new organization in most countries. In some countries, a declining interest of workers in unions inhibits new organization. Workers increasingly see other institutions as the source of improvements in working conditions. In particular, the growing responsibility of states for many benefits once found only in union contracts makes it difficult for unions to differentiate their product from nonunion workplaces. Finally, expanding international trade has not been the only source of increased competitive pressure. The deregulation of domestic industries in several countries has reduced or eliminated regulatory barriers to entry that previously produced rents available for capture by unions.

Unionization data from around the world do not reveal an obvious connection between free trade policies and union representation. The figures in table 4.2 compare union density rates for 1985 and for the late 1990s for open and closed economies (according to the Sachs–Warner criteria). When each country is weighted equally, open and closed countries have essentially identical unionization rates in 1985, but rates decline more rapidly in closed economies over the next 10–15 years.[4] When each country is weighted by the size of its labor force, however, unionization is distinctly higher in closed economies. But the weighted estimates also show that unionization rates declined substantially in closed economies at the end of the twentieth century, while remaining virtually unchanged in open economies. Overall, union density rates converged during this period, but the convergence is more

Table 4.2
Union Density Rates, Open and Closed Economies

	Unweighted		Weighted*	
	Open	Closed	Open	Closed
Union density, 1985	31.7	29.3	20.6	48.8
Union density, late 1990s	29.1	22.6	19.0	34.5
Change in union density	−2.6	−6.7	−1.6	−14.3

* Labor force weights

Source: Visser 2003

precisely determined in the weighted than the unweighted data. More generally, globalization has surely constrained some unions, but it does not appear to be the primary force behind declining union representation around the world in the late twentieth century. In short, even after holding the effects of a country's level of development and institutional structure constant, openness to international trade is associated with superior civil liberties. Moreover, while free trade may reduce the bargaining power of some labor unions, there is no convincing evidence that it accounts for much of the worldwide decline in unionization in the late twentieth century.

Forced Labor

Forced labor continues to be measured in two ways: Bales's estimates of the number of slaves in each country at the end of the twentieth century and the number of the top four varieties of forced labor present in each country at that time. In simple comparisons, countries with large trade shares have fewer slaves and fewer varieties of forced labor, as we saw in chapter 2. After holding the effects of growth and institutions constant, however, there is no reliable difference between open and closed economies in the estimated number of slaves, although open economies have significantly fewer varieties of forced labor. Evidence that countries with higher trade volumes or open trade policies have less slavery, ceteris paribus, does not survive instrumental variables estimation. That is, open economies appear to have neither more nor less forced labor than closed economies after controlling for level of development, institutional structure, and for the possibility of reverse causation.

Taken as a whole, the evidence indicates that greater participation in international trade or the adoption of more open trade policies improves most working conditions and labor rights. Countries that adopt open trade policies have higher wages, greater workplace safety, more civil liberties (including workplace freedom of association), and less child labor. Only in the case of gender wage discrimination is there an indication of a possible adverse effect from free trade policies, and openness appears to have a neutral effect on measures of forced labor. The conclusions about these labor conditions rest on cross-section evidence only. Unfortunately, data that permit analysis of changes within countries over time do not yet list these labor rights. The country-level econometric evidence presented here is consistent with findings in microdata case studies of individual countries. These findings strongly caution against the use of trade sanctions to induce superior labor conditions. Such sanctions thwart their own objectives and may worsen conditions in the countries imposing them as well.

A Race to the Bottom in Labor Conditions?

The evidence that countries with open trade policies generally have superior working conditions and labor rights would seem to undercut the hypothesis that countries degrade labor conditions to improve export performance. But this hypothesis merits a direct appraisal, particularly in view of evidence that countries sometimes suspend or limit labor regulations in EPZs. The hypothesis begins with the assumption that superior labor conditions are costly, placing countries with superior conditions at a competitive disadvantage in international markets.[5] From here it is a short step to make two arguments: (1) companies degrade working conditions in order to increase their exports, and (2) national governments deny labor rights and provide little political support for superior labor standards both to expand exports and to attract foreign direct investment.

The race-to-the-bottom hypothesis fails at its first step—the assumption that superior labor conditions are costly in a way that interferes with export sales. The previous chapter reported and demonstrated how higher wages are supported by higher productivity. Poor labor conditions also signal low labor productivity, and low productivity raises unit labor costs, making exports more difficult to sell. Even before looking at evidence on the relationship between labor conditions and export performance, this aspect of the race-to-the-bottom hypothesis seems dubious.

Looking across countries, the ratio of exports to GDP ranged from 1.4 percent (Bangladesh) to 66 percent (Belgium) across a sample of about 80 countries in 1980–84. Many factors other than labor conditions may influence a country's export performance, including its sources of comparative advantage, the costs of conducting trade, and the relative price of its exports. One must also control for these "baseline" influences when testing for the role of labor conditions. An analysis for 1980–84 finds that the baseline variables discussed above account for 63 percent of the international variance in export performance among the 80 sample countries and generally have the expected signs. High relative export prices and larger distances from major markets reduce the export share of GDP, while labor intensity and human capital investments raise exports. Contrary to the view that countries with large reserves of unskilled labor gain competitive advantage in international markets, export shares are *larger* in countries with *high* educational attainment by the population (Flanagan 2003).

But do poor labor conditions improve a country's export performance, ceteris paribus? Adding measures of working conditions and labor rights to the baseline empirical model of how export performance varies among countries produces a surprisingly simple conclusion: labor conditions in a country are not significantly correlated with the country's share of exports in GDP. Contrary to globalization skeptics' expectations, countries with more child labor, fewer civil liberties, and shorter life expectancy do not have superior export performance. Indeed, labor conditions appear to be statistically unrelated to exports. We have seen that international real labor cost differentials mainly reflect international productivity differences. Nevertheless, country-specific factors can raise or lower labor costs relative to productivity, raising the question of whether countries with low (high) wages relative to productivity experience superior (inferior) export performance. The final analysis of export performance addresses this question by substituting a variable for actual minus predicted labor costs in manufacturing for the measures of ratifications and other labor conditions discussed earlier. (A country's labor cost per employee is predicted on the basis of its labor productivity and price level.) This variable is marginally significant, but the sign is the *opposite* of the race-to-the-bottom hypothesis (Flanagan 2003). Countries in which labor costs per worker are high relative to labor productivity and prices have a higher share of GDP in exports. In summary, the cross-country analyses offer no support for the view that countries with poor labor conditions enjoy superior export performance. Instead, the factors determining comparative advantage and the costs of conducting trade influence export patterns.

Trade Sanctions or Adjustment Policies?

The evidence that free trade advances working conditions and most labor rights around the world undermines proposals that international organizations apply trade sanctions to induce countries to improve labor conditions. If the objective is to improve working conditions and labor rights, trade sanctions are illogical. Raising barriers to free trade between countries thwarts an effective mechanism for improving poor working conditions and for reducing the inequality of real wages and most other working conditions around the world. We return to this theme in the discussion of labor standards in chapter 7.

Beneath the generally positive average effect of trade on labor conditions are patterns of gainers and losers in each country, the identity of which varies from country to country. Concern over such distributional consequences is the source of much of the tension over open trade policies. Moreover, the benefits of trade are often more dispersed across a population than are its losses. Individual losers then have a more powerful incentive to organize to resist change than beneficiaries have to support it. There is a real risk in most countries that the concerns of losers may thwart the much larger benefits to a country from open trade policies. Since the earliest efforts at globalization, the underlying distributional conflict has produced a fundamental policy challenge to find productive, socially acceptable ways to compensate losers with society's net gains from the structural changes that accompany economic transitions.

Traditional economic thinking stresses that open trade policies are but one source of structural change in a country's output and employment. Changing consumer tastes, varying income elasticities of demand, technical change, and other factors all produce patterns of industrial change that force layoffs in some industries and new hiring in others. As a practical matter, it is generally impossible to decompose observed structural change into its "causes" with any reasonable precision. In a normative sense, it is unclear why one source of economic change merits higher status than others. The needs of an unemployed worker do not rest on whether trade or technical change accounted for a layoff. Cushioning the effects of one type of economic change in principle deserves no more priority than others.

Most countries have a traditional approach to providing monetary support for worker transitions to new jobs—unemployment insurance. Under unemployment insurance programs, workers receive benefits (usually a fraction of their most recent wage) for a time period that is specified in the law. The exact provisions of unemployment insurance programs vary substantially across countries, providing an opportunity to determine whether the job-seeking behavior of the unemployed depends on details of a nation's policy. The general conclusion of the many studies of this question is that unemployment insurance systems often retard rather than accelerate worker adjustments to structural change. Policies regarding unemployment insurance present a typical conflict between risk-reduction and incentives, raising significant moral hazard problems: providing support for unanticipated periods of joblessness also reduces the incentive to accept a new job rapidly. Many studies show that the duration of joblessness increases with the fraction of the wage replaced by unemployment insurance and with the duration for which benefits are available. Indeed, there is often a "spike" of job acceptance just before benefits are terminated. In short, the more generous the support offered by a nation's unemployment insurance policy, the higher the country's equilibrium unemployment rate.

Countries have also experimented with nonmonetary approaches to helping workers adjust to change. Scandinavian countries pioneered in the use of government retraining programs that later were emulated by many other countries. The results of this approach has been decidedly mixed. Government agencies can't predict what skills will be demanded in the future; potential employers sometimes interpret participation in a government program as a signal of inferior productivity; and long-run returns to participants in public programs rarely exceed those of nonparticipants. The postwar history of such active labor market policies has inspired titles such as "The Rise and Fall of Labor Market Programs." One review of public job training programs concluded, "Training should be used sparingly," and "policymakers appear to underrate the ability of most workers to acquire substantially more human-capital-enhancing knowledge on the job rather than in the classroom" Jacobson (1998, p. 505). Periods of rapid technical change have also produced private and public experiments with relocation allowances to move workers from areas of declining opportunities to areas of expanding opportunities, but such policies have generally failed with all but the youngest workers who can anticipate the highest present values from such investments.

Policies that enhance rather than retard adjustment to change are clearly needed. Two examples of such policies are reemployment bonuses and "wage insurance." Reemployment bonuses provide lump-sum payments to unemployed job seekers who accept a job a certain time before they exhaust their unemployment insurance benefits. The bonus program is designed to reduce the length of unemployment spells by encouraging more intensive job search behavior, to reduce unemployment insurance expenditures, and reduce employer payroll taxes for unemployment insurance. Four experimental programs conducted in parts of the United States yielded mixed results. The programs generally had the predicted effects, but in some cases the expenditures of the bonus program exceeded the reductions in unemployment insurance payments (O'Leary, Decker, and Wandner 1998). This may be too limited an assessment for programs designed to effect adjustments to policy changes, such as liberalized trade, that produce net benefits for society. Certainly, a full assessment would consider the wages and other aspects of job quality that workers attained under alternative adjustment programs.

Wage insurance policies compensate laid-off workers for a fraction of the wage loss that they incur when they accept a new job. "The fraction [of the wage loss] could vary by age and tenure of the worker. Payments begin only when a worker has a new (full-time) job and could continue for up to two years following the initial job loss, as long as the new job paid less than the old job. Annual payments could be capped" (Kletzer 2004). To provide incentives for rapid job acceptance, policy parameters may be set so that the wage on the new job plus wage insurance replaced a larger fraction of the previous wage than would unemployment insurance benefits. Higher wage insurance replacement rates provide stronger incentives to search for some job but weaker incentives to search for a higher paying job. Wage insurance is likely to be most valuable for workers with company- or industry-specific skills, who have the most to lose from job displacement and who would otherwise remain unemployed longest trying to replace wages that were unique to their prior employment.

Summary and Conclusions

Predictions that free trade will degrade working conditions stand in stark contrast to the predictions of the leading theories of international trade reviewed early in this chapter. Those theories hold that the reallocation of resources to industries in which a nation has a comparative advantage or captures significant economies of scale raises productivity, thereby increasing the scope for improved monetary and/or nonmonetary working conditions. Higher productivity raises economic growth, which we have seen to have a powerful influence in improving working conditions and labor rights. Pro-growth policies improve labor conditions, and open trade policies enhance growth. Through its effect on growth, openness promotes higher pay, lower work hours, and safer working environments. Openness also supplements the role of growth in reducing child labor and in improving freedom of association rights and other civil liberties.

Though most of the effect of open trade policies on working conditions flows from improved per capita income, openness also leads to changes in labor market structure and institutions that can directly improve some labor rights. Countries with open trade policies have superior labor rights, and labor rights improve over time in countries that adopt open trade policies. Looking forward from the period covered by this analysis, great scope remains for improving labor conditions through greater openness. Three of the world's more populous nations—China, India, and Pakistan—were on the diminishing list of countries with closed trade policies in the 1990s. As these countries shift to more open policies, a large fraction of the world's workers could experience improved labor conditions.

The discussion in this chapter clarifies the scope of claims that "trade degrades labor conditions" in surprising ways. Neither theory nor empirical evidence supports the view that trade degrades labor conditions in developing countries. Most less developed countries are net exporters, and more open trade policies typically raise the demand for exports and the labor that produces them. The effect of increased labor demand on compensation (in the broadest sense) then depends on labor supply conditions—the quality of the alternative jobs available to workers. It is difficult to construct any situation that produces declining compensation in this environment, and the evidence instead indicates superior labor conditions in export firms. The view that exporters degrade labor conditions confuses the compensation of labor with the labor cost of output (labor compensation of labor divided by labor productivity). Exporters can reduce the labor cost of output in two ways: improving productivity and/or reducing labor compensation, broadly conceived. The latter approach risks reducing productivity by inducing fatigue, lowering morale, or raising labor turnover. The former approach provides scope for wage increases. Evidence presented in this chapter indicates that rather than degrading labor conditions, exporters seek to raise productivity and often succeed. To be clear, this does not deny the truth of some anecdotes linking specific exporters with poor working conditions, but the linkage does not seem to be true of international labor markets generally.

Open trade policies instead most directly threaten the working conditions of workers in import-competing industries during periods of adjustment to new trade patterns. This concern mainly challenges more industrialized countries, where imports from countries with a comparative advantage in unskilled labor threaten the working conditions of unskilled native workers. If trade threatens working conditions, the threat is strongest for some workers in the richest countries, not the poorest countries. The evidence suggests that trade has a small negative impact on the wages of unskilled workers in industrialized countries. Even as more open trade may be threatening the working conditions of some workers in industrialized countries, it is also benefiting other workers who are employed in the export industries. Indeed, this is the process that ultimately induces labor and other resources to shift to more efficient production. As this process moves forward, labor conditions improve for those who are initially threatened or their children.

Correctly framed, the issue is not whether trade produces a general deterioration of labor conditions. In the short run, trade enhances the working conditions of some workers and threatens the conditions of others. What is the net effect? As noted above, the cross-country and panel analyses reported in this chapter never find that free trade is associated with poorer working conditions. Instead, by raising per capita income, free trade has a net positive effect on working conditions and labor rights, except for gender discrimination, where the effect is neutral. Through other mechanisms, free trade produces further advances in most labor rights.

With no evidence that openness is associated with inferior labor conditions, the claim that companies or countries degrade their labor conditions to improve export performance appears to lack a foundation. Nonetheless, the chapter tests for but does not find significant links between export performance and labor conditions. Again the story is quite simple: The cross-country econometric analysis uncovers no significant connection between the characteristics of a country's working conditions or labor rights and the share of exports in the country's GDP.

As important as the level of development and open trade policies are for labor conditions, they leave much of the international variation in working conditions and rights unexplained. Much room remains for more targeted policies to improve national working conditions. The evidence presented in this chapter warns of counterproductive policies that might tempt the international community. In particular, trade sanctions are likely to (further) worsen labor conditions in developing countries. The analysis of the differential effect of free trade in exporting and importing industries strongly implies that trade sanction proposals are advanced more to protect the conditions of some workers in rich countries than to advance the conditions of workers in poor countries. Policy activity should instead focus on expanding opportunities for workers, for example by encouraging further development of human capital in poor countries and by facilitating adjustment for workers threatened by trade in rich countries.

Free trade is by no means the only mechanism for equalizing working conditions around the world. Historically, a very effective alternative has been international migration, which we consider in the next chapter.

CHAPTER 5

International Migration and Labor Conditions

A most puzzling aspect of modern discussions of globalization and labor conditions is their inattention to the role of international labor markets in altering working conditions. This is puzzling both because international labor markets have historically provided options that enabled workers in poor countries to improve their lot and because modern interferences with this demonstrably effective mechanism for improving adverse labor conditions come from easily identified national public policies. Yet critics concerned that free trade encourages sweatshop working conditions remain virtually silent about the national immigration barriers that prevent many workers from moving to superior jobs in other countries. They are at least consistent in revealing a primary concern with working conditions in rich countries.

The mass transatlantic migrations that were part of the first wave of globalization provide the clearest evidence of the how international labor markets can reduce international inequality in working conditions. This chapter first reviews how mass migration in the late nineteenth and early twentieth centuries narrowed real wage differences between the Old World and the New World. Paradoxically, the consequences of that migration also prompted the development of restrictive national immigration policies that constrain the level and pattern of international migration a century later.

Why thwart a mechanism known to equalize working conditions around the world? The earliest restrictions emerged in major destination countries of migrants and reflected the very different impact of migration on working conditions in sending (origin) and receiving (destination) countries. Subsequent restrictions reflected additional concerns in destination countries, including the social and cultural influence of migrants, the effect of migrants on public budgets, and, most recently, fears about the spread of HIV/AIDS. The second part of the chapter examines the very different setting of international migration in the late twentieth and early twenty-first centuries, exploring how incentives for international migration have changed and how national immigration policies alter these incentives. Sending countries also develop concerns about international migration, and the chapter considers whether international migration harms sending countries by producing a brain drain that limits their growth prospects.

As we saw in the previous chapter, international trade itself may alter labor conditions at both ends of a trading relationship, even if there is no international migration. Restrictive trade barriers have gradually diminished over the past 60 years in the wake of a sequence of international negotiations over tariffs and trade. In a world of freer trade, is migration necessary to improve labor conditions? Can a reduction in trade barriers substitute for reductions in migration barriers? Does trade or migration have a more powerful effect on labor conditions? The final part of the chapter considers the relationship between trade and migration.

Migration during the First Wave of Globalization

The huge changes in the scale of global economic activity between the mid-nineteenth century and the onset of World War I provide attractive opportunities for searching for links between globalization and labor conditions. By the middle of the nineteenth century there were dramatic differences in labor conditions between the land-rich, labor-scarce countries of the New World and the labor-abundant, land-scarce countries of the Old World. Real wages (for urban, unskilled, male workers) in the United States were more than four times those in Sweden, and Australian wages were more than three times those in Ireland. Wages in Canada and in South American countries were also multiples of European wages (Hatton and Williamson 1998). However unpleasant the working conditions faced by immigrants to the New World, they were distinctly superior to the conditions they left behind. The slave trade, the main source of labor for the Americas in the eighteenth century, had ended, although slavery had not. Future increases in the New World labor supply had to come through free migration.

How might international migration alter the dramatic international differences in wages and other working conditions? The migration of workers from countries with poor working conditions to countries with superior conditions influences conditions in both the source and destination countries. Migrants themselves move to access higher wages in destination countries. By diminishing labor supply in the source country, migration also raises the wages of the workers who remain behind. Immigration increases labor supply in destination countries, however, reducing or slowing the growth of wages of native workers with similar skills. Migration also affects returns to capital, land, and other inputs that complement immigrants. As migrants flow into destination countries, capital, land, and skill become relatively scarce, and their value in the productive process increases. Immigration raises returns to the owners of land and capital and possibly skill in destination countries. Of course, emigration has the opposite effect on the owners of these "complementary" inputs in source countries. As labor leaves the country, capital and land become abundant relative to labor, and their return falls. These diverse economic effects inform the political divisiveness of immigration.

International migration also may affect labor rights. Labor unions, a labor market expression of freedom of association, have historically gained members and achieved more gains in strong labor markets and lost ground in weak labor markets. By reducing labor supply relative to demand, emigration should tend to strengthen unions in sending countries. Conversely, substantial immigrant flows, particularly of unskilled workers, tend to undermine the ability of unions in receiving countries to maintain a floor under wages and other working conditions. Indeed, during the mass transatlantic migrations of the late nineteenth century, only unions of skilled craft workers survived in the United States, in large measure because they were able to limit the supply of particular skills by controlling admission to apprenticeship programs. Unions of unskilled workers wilted in the face of mass immigration and recessions.

Patterns of discrimination against labor market minorities have also proved vulnerable to labor surpluses and shortages. Periods of labor shortage tend to erode discriminatory practices, as the employment and wage gains made by women and nonwhite workers in the United States during World War II illustrate. From this perspective, migration should tend to break down discrimination in sending countries but may slow the progress of minorities in destination countries. By relieving poverty in sending countries, international migration also may eventually reduce child labor.

Open international migration also limits some types of forced labor—notably trafficking in humans. Modern trafficking in humans stems from *barriers* to free movement across national boundaries. Immigration barriers raise the demand for evasion, and traffickers offer to meet that demand for a significant fee. Overall, international migration tends to improve labor rights in sending countries, but may erode rights in receiving countries, absent legal protections. Migration barriers tend to have the opposite effects.

Migration Incentives

Migration during the first wave of globalization primarily reflected the influence of economic incentives—a balancing of the benefits and costs of moving to and working in another country. As with many investment decisions, migration costs are largely incurred up front when the migration occurs, while the returns are distributed over time as migrants earn higher wages in destination countries. The large wage differentials between countries in the New and the Old Worlds offered attractive returns, but the costs of migration and other human capital investments are famously difficult to finance: one cannot offer oneself as collateral for loans in nonslave societies. Economically motivated migration occurs when would-be migrants decide that the net benefits of migration are positive—that the present value of the returns minus the costs is positive—and can afford the costs.

The major return to migration is higher expected income in the destination country. In the late nineteenth and early twentieth centuries, most income was from work, and the huge international real wage differences between the New World and the Old World appeared to provide attractive returns to migration. But for a given wage differential, the returns were greatest for those with the longest prospective work life. Young, healthy, male workers had the strongest incentive to migrate—if they could cover the costs of transport.

Balanced against the returns were significant monetary and nonmonetary migration costs. For long periods of time, transport costs provided the major monetary barrier to migration. These costs increased with distance from a host country, so that larger wage differences were required to attract migrants from more distant locations. Even those who could afford transport faced costs of job search and settlement in the new country, while separated from normal social and economic networks. The settlement costs included adjusting to the norms of a new culture and, for some, learning a new language. For long periods of time, the costs outweighed the benefits of migration. In the last two-thirds of the nineteenth century, however, the costs of transatlantic freight and passenger transport fell dramatically relative to real wages, stimulating migration for those who could afford the transport and were willing to incur the nonmonetary costs.

The expense of migration was still sufficiently large that the lowest wage workers, who had the most to gain from migrating, often could not afford the trip. The earliest migrants did not come from the bottom of the income distribution.

Early migrants reduce migration costs to future migrants from their country in two ways. First, migrants often send back a portion of their earnings as remittances that may finance subsequent migration by relatives and friends. Second, early migrants develop communities and networks of information in the destination country that can reduce the costs of finding employment and housing and of coping with a strange environment and culture. In short, the earliest migrants from a particular sending country incur the highest costs but make later migration from that country easier. The role of early migrants in reducing much of the uncertainty connected with the nonmonetary costs of migration explains the path dependence in the destinations of migrants from different nations.

Transatlantic Migration

L ate-nineteenth and early-twentieth-century migration illustrates most of these forces. Research by economic historians shows that the earliest transatlantic migrants were not those who would have benefited the most from migration. Wage benefits notwithstanding, most workers in the lowest wage countries simply could not afford even the falling costs of getting to the New World. Many would-be migrants had to wait for remittances from the trailblazers who could afford to make the trip (Hatton and Williamson 1998). Consistent with differences in the present value of migration returns, migrants were also younger and had a higher labor force participation rate than home-country populations.

The huge differences in labor conditions between the Old World and the New World induced annual migration flows from Europe as high as 1.4 million people in the early twentieth century (Hatton and Williamson 1998, p. 8). With so many migrants actively in the labor force, international migration was bound to have notable effects on labor markets in both the sending and receiving countries. Economic historians Kevin O'Rourke and Jeffrey Williamson (1999, table 8.1, p. 155) have calculated that by 1910 the cumulative effect of international migration was to increase the New World labor force by 40 percent and reduce the much larger Old World (European) labor force by 13 percent. Migrants increased the size of the labor force in Argentina by 86 percent, Canada by 44 percent, Australia by 42 percent and the United States by 24 percent. Labor force reductions in source countries were equally dramatic, ranging from 45 percent in Ireland and 39 percent in Italy to the low single digits in France, Germany, and the Netherlands.

Migration produced a substantial convergence of unskilled real wage rates between sending and receiving countries (Hatton and Williamson, 1998; Chiswick and Hatton, 2003). Without the transatlantic migration, wages and labor productivity would have been much higher in the New World and much lower in the Old World. Lindert and Williamson (2003) write, "In the absence of the mass migrations, real wage dispersion would have increased by seven percent rather than decreasing by 28 percent, as in fact it did" (p. 243). Unfortunately, the relationship between migration and nonmonetary working conditions during this period has received little attention.

Migrants and Native Workers

R eal wage convergence between Europe and the New World mainly reflected predictable adjustments in wages for unskilled workers on both sides of the Atlantic. Most European migrants were substitutes for unskilled native workers, and unskilled real wages grew more rapidly in origin than in destination countries (table 5.1). Yet, the mass migrations in the first wave of globalization did not produce real wage *losses* for unskilled native workers in the receiving countries. Real wages continued to grow, although

Table 5.1
Real Wage Convergence, 1870–1913

	Real wage, 1870 (U.S. = 100)	Percentage increase in real wage, 1870–1913
Destination countries		
Argentina	53	51
Australia	110	1
Canada	86	121
United States	100	47
Origin countries		
Ireland	43	84
Italy	23	112
Norway	24	193
Sweden	24	250

Source: Krugman and Obstfeld (2003, p. 165), compiled from data in Williamson (1995, table A2.1)

at rates that were reduced by migration. Some of the gains of migrants come at the expense of native workers with similar skills.

Immigration should raise the returns to inputs used in tandem with migrants. Migration raises the marginal product and returns to complementary inputs by making them relatively scarce. One can see this effect in the returns to nonlabor inputs, such as land and capital in the New World during the transatlantic migrations, a development that shifted income distributions in New World countries away from labor (O'Rourke and Williamson 1999; Chiswick and Hatton 2003). Judging by wage behavior, however, European immigrants were not complements with skilled labor in the New World. Economic historians find no evidence that immigration raised the productivity and wages of skilled workers. The fact that migrants and native workers were mainly substitutes drove both the transatlantic convergence in unskilled real wages and the eventual political backlash to migration in receiving countries.

The political backlash began modestly in the 1880s and eventually evolved to full-scale quotas based on national origin during the interwar retreat from globalization. In the 1880s and 1890s, subsidies and related incentives to attract migrants were modified or dropped first by Australia and New Zealand and then by Argentina and Chile. In the United States, a Chinese exclusion law passed in 1882 was followed by barriers to Japanese and other Asian immigration in 1908 and 1917. The United States also instituted a literacy test in 1917 followed by national origin quotas in 1921 and 1924 (Chiswick and Hatton, 2003, pp. 97–100).

Summing Up the First Wave

The history of the first wave of globalization dramatically clarifies how migration can be a force for global equalization of working conditions among nations that participate in the migration process. As both international trade and migration expanded, real wage differences between the richer and poorer nations in the transatlantic community narrowed. Which mechanism of globalization had the more important effect on working conditions? After an extensive study, O'Rourke and Williamson conclude that "the econometric evidence suggests that mass migration, not trade, seems to have played the critical globalization role in the late nineteenth century" (1999, p. 182). The effects on nonmonetary working conditions during the period remain less well documented. Though workers may choose to take some increases in compensation in the form of shorter working hours or safer jobs, as discussed in chapter 2, there is little information on the extent to which they did so in this period.

Things did not go nearly so well for the peripheral nations that did not participate in the international migrations. Though most of the transatlantic community benefited from migration and trade during the first wave of globalization, overall world inequality increased (Bourguignon and Morrisson 2002). Labor conditions did not improve in those nations of the Atlantic community that did not participate in global markets (O'Rourke and Williamson 1999). Nor did conditions improve in the Asian and African nations that remained largely outside the globalization process.

The onset of World War I marked the end of a golden age of economically motivated mass migrations. Even before the higher costs of travel imposed by two world wars, political responses to the predictable distributional consequences of migration reduced the primacy of economic motivations in the international allocation of labor. The immigration barriers that emerged from the political backlash permanently weakened migration as a force for equalizing working conditions around the world.

International Migration during the Postwar Globalization

Lower migration rates accompanied the general retreat from globalization between the two world wars, reflecting the accretion of increasingly restrictive national immigration policies as well as the distinctly higher costs of movement during periods of international conflict. International migration recovered somewhat following 1950 and increased into the 1990s. Unlike international trade and capital flows, however, international migration has not returned to heights attained late in the first wave of globalization in most New World countries (table 5.2). These countries remain major migration destinations. According to the ILO, the United States now absorbs more than 81 percent of the new migrants from developing countries, and Canada and

Table 5.2
Foreign-Born Percent of Population

	1910	1930	1960	2000
New World	15.5	12.0	6.7	13.7
Australia	17.7	5.4	16.6	24.6
Canada	22.0	22.2	15.4	18.9
New Zealand	30.3	5.0	14.1	22.5
United States	14.7	11.6	5.2	12.3
Western Europe[a]	2.3	2.7	4.6	10.3

[a] Belgium, France, Germany, Italy, Luxembourg, and Switzerland.

Source: U.N. Department of Economic and Social Affairs (2004), p. vii.

Australia account for 11 percent. Martin and Widgren write that "Canada and the United States include about 5 percent of the world's population, but they receive more than one-half of the world's immigrants" (2002, p. 9). France, Germany, Italy, and the United Kingdom are the major receiving countries in the European Union. But as the ILO notes, almost half the 10 million people who crossed borders annually in the last decade of the twentieth century moved "from one developing country to another. Indeed, considerable migration for employment takes place between and among countries where differentials in wages are not very large" (2004b, p. 5). At the beginning of the twenty-first century, there were about 175 million people living outside their country of birth, or about 3 percent of the world's population of 6.1 billion people (UN Population Division 2002).

The migrations in the late twentieth century involved origins and destinations notably different from those of the mass migrations during the first wave of globalization. Although Europe was the primary sending area during the first wave—indeed, migration reduced the European labor force by about one-eighth—it became a significant receiving region after World War II. Transport costs between the Old World and the New World continued to diminish, but prior migration and trade as well as rapid postwar economic growth in Europe had greatly narrowed income differences between the two regions, diminishing incentives to migrate. Most important, Europe's domestic labor force could no longer satisfy the demands of rapid economic growth.

By the late twentieth century, Europe has also developed a fiscal need for migrants. Aging populations raised the cost of public social security systems. At the same time, falling fertility rates in the native populations reduced the natural increase in the domestic labor force—the source of the tax revenues needed to finance social security expenditures. From a purely fiscal perspective, migrants supplement the domestic labor force, generate tax revenues to help finance social security systems, and typically have higher fertility rates than natives. Nor do they draw on national welfare systems to a greater extent than native workers, given their characteristics (see below).

In the last decades of the twentieth century, Third World countries became the major source of migrants. Even southern European countries such as Italy shifted from net emigration status in the early postwar years to net immigration by the end of the century, receiving significant numbers of migrants from Africa, Asia, and Latin America. Latin America, an important destination for European migrants during the first wave of globalization, shifted from net immigration to net emigration status by the late twentieth century (Hatton and Williamson 2006). Migration from eastern and central Europe followed the end of the Cold War and the expansion of the European Union.

Postwar growth patterns also produced new destination countries. Massive development projects in oil-rich Middle Eastern countries drew such large flows of migrant workers that foreign labor constituted almost half the labor force in several countries—the highest migrant shares in the world. South Africa, one of the few economic bright spots on the African continent in the late twentieth century, attracted migrants from many neighboring countries—and was almost alone on the continent in erecting significant legal restrictions on immigration (Hatton and Williamson 2006, chap. 12).

As a result, the geography of international migration looked very different almost a century after the end of the first wave of globalization. Understanding why the influence of international migration on labor conditions diminished during the second wave of globalization requires understanding how the shifting structure of incentives and public policies has altered the geography of international migration and the efficacy of migration as a tool for producing international convergence of labor conditions.

Migration Incentives in the Late Twentieth Century

We have seen how nineteenth-century transatlantic migration was largely economically motivated. How had migration incentives changed by the onset of the second wave of globalization? Except during the interwar years, transportation costs continued to decline during the twentieth century, reducing the most prominent monetary cost of migration. Though the costs of moving from developing countries to industrialized countries still exceeded the costs of moving between industrialized countries in the late 1990s, the differences were not large relative to the potential returns from migration discussed below.[1] The story on shifting migration incentives is in the pattern of returns.

INTERNATIONAL PAY DIFFERENTIALS. Changing patterns of international real wage differences that provided the main stimulus for earlier transatlantic migration help explain the changing geography of migration during the second wave of globalization. The sheer volume of nineteenth-century migration eventually produced a convergence of real wages between countries in the Old and New Worlds that participated in global markets at that time. The convergence itself gradually diminished one of the most important incentives to migrate between these regions. By the last half of the twentieth century labor conditions had largely equalized between the source and destination countries of the earlier migrations.

Within Europe, the muted role of migration incentives was even clearer. In the 1957 Treaty of Rome, six European countries dropped most barriers to cross-border migration and trade. (The number of nations in the European Union (EU) increased over subsequent decades, reaching 25 by 2004.) The early years of the EU saw neither a burst of internal migration nor a convergence of real wages between member countries. For most European workers, intra-European differences in wages and working conditions were not sufficiently large to offset language differences and other migration costs (Flanagan 1993). The notable increase in migration during the period came from poorer countries outside the EU. For residents of these countries, the prospective wage gains were larger than migration costs, and the ensuing migrations produced some wage convergence between the sending and receiving region.

By the late twentieth century, workers in countries that did not participate in the first wave of globalization faced the strongest incentives to migrate. Manufacturing compensation ratios between industrialized nations and many Third World countries clearly exceed the ratios of three or four to one that stimulated nineteenth-century migration (table 5.3). The changing pattern of returns alone predicts a changing geography of migration flows.

Wages are not well documented in some of the poorest countries, but painstaking efforts to examine incentives to migrate from areas like sub-Sahara Africa conclude that the incentives far exceed those that stimulated nineteenth-century migration. Most current African migration is within a region, not across continents. When economic historians Timothy Hatton and Jefferson Williamson (2001, 2006) apply a model first used to explain transatlantic migration during the first wave of globalization to contemporary migration, they find that Africans are as responsive as the first wave of migrants to key incentives. Stalled growth in sub-Saharan Africa has widened relative wage differences with industrialized countries, and high birthrates have increased the size of the working-age population (subject to mitigation by the HIV/AIDS epidemic). Both factors stimulate migration.

Strong tribal and kinship ties tend to counter these forces. (Refugees from tribal and political conflict tend to return to their homes as soon as conflict subsides, for example.) Hatton and Williamson conclude, "Rapid economic development in Africa would stem future emigration pressure, but it would have to be a spectacular improvement over past performance" (2003, p. 482). They find it more likely that "by 2025 Africa will record far greater mass migrations than did nineteenth-century Europe" (2003, p. 483). Two important factors may mitigate these conclusions: the future course of the

Table 5.3
Relative Hourly Compensation*

	2002[a]	1995–99[b]
United States	100	100
Australia	72	90
Canada	75	98
Belgium	107	83
Germany	114	115
Netherlands	102	119
Norway	127	133
Switzerland	113	—
Portugal	24	26
Spain	56	67
Brazil	12	49
Mexico	12	26
Hong Kong	27	—
Korea	42	37
Singapore	34	74
Sri Lanka	2	2
Taiwan	27	

* Percent of U.S. manufacturing production worker compensation

Sources: [a] http://www.bls.gov/fls/ichccreport.pdf
[b] UNIDO

HIV/AIDS epidemic in Africa and immigration restrictions in developed countries.

ROLE OF GOVERNMENT BENEFITS POLICIES. During the first wave of globalization, national governments had limited direct influence over monetary incentives to migrate and offered few direct barriers to international migration. By the last half of the twentieth century, both types of government influence had become all important. Government social benefits and labor regulations now influence many of the returns to work, conditions of work, and general social protections. Monetary compensation, work time, and protection from employment risks reflect government policies on social benefits, vacations and holidays, and compensation for unemployment or work injuries. Both the generosity of these benefits and their availability to migrant workers alter migration incentives for some workers. Social security policies, including unemployment insurance, sickness benefits, and old-age support, have broader scope and greater generosity in industrialized countries than in less-developed ones (Botero et al. 2004).

Popular discussions of the interactions between social benefits and migration often take for granted that countries that raise benefit levels attract more migrants. In fact, the effect of benefit levels on migration is more nuanced, because workers must also pay the taxes that finance the benefits. Improvements in social benefits generally establish a more equal distribution of income in a country, because most social benefits disproportionately help low-skill, low-wage workers. A country providing some of the benefits noted above therefore offers more attractive expected incomes to low-skill workers but less attractive expected incomes to high-skill workers, who must pay higher taxes to finance the benefits. If one imagines a world in which only one country offers benefits, that country will attract more unskilled migrants but fewer skilled migrants. In short, the more egalitarian benefit system alters the composition of migration, increasing the proportion of low-skilled migrants; it attracts or "selects" migrants whose characteristics are most likely to qualify them for benefits. If other countries adopt even slightly less generous social benefits, they may not encounter this "selection" phenomenon. Countries with lower benefit levels will not be attractive destinations for unskilled migrants. This analysis provides some basis for concerns about a potential race to the bottom in social benefits in a world of unrestricted migration. The concern is in many respects a variant on the concern that migrants slow real wage growth for substitute workers in destination countries. Generally speaking, unskilled migrants are attracted to more egalitarian countries because they provide generous benefits, while skilled migrants are attracted to less egalitarian countries where their taxes are lower (Roy 1951).

National governments also provide extensive social benefits that are not attached to labor force status. Because there were no well-established national welfare systems in the first wave of globalization, migration offered few returns to nonworkers, and transatlantic migrants were disproportionately young male workers attracted to higher wages. With the social welfare systems now in place in industrialized countries, migration is less likely to be motivated exclusively by work incentives. Even in the absence of national immigration restrictions, broadening government safety nets have changed the composition of modern migration flows, reducing the proportion of active labor force participants. National governments often try to defend against welfare shopping by migrants. A study of the European Union noted that:

> Several provisions in the legislation of the EU and its member states are designed to protect national social security systems against welfare shopping: nationals from other EU countries are only admitted if they can prove that they are able to finance their living out of their work or other financial means. Job seekers are not entitled to any welfare benefits in the host country. Claims against social insurance such as unemployment benefits are only accepted after certain periods of payment. This also holds true for family reunification. . . . [However,] workers from other EU countries and their

families are in practice entitled to the same set of social welfare benefits as natives once they have been employed in another EU country for a certain period of time. (Brucker et al. 2002, p. 44)

This study also found that migrants to European countries were more likely than native Europeans to have characteristics that would qualify them for benefits. The study asked if migrants tended to make greater use of benefit systems (given their characteristics). Here the evidence was mixed, with migrants making disproportionately more use of the unemployment insurance and family benefits than natives, but less use of pension schemes (in part because migrants are younger than natives). Overall, the evidence of welfare shopping by migrants among European countries was rather weak.

To summarize, postwar monetary incentives for migration are even larger than during the first wave of globalization, but they imply a very different set of sending and receiving countries. Where market incentives are permitted to operate, migration continues to narrow differences in labor conditions among countries. Government social welfare policies now supplement the market incentives, with three major consequences. Social benefit policies and the taxes that must be paid to finance them influence the skill composition of the migrant labor force attracted to each destination country. Second, the breadth of social benefit systems renders migration more attractive to nonworkers than a century ago. Not all migration will be a force for international convergence of working conditions. Finally, the bills for social benefits must be paid, and tax bills for social benefits are more broadly distributed than are the immediate effects of migration on the labor market. Concerns about migration's fiscal effects increasingly condition political responses and help to account for the persistence of national immigration barriers in a world of falling trade barriers. But there are now relatively few regions in which economic incentives are permitted to operate unimpeded.

ROLE OF NATIONAL IMMIGRATION POLICIES. Modern migrations occur in a world of significant national restrictions on immigration, many of which emerged in reaction to immigration's effects on native workers during the first wave of globalization. National immigration policies now determine the size and composition of legal migration flows. Some policies place absolute restrictions on immigrant flows, limiting the worldwide convergence in working conditions possible through international migration. Others influence the composition of immigration by establishing and enforcing criteria for legal immigration. By favoring some skill groups over others, national policies can influence the *patterns* of convergence; convergence is limited to the countries permitted to send migrants and to the skills permitted to migrate.

In the earliest postwar policy regime, sending and receiving governments carefully arranged core/periphery migrations. Labor shortages in the richer

European countries stimulated a series of bilateral agreements with less wealthy southern European countries that permitted inflows of temporary "guest workers," who were expected to return to their countries of origin after the shortages eased (Martin 2005). Weak enforcement of the time limits transformed many "temporary" migrants into permanent residents and stimulated subsequent migration motivated by family reunification.[2] The ILO has emphasized the important "role played by States in organizing and closely supervising recruitment, employment, and return. Employers seeking foreign workers sent their request to local public employment offices, which then relayed it to public employment authorities abroad, where workers were recruited, tested, and selected. Between 1960 and 1966 the *Gastarbeiter* program brought some 3.6 million foreign workers to West Germany, and 3 million returned home as expected" (2004b, p. 15). In the United States, a *Bracero* program admitted around 5 million workers from Mexico for agricultural work between 1942 and 1966.[3] In both of these cases, the migrants were mainly unskilled workers, and as in nineteenth-century migration, the arrangements produced some convergence of unskilled wages between sending and receiving countries.

Later, international migration policies tended to be developed unilaterally, reflecting a variety of monetary and nonmonetary motivations. Over the postwar years, there has been a shift from national origin quotas to more egalitarian worldwide quotas. Social and political events have also increasingly influenced migration decisions in the late twentieth and early twenty-first centuries. Wars, famines, and the persecution of political minorities gravely raise the costs of remaining in one's home country. The migration of refugees from civil wars or from political oppression is increasingly common. Humanitarian considerations, including the need to shelter political refugees and reunite families, now receive considerable weight in granting visas.

These preferences, which did not accompany migration during the first wave of globalization, further reduce the importance of economic motivations in modern migrations, and, along with overall quotas, they reduce international migration as a force for narrowing international differences in working conditions. Most recently, some countries have experimented with skills-based immigration quotas, an approach that presents the prospect of limiting immigration flows to skills that are complementary to (and hence would raise the returns to) the skills of native workers (Chiswick and Hatton 2003; ILO 2004b). With skill-biased immigration policies, international migration may still produce convergence of labor conditions for skilled workers, but it is not available to equalize worldwide labor conditions for unskilled workers.

The web of rules that constitute national immigration policies defies easy summarization, and no international organization publishes comparative indicators of immigration restrictions. Even if an index of de jure restrictions existed, it would provide a poor guide to effective restrictions produced by variations in government enforcement activities. The ease with which a company can employ foreign workers provides one indicator of the practical impact of immigration restrictions. For many years, executives around the world have been asked whether national immigration laws prevent their companies from "employing foreign skills." Between 1992 and 2003, responses to this question indicated a general, if not uniform, increase in the perceived restrictiveness of national immigration laws. In 21 of 34 countries, executives indicated that it became more difficult to employ foreign workers. Not surprisingly, most of these countries were industrialized destination countries. In contrast, immigration restrictions were perceived to ease in a number of net emigration countries (IMD 1992, 2003). By this indicator, recent trends have been toward more restrictive immigration policies.

By significantly limiting the ability of workers around the world to respond to prevailing economic incentives, national immigration policies also influence both the size and composition of illegal migration flows. In restricting legal economic opportunities for workers in sending countries, the policies establish strong economic incentives for illegal migration. The rise of illegal migration is tied to the development of significant limitations on legal migration since the first wave of globalization. So is the rise in some forms of trafficking in humans. Missing from most critiques of globalization is a condemnation of the barriers to international migration that limit opportunities in the poorest regions.

Effect on Native Workers

Early in this chapter I emphasized that the initial effect that an influx of immigrants into the labor market has on native workers depends on whether the native and immigrant workers have the same skills. Native substitutes perceive immigration as a threat to their wages or job opportunities. Along with the owners of capital and land, native workers with skills that complement the skills of migrants may see immigration as an opportunity, however. Unskilled immigrant workers may threaten the working conditions of some native workers but improve the labor market prospects of others.

The increasing restrictiveness of immigration laws implies that the larger effect has been on substitute workers (or that they are more effectively organized for political action). But how large is the effect on native workers? Evidence from the first wave of globalization indicated that transatlantic migration did not reduce the real wages of unskilled American labor but did slow their rate of growth.

When governments and labor unions play a small role in wage determination, as was the case during the nineteenth-century globalization, the threat to native workers with similar skills consists of lower wages. Unions have waxed and waned in industrialized over the past 60 years, but even as their membership now declines in most OECD countries, the remaining effects of collective bargaining limit downward wage flexibility—particularly in Europe. Government minimum wage policies also limit wage adjustments at the bottom of the wage distribution, where unskilled migrant workers are most likely to have an impact. With institutional limits on wage adjustments, immigration is more likely to raise unemployment of native workers, immigrants, or both. Faced with the prospect of lower wages or higher unemployment, small wonder that substitute workers in destination countries seek political responses to limit the threats. More mysterious is the failure of employers, landowners, and skilled labor to resist restrictions on immigration. This diffidence must be explained later in the chapter by looking beyond the labor market effects of migration.

The political instinct to restrict immigration rests on an incomplete economic analysis, however. The immigrant flows that threaten the wages or employment of unskilled labor by increasing its supply also create a relative scarcity of capital, raising its return. With fluid capital markets, the higher returns should attract more capital to complement the inflow of unskilled labor. Such shifts in the demand for labor mitigate and may eliminate adverse wage or employment consequences.

What do empirical studies of postwar international migration find? In fact, the estimates in various studies are quite scattered and include both positive and negative effects on native workers. A recent review and meta-study of almost 350 impact estimates reported in 18 studies covering the main destination areas (North America, Europe, Australia, and Israel) concluded that "a negative but small effect of immigration on wages of native groups with similar skills appears rather robust" (Longhi, Nijkamp, and Poot 2004). By "small" the authors mean that on average across the studies, a doubling of the population of immigrants in the labor force would reduce wages by about .6 percent. The effect is somewhat more negative for men than women and largest for low-skill workers. The same study indicates that the negative effect on wages is largely restricted to other (prior) immigrant workers in the destination country: "Immigrants are more in competition with other immigrants than with natives" (p. 19). Taken at face value, the conclusion implies that on average, capital flows and output adjustments do not completely offset the effect of increased labor supply on wages.

Studies find smaller effects on native workers in the United States than in Europe. This may be because the effect on wages becomes more difficult for statisticians to observe in countries, such as the United States, with well-functioning labor markets. Downward wage pressures and job competition from immigrants in one labor market encourages some workers to escape the impact of immigrant competition by moving to another area. Labor mobility diffuses immigration's effects more widely, rendering it more difficult to observe than in labor markets with a high concentration of immigrants. In short, though immigration appears to have a small negative effect on the wages of native workers, one cannot speak confidently about how immigration's effects on labor markets differ among destination countries.

Effect on Workers in Sourcing Countries

Theoretically, emigration should also improve wages and/or replace the unemployment of workers who remain behind by reducing labor supply in source countries. Initially, the effect should be strongest on the wages of workers with the same skills as emigrants, but some of the wage benefits should eventually flow to other groups as employers alter their production methods to reduce their need for workers with the largest relative wage increases.

How important is the effect on source country workers in practice? In contrast with the vast amount of research in how immigration affects workers in high-wage receiving countries, there are few studies of the consequences for workers in low-wage sending countries. Simulation exercises indicate substantial pay increases in some European sending countries during the late-nineteenth-century transatlantic migrations (O'Rourke and Williamson 1999). Two studies of the effect on wages of migration from Mexico to the United States appear to provide the only evidence from late-twentieth-century globalization (Mishra 2003; Hanson 2005). Most emigration from Mexico consists of relatively educated and experienced workers. Within Mexico, there are also notable regional differences in the extent of emigration. These two studies detect comparatively large increases in wages in the skill groups and regions in which emigration most reduced domestic labor supply. One of the studies also finds a spillover effect on wages in regions with relatively little emigration.

Of course, emigration's effects can be much broader than changes in the wages of workers who remain at home, particularly in countries, such as Mexico, with a high out-migration of skilled workers. This raises the question of brain drain, to which we now turn.

Does International Migration Harm Developing Countries?

Decisions to migrate may be rational for individual emigrants, but can emigration harm sending countries? The answer to this question varies with the skill level of emigrants. Source countries lose the output that would have been produced by emigrants and the taxes they would have paid, but they save the social expenditures that would have been made on the emigrants' behalf. From this perspective, emigration of unskilled workers is most likely to produce positive net benefits for sending countries. Most developing countries have excess supplies of unskilled workers with little education and low productivity. Labor market competition forces unskilled wages down to low levels that often are determined by social minimum wages. The low wages yield little tax revenue, and minimum wages may contribute to unemployment or underemployment among the unskilled. The unemployed draw on what social benefits are available. In this environment, migration by unskilled workers is a positive development for source countries, particularly when migrants send remittances (discussed below) from their foreign incomes. Remittances aside, emigration of the unskilled eventually puts upward pressure on the working conditions of unskilled workers who remain in the developing countries. Indeed, this was part of the mechanism producing a convergence of wages between the Old and New Worlds during the mass migrations of the late nineteenth century.

The migration of skilled labor produces a rather different calculus for developing countries, which spend scarce public resources to fund educational systems that build skills. There is no shortage of jobs for skilled workers in less developed countries, and their relatively high wages produce significant tax revenues that defray the costs of public education. When the most skilled workers, rationally responding to current economic incentives, migrate abroad, taking their locally funded skill investments with them, developing countries confront the general training problem writ large: less developed countries incur the cost of providing skills, but international migration denies them a return on their investments in skills that may be applied throughout the world. As the ILO noted, "the emigration of African doctors and nurses leads to poorer health care in Africa at a time when there is a greater need for it because of HIV/AIDS and recent initiatives to improve immunization rates" (2004b, p. 21). There are limits to this argument. Many residents of less developed countries acquire at least some of their higher education abroad. More than half of the 1.5 million foreign students in OECD countries originate outside the OECD. Their home government does not always support their education in foreign universities, and some of the students return to their home countries with skills developed from their foreign education.

Nevertheless, the skill bias of late-twentieth-century immigration policies in some major destination countries exacerbates the potential for brain drain while deterring legal unskilled migration that might be beneficial for developing countries.[4] The migration of the most able human capital to other countries can diminish national growth prospects. The pro-skill bias in the immigration policies of developed countries limits the convergence in labor conditions attributable to migration to the highest skilled workers.

How important is the brain drain phenomenon? Until recently, the difficulty of obtaining data on migrants' educational attainment impeded answers to this important question. Recent IMF and World Bank studies have estimated migration rates to OECD countries by level of education, however (Carrington and Detragiache 1998; Docquier and Marfouk 2004). The more recent of these studies tabulates an overall migration rate—defined as the fraction of people age 25 or older who were born in each of 190 countries and lived in an OECD country in 2000—and a skilled migration rate (the fraction of each country's population with a tertiary education (more than high school) living in an OECD country in 2000).[5] The study shows significant brain drain in the sense that the emigration rates for individuals with tertiary education typically exceed the emigration rate for all education levels in each country—often by a very large margin. (Compare columns 1 and 3 in table 5.4.) Brain drain is particularly notable in some smaller African and Caribbean regions. In many regions, brain drain continued to grow during the 1990s (column 2). An OECD study, which measures brain drain as the ratio of high-skilled emigrants to the high-skilled native-born population of a country, confirms that the highest brain drain rates observed in migration flows to OECD countries come from African and Caribbean countries with English or Portuguese colonial histories (Dumont and Lemaître 2005).

The cumulative effect is quite impressive. According to the World Bank study, "In 1990, high-skill immigrants represented 33 percent of the OECD immigration stock whilst only 9.1 percent of the world labor force was tertiary educated. Between 1990 and 2000, the percentage of skilled immigrants increased to 37 percent" (Docquier and Marfouk 2004, p. 22). The regional averages in table 5.4 obscure the most dramatic country-level cases of brain drain. In 20 (mostly small) developing countries, more than half the skilled

Table 5.4
Emigration Rates, 2000

	Tertiary education		
	Rate	1990–2000 change	Overall rate
North America	1.0	0.2	0.8
Central America	16.1	3.1	11.0
The Caribbean	40.9	−0.5	13.9
South America	5.7	1.0	1.5
Northern Europe	14.3	−1.9	6.8
Western Europe	7.3	−3.2	3.2
Southern Europe	9.0	−2.2	6.2
Eastern Europe	4.5	2.2	2.2
Northern Africa	6.2	−0.6	2.5
Central Africa	13.3	3.5	0.8
Western Africa	26.7	0.8	6.0
Eastern Africa	18.4	3.0	0.6
Southern Africa	5.3	−1.6	0.9
Western Asia	5.8	−1.1	3.2
South–Central Asia	5.1	1.1	0.5
South–Eastern Asia	9.8	−0.5	1.7
Eastern Asia	4.3	0.2	0.5
Oceana	6.6	0.6	4.3

Source: Docquier and Marfouk (2004, table 2).

labor force had emigrated to OECD countries by 2000. The rates for this group ranged from 51 percent (Belize) to 89.9 percent (Suriname). In contrast, the skilled migration rate from the United States is 0.5 percent, the second lowest in the world (Docquier and Marfouk 2004, table 3).

Three factors may offset the costs of this emigration to developing countries—subsequent remittances from emigrants, return migration, and the effect of migration opportunities on incentives to invest in education and other human capital in source countries. These countervailing factors can be quite significant. International remittances amounted to $72.3 billion in 2001 and have exceeded flows of official development assistance since the mid-1990s. Only foreign direct investment provides a larger source of external funding for developing countries. By any reasonable measure, remittances are most important to the lowest income developing countries. Though large developing countries such as India, Mexico, and the Philippines receive the largest flows of remittances, the economic impact is greatest in smaller countries such as Tonga (37 percent of GDP), Lesotho (26.5 percent), and Jordan (23 percent). Remittances average around 7 percent of GDP in Middle East and North Africa, 4 percent in transition economies and Central Asia, almost 4 percent in Sub-Saharan Africa, and about 2 percent in Latin America and the Caribbean (World Bank 2003, chap. 7). The main destination countries of migrants constitute the main sources of remittances—the United States (39 percent of all remittances), Saudi Arabia (21 percent), and Germany, Belgium, and Switzerland (each 11 percent).

For recipients, remittances constitute income support for migrants' families, contributing to poverty reduction and resources for additional migrants, as they did in the mass migrations of the late nineteenth century. A study of more than 7,000 Guatemalan households and more limited studies in Egypt and Mexico confirm that remittances from both international and internal (rural-to-urban) migrants reduce the severity of poverty in sending countries (Adams 2004). Rural-to-urban migration by Chinese youth also produces remittances—often exceeding annual rural incomes—that improve the quality of life of their parents and relatives (Chang 2005). The World Bank reports that "there is some evidence that remittances have increasingly been for investment purposes in developing countries, especially in low-income countries" (2003, pp. 161, 164). Remittances also provide a comparatively stable source of foreign exchange for sending countries, despite some sensitivity to changes in immigration laws and changes in oil prices (for migrants to Saudi Arabia and other Middle East countries). According to the World Bank report, "Remittances also more than offset the loss of tax revenue in most developing countries" (p. 164).

Developing countries' concerns about the effects of skilled migration raise the question of whether skilled migrants remit more than unskilled migrants. Skilled workers receive higher earnings and hence might be expected to remit more, offsetting some of the costs of their migration from their home country. Yet remittances are usually directed at families, raising the difficult-to-answer question of whether skilled or unskilled migrants are more likely to have families remaining in their home country. There is little direct evidence that skilled workers remit more than unskilled workers. Remittances generally decline with the length of a migrant's stay in another country, and skilled migrants typically remain longer than unskilled migrants. One effort to infer the effect of skill on remittances regressed remittances per capita to the sending country on its stock of migrants (more migrants mean more remittances), per capita GDP (wealthier sending countries receive fewer remittances from altruistic migrants), and measures of the migrants' skill levels. Remittance measures were weakly negatively correlated with the proportion of a country's population living abroad that had a tertiary education. No such correlation emerged for migrants with a secondary education (Adams and Page 2003). Evaluating whether remittances effectively counter the losses associated with the migration of a country's skilled labor is clearly a complicated business. One rough estimate finds that remittances compensate for source-country GDP losses from migration on average, although outcomes naturally vary among countries (Hatton and Williamson 2006, chap. 15).

Return migration, possibly with enhanced skills, also provides a potential mitigation of the costs of emigration and particularly brain drain to developing countries. If skilled migrants return home after acquiring new skills in a host country, they reverse the general training phenomenon to the advantage of developing countries. As yet there is no definitive evidence in this regard, although findings that migrants from developing countries who earn Ph.D.s are more likely to remain in the developed countries where they obtain their degrees and that the education attainment of returning migrants is lower than remaining migrants imply that more highly skilled emigrants tend to remain abroad.

In one respect, emigration may produce a "brain gain" that counters the brain drain in developing countries. The fact that migration policies offer well-educated workers a choice of employment abroad as well as at home raises the incentive to acquire more education. Since only a fraction of those who acquire the education migrate, the country's stock of skill may increase, notwithstanding some emigration. The limited evidence now available on this point is not very supportive. One study found that "the tertiary enrollment ratio in sending countries is negatively associated with the skilled content of migration," a finding that casts doubt on the idea that the possibility of migration may increase educational attainment in sending countries (Faini 2003, p. 2). Yet to the extent that migration opportunities stimulate more schooling, the world supply of skill increases.

A definitive conclusion on the net benefits of skilled migration from developing countries continues to elude students of the development process. Some Caribbean and African countries are most likely to incur negative net benefits. Whatever the exact numbers, skill-biased immigration policies in destination countries threaten the benefits that migration can bring to sending countries by limiting the emigration of unskilled labor.

Twenty-First Century Migration Policy

Migration's effects on convergence of labor conditions around the world have been much weaker during the second wave of globalization not because of weaker economic incentives to migrate but because of national immigration restrictions. The policies of the major host countries have reduced the usefulness of international labor markets as a mechanism for producing a convergence of labor conditions for unskilled workers. Incentives to cross borders remain strong, but absolute limits on the number of immigrants along with the rise of family reunification and asylum as criteria for legal entry have reduced the importance of economically motivated international migration during the postwar globalization. To the extent that international labor markets produce real wage convergence, they work best for the most educated workers, given the pro-skill bias in some national migration policies. At the same time, some developing countries feel threatened by policies that encourage the migration of skilled workers.

How much could the world gain by freeing up international labor markets? What factors inhibit the attainment of the gains by eliminating national immigration restrictions? In a world of increasing free trade, should policy makers worry about immigration barriers? Can free trade attain the same results? These policy concerns occupy the rest of the chapter.

Dropping Immigration Barriers

Total world output increases as labor moves from countries where its value is low to countries where it is higher. Migrants receive higher wages in destination countries because the value of what they produce there exceeds the value of the output lost by the country they leave. Studies of the aggregate economic gains from removing immigration barriers find that substantial gains in world output and income would accompany unrestricted international migration. Though estimates vary with the exact assumptions used to build and calibrate such "computable general equilibrium" models, studies agree that the gains would be large.

The most recent study divides the world into eight broad regions and variously assumes that the labor force of each region consists of a single skill or of both skilled and unskilled workers (Iregui 2003). Given current interregional wage differences, the study estimates gains from unrestricted migration equal to 54 percent of world GDP under the single skill assumption or 48 percent if there are two skills of labor and both skills migrate. Under alternative wage definitions, the gains to unrestricted migration range from

15 to 67 percent of world GDP. The exact estimates are much less important than the conclusion that the gains to unrestricted migration are quite large. This conclusion is consistent with the results of an earlier study, which estimated even larger returns to free migration (Hamilton and Whalley 1984). Another study estimates that liberalization of labor mobility to the level of 3 percent of the workforce of OECD countries could result in global welfare gains of up to $150 billion a year (Winters et al., 2003).

The study by Iregui also estimates the effects of unrestricted migration on real wage convergence between countries. Consistent with theoretical predictions and experience during the first wave of globalization, unrestricted migration produces real wage convergence (as well as the net gains described above), but not everyone gains. In the industrialized receiving countries, workers with the same skills as the migrants incur some real wage losses. But the losses turn out to be small in comparison to the huge wage gains in the sending countries—the world's least developed and lowest wage countries. Nonetheless, the prospect of losses to some workers motivates political restrictions on migration in some receiving countries.

Barriers to More Open Migration Policies

What are the foundations of current political barriers that thwart such large potential gains to unrestricted migration? Where does the opposition to migration come from? Why are the resulting inefficiencies more difficult for the international community to address than the inefficiencies from protective trade barriers?

PUBLIC OPINION. Current national immigration policies may reduce world output and income, but they are still less restrictive than the public would prefer. Chiswick and Hatton (2003) report that public opinion polls "regularly find that two-thirds of the population would prefer less immigration" (p. 105). Surveys rarely capture how opinion differs with the reasons for migration: economic opportunities, family reunification, refugees. There is an important difference between European and American attitudes toward migration, however. In Europe, a majority of respondents to opinion polls prefer no increase in the stock of migrants, whereas in the United States, respondents prefer no increase in flows but appear to accept the fact that the stock of migrants will increase (Brucker et al. 2002).

Does public opposition to immigration reflect economic self-interest? Self-interested workers should be divided in their attitudes toward immigration, which threatens the wages of host-country workers with similar skills and enhances the wages of host-country workers with complementary skills. Unskilled immigrants put downward pressure on the wages of unskilled resident workers, but they raise the demand for and wages of complementary skilled workers. Consistent with these economic effects, high-skilled U.S. workers, the country's relatively abundant factor, are less likely than low-skill workers to support restrictive immigration policies (Sheve and Slaughter 2001). Looking across countries, the attitude of any skill group toward immigration policy should vary with the skill level of migrants.

Empirical evidence supports economic self-interest as an important determinant of attitudes toward immigration policy, at least to the extent that Heckscher-Ohlin arguments characterize economic self-interest. The International Social Survey Program National Identity Survey of 1995 provides information on opinions toward trade and immigration for 24 OECD and transition countries, respondents' skill levels, and considerable economic information.[6] There are no African or Latin American countries in the sample, and the only Asian countries included are the Philippines and Japan. As in other surveys, the mean response in every country favors less immigration, with the strongest anti-immigrant sentiment found in countries in transition from central planning to market oriented economies. (In every country except Japan and the Netherlands, the mean response also favors fewer imports.) A regression analysis relating attitudes toward immigration and free trade to economic and social characteristics finds that although nationalism and other measures of ideology strongly predict anti-immigrant and protectionist sentiment, economic self-interest also plays a strong role. Consistent with predictions of international trade theory, skilled workers are most likely to favor immigration (and free trade) in rich countries and to oppose it in poor countries. More generally, respondents who desire restrictions on immigration also prefer more protection. Respondents apparently view free trade and migration as substitutes in threatening or enhancing their working conditions (O'Rourke 2003).

Why, then, do political responses favor freer trade over freer migration? In modern times, public concerns over the fiscal effect of migrants provide the most likely explanation. A native labor force that is divided by skill over the effect of immigration on the labor market will unite in opposition if migrants are believed to take more than they contribute to public social benefits systems. (Several European countries report that the welfare dependency of immigrants exceeds that of natives [ILO 2004b, p. 35].) Taxpayers outside the labor force will add their opposition to open immigration. To these fiscal concerns, one must also add a role for discriminatory tastes. The changing geography of postwar migration has increased the cultural distance between migrant and native populations beyond anything experienced in the first wave of globalization. Differences in language, religion, and race no doubt play a larger if less measurable role in conditioning modern resistance to immigration. Politically, countries find it easier to accept the "indirect" challenge from imported goods than the direct challenge from the presence of workers from distinctly different cultures and traditions. In modern times, such fears and prejudices are surely strengthened when immigrant flows are from regions plagued by HIV/AIDS or other serious, transmittable health problems.

TIMIDITY OF INTERNATIONAL ORGANIZATIONS. On February 24, 2004, the United Nations' International Labor Organization, the only major international agency focusing on the welfare of the world's workers, released the long-awaited report of its World Commission on the Social Dimension of Globalization (2004a). The report is notable mainly for its remarkable failure to include international migration in its list of "key characteristics of globalization" and its gift for understatement in observing that "there is a strong polarization of views on the desirability of expanding opportunities for international migration" (p. 97). Why would the international agency that specializes in world labor conditions ignore the historically important role of international labor markets in reducing differences in labor conditions around the world? This telling failure speaks volumes about the willingness of international agencies to settle for weak, second-best solutions in the face of perceived political opposition to first-best solutions.

International organizations, so important in the postwar reduction of trade barriers, avoid parallel efforts to reduce immigration restrictions, despite the huge potential gains to greater migration noted earlier. Instead of emphasizing the role of immigration barriers in limiting the advance of working conditions around the world, the ILO focuses on protecting the conditions under which legal migrants live and work in destination countries.[7] There are grounds for concern about these conditions: news reports regularly provide examples of degrading, discriminatory treatment of legal migrants and their lack of legal recourse in some major destination countries.[8] But the voluntary international labor standards issued periodically by the ILO have proved to be an ineffective response to the underlying problems. For example, the two ILO labor standards addressing problems faced by migrants in destination countries have mainly been ratified by a few high-emigration nations and ignored by destination countries.[9] Issued in 1949, the first labor standard calls for nondiscrimination against legal immigrants and encourages bilateral agreements regarding the level of migration and the treatment of migrants. The second labor standard, issued in the 1970s, a period of weaker labor markets, calls on member countries to respect the rights of migrants, but focuses on controlling illegal migration. Chapter 7 contains a broader discussion of the difficulties encountered in trying to improve labor conditions via international labor standards.

Some of the ILO's difficulty in coming to grips with the fundamentals of the migration issue no doubt reflects its tripartite structure. Representatives of labor, management, and national governments deliberate and formulate labor standards—a process that has no exact parallel in other international organizations. The compromises that emerge from the conflicting national interests—between countries of emigration and immigration and between different interest groups within each set of countries—more or less guarantee a lack of consideration of the gains to the world community from more open migration.

Why have the international organizations that achieved notable reductions in trade barriers failed to mount a parallel effort to reduce restrictions on international migration? Perhaps the greatest impediment to coordinated international action is the difficulty of implementing the principle of reciprocity that has been so important in negotiating successive reductions in trade barriers. Virtually all parties to GATT and later WTO negotiations began the process with tariff and nontariff barriers to negotiate away. The ubiquity of trade barriers provided a basis for reciprocal actions—a quid pro quo that provided a veneer of fairness to promote political commitment and closure.

International migration does not provide a parallel opportunity for political reciprocity. The political economy of immigration guarantees that immigration barriers will mainly emerge in destination countries. Countries of emigration have little to offer in exchange. In some destination countries, declining immigrant quality may provide another barrier to removing immigration restrictions.

Trade versus Migration

This chapter tells a simple story: international migration played the dominant role in the convergence of wages during the first wave of globalization, but politically determined immigration regulations muted the role of migration as an instrument for equalizing labor conditions during the postwar globalization. Historically, this key mechanism of globalization improved the poorest working conditions in globally integrated countries; more recently, barriers to this aspect of globalization appear to limit the improvement of the world's worst working conditions.

Appearances may be deceiving. After all, the conclusion that migration barriers inhibit improvement of the poorest working conditions overlooks some key results of economic theory discussed early in chapter 4. These results—the famous "factor price equalization" theorems—hold that even in a world with no international labor mobility, trade in goods would equalize compensation across countries. Emigration will improve wages in poor countries, but so will the export of labor-intensive products to capital-rich, labor-scarce, high-wage countries. Rich countries may either import unskilled labor-intensive product or admit unskilled migrants to produce the goods. Free trade effectively moves jobs to workers, rather than workers to jobs. With free trade, the presence or absence of immigration barriers influences the location of production activities rather than the level of labor conditions. If trade and migration are substitutes, immigration restrictions alone may not protect working conditions in high-income countries; nor will trade barriers by themselves. The question of whether migration barriers have a benign effect on world labor conditions if trade in commodity and services remains free is of enormous relevance to twenty-first century policy debates.

One can see examples of how trade flows may substitute for migration flows in the postwar economic experience. Although the European Union reduced both trade and migration barriers between member countries, only the trade flows accelerated to narrow the initial pay differences between countries. The more recent phenomenon of offshore outsourcing in the United States provides a more graphic illustration of substitution. Consider the case of Indian programmers. Absent immigration barriers, the programmers could migrate to the United States, increasing the relative supply of programming skills and mitigating upward pressure on programmer wages. Such migration in fact occurred, but ultimately was limited by immigration restrictions. What was the international market response to the restrictions? Skills that could no longer be supplied through migration now arrive through trade in services. Programming services are performed in India (rather than on site) and transmitted to clients in the United States and other countries. The demand for native programmers and their working conditions are essentially the same, whether foreign labor input arrives migration or trade. But do trade flows substitute for migration flows in general?[10]

Postwar policy choices imply a prevailing political view that trade and migration are substitutes. The general objective of the international community during this period was to reverse the interwar retreat from globalization. If international trade and migration are viewed as substitutes, restrictions on only one policy need be relaxed to achieve greater economic integration. If viewed as complements, both trade and migration must be liberalized. At the highest levels of international policymaking, the substitution view clearly dominates. A long sequence of negotiations in GATT and its successor, the WTO, have focused on the elimination of national trade barriers while ignoring national restrictions on immigration. No other international organization has adopted the cause of liberalizing immigration. At the regional level of decision making, the evidence is mixed. The North American Free Trade Agreement and other regional negotiations conducted by the United States follow global negotiations in reducing trade barriers while leaving immigration restrictions in place. The U.S. Commission for the Study of International Migration and Cooperative Economic Development clearly view trade and labor flows as substitutes. In its 1990 report it concluded that "expanded trade between the sending countries and the United States is the single most important remedy" for unwanted migration (p. xv). Only the European Union from its inception liberalized both product and labor markets, consistent with the complementary view.

Neither international trade theory nor empirical studies support substitution as the general case, however. The prediction that either trade or migration flows will equalize wages rests on the assumption that differences in factor endowments are the sole basis of trade. A significant economic literature, reviewed in O'Rourke and Williamson (1999, pp. 252–254), makes the point that trade and migration can be complements when there is some other basis for trade, such as international differences in technology. When the flows are complementary, the policy implications change drastically: a barrier to either flow will reduce the other flow because they are connected. The theoretical results also overlook how the costs of conducting trade and of migration limit the extent to which either flow can by itself equalize international differences in wages and working conditions.

The idea that trade and migration are substitutes finds no support in the transatlantic economic integration of the late nineteenth century, as O'Rourke and Williamson note. "Overall, the history of the Atlantic economy between 1870 and 1940 rejects the thesis that trade and factor mobility were substitutes. It is a little more comfortable with the thesis that they are complements" (1999, p. 268). Evidence of a complementary relationship emerges for less than half the countries. No statistically discernable relationship exists for the other countries. The economic historians also argue that the public policy choices made by national governments were consistent with a view that the flows were complementary. The earliest restrictions on globalization were trade barriers; only later did immigration restrictions emerge.

In modern times, several practical realities limit the ability of free trade to equalize labor conditions around the world. Even if all remaining trade barriers were removed, significant differences in technology and resources between rich and poor countries limit the prospects for a complete convergence of working conditions via trade. So do the costs of conducting trade. The spectacular decline in some costs of conducting international business over the past 150 years sometimes obscures the fact that significant costs remain. A recent study finds that total trade costs approximate a 170 percent ad valorem tax for rich countries, after removing the effects of tariff and nontariff barriers. "Representative retail and wholesale distribution costs are set at 55 percent, close to the average for industrialized countries" (Anderson and van Wincoop 2004, p. 693). The remaining ad valorem tax equivalent arises from the costs of transportation and border costs associated with international trade. Transportation costs (amounting to a 21 percent tax equivalent) include directly measured freight costs and a 9 percent tax equivalent of the time value of goods in transit. Border-related trade barriers (other than tariff and nontariff policy barriers) include language differences (7 percent), costs from using different currencies (14 percent), information costs (6 percent), and security (3 percent). Trade costs can be much higher in less developed countries, where relatively poor institutions and infrastructure raise distribution costs.

To these costs, a practical discussion must at least note the remaining political trade restrictions. Trade in agricultural products, the most important source of employment for Third World workers, is still heavily distorted by agricultural subsidies in advanced countries to the detriment of less developed countries. Free trade in agricultural products would reduce pressures to migrate from the least developed countries. In short, there are enough real world limitations on the full promise of factor price equalization theorems to leave a significant role for international migration in equalizing labor conditions around the world.

Much the same may be said of unrestricted international migration. Even if the world could return to a regime of unrestricted international migration, there are important practical limits on equalizing labor conditions through migration. Private transport costs declined during the twentieth century, but the costs of moving between cultures remain. A recent study of mobility between OECD countries demonstrates the effects of these costs (Belot and Ederveen 2005). Many workers in this sample live in the European Union, where national policies do not restrict their cross-border movement. After controlling for the effects of many standard economic influences on gross migration, the study nonetheless finds that linguistic and religious dissimilarities between countries significantly inhibit migration. Moreover, the brain drain discussion reminds us that from the perspective of developing countries, emigration may include significant social costs. Countries suffering from brain drain prefer trade to migration as the mechanism of convergence.

Differences in technology and resources and the continued significance of the costs of conducting trade limit the literal application of factor price equalization theorems to worldwide labor conditions. Even with the removal of remaining trade barriers, free trade would produce convergence but not equalization. Much the same can be said of international migration. The potential for convergence is great, but a combination of significant monetary and nonmonetary migration costs, immigration barriers in receiving countries, and concerns about the quality (including health) of migrant human capital will limit equalization before equality is achieved. Will reducing trade barriers or migration barriers produce more factor price equalization? With only rough measures of trade costs and even rougher measures of migration costs, the research community has not yet been able to provide an answer to this question.

Conclusions

This book began by listing frequently voiced concerns about how globalization might degrade labor conditions. Chief among these is the fear that global competition will encourage sweatshop labor in the poorest countries. This chapter has challenged that view by showing the powerful role of international labor market competition in narrowing differences in labor conditions between countries that remain open to migration. Mass migration was the major factor equalizing real wages between Europe and the New World during the first wave of globalization. In modern times, the incentives to move across international borders remain huge, and migration has continued to narrow differences between the haves and the have-nots when international labor markets have been permitted to function. At the beginning of the twenty-first century, the scope for further gains from migration remains large. Despite incentives to move, surviving restrictions on international labor markets limit the prospects of the migration mechanism for improving working conditions around the world. Even a modest relaxation of migration barriers would produce large gains.

Like trade, migration produces both winners and losers in the short run amid the aggregate gains. During the first wave of globalization, the huge convergence in real wages between the Old and New Worlds occurred with slower wage growth to unskilled workers in destination countries. More recently, estimates of the impact of immigrants on the wages of native workers vary widely, with the most probable outcome a small negative effect. In the short run, migration may provide a small threat to the wages and working conditions of some workers in the richest countries, but it clearly offers major opportunities to workers in the poorest countries. Though current suspicion of globalization flows from groups concerned about the plight of labor in the poorest countries, concerns about the short-run effects of migration on low-wage workers in the richest countries motivate most immigration restrictions.

However small the actual effect on native wages, fears that immigrants will lower wages and worsen working conditions have provoked restrictions on immigration in destination countries since the nineteenth century. By limiting the volume of international migration and altering international patterns of migration, these policies effectively mute migration's potential as a force for greater equalization. When it comes to international labor markets, it is not globalization but a retreat from globalization that perpetuates poor working conditions. It is striking that a reduction in barriers to international migration receives so little attention, let alone emphasis, by those who express the greatest concern about global labor conditions.

Even in an environment of more liberalized trade, the absence of this powerful mechanism for equalizing labor conditions surely has slowed the international convergence in labor conditions. Reducing international migration barriers would produce several benefits. First and foremost, the experience from periods when barriers were low demonstrates that immigration improves working conditions in the poorest countries and reduces income inequality between nations. It also narrows income differences in source countries and increases income inequality in destination countries. Unskilled immigration therefore raises incentives to acquire more human capital in the latter countries.

Second, removing barriers to immigration reduces illegal flows of immigrants and diminishes the demand for trafficking in humans; exploitation and forced labor declines. Diminishing the scope of illegal migration frees up enforcement resources and spares countries awkward political decisions on how to treat illegal migrants who have lived and worked in a destination country for several years. The frequent amnesties for such workers signal a de facto recognition that the distinction between legal and illegal immigration is arbitrary and poorly correlated with the contributions of the two groups to destination countries.

Third, balanced against the traditional fiscal concern that migrants fail to finance the public services that they consume in destination countries is a view that migration may provide at least transitory fiscal benefits to many destination countries with aging populations and low birthrates. When new labor force entrants cannot replace workers who retire or otherwise leave the labor force, countries face lower growth rates and increasing difficulties in meeting their pension and other social insurance obligations. The younger age distribution and higher birthrates of immigrants provide short-term mitigation of the fiscal pressures.

Restrictive immigration policies would be unnecessary in a world with smaller economic incentives to migrate. For countries wary of immigration, policies that diminish migration incentives provide an alternative to direct barriers. Improving economic and social opportunities in countries of emigration through more rapid economic growth provides an attractive if difficult option. After all, strong postwar economic growth transformed Europe from a region of net emigration to a region of net immigration. Latin America's weak growth produced the opposite reversal of migration flows. Stimulating economic growth in source countries is beyond the means of any single country. It requires coordinated action through international organizations. Moreover, this approach has a spotty record (Easterly 2002), and even the rare successes require a long gestation period to narrow the productivity and wage differences that stimulate international migration. Indeed, initial source-country income gains may provide would-be migrants with the resources to finance a move to another country. Eventually, higher source-country income should reduce migration flows.

With migration off the table, international government and nongovernmental organizations have searched for alternative mechanisms for improving labor conditions. The search for alternative mechanisms has led some wealthier nations in the international community to champion regulation—particularly the establishment and enforcement of international labor standards. Whether this default approach provides an adequate substitute for international migration is the subject of chapter 7. But first we must assess the effect of multinational companies on worldwide labor conditions.

CHAPTER 6

Multinational Corporations
and Labor Conditions

Few indictments of the human effects of globalization omit a critique of the role of multinational companies. Their critics see multinational corporations, either directly through their foreign affiliates or indirectly through their overseas contractors, as engines of worker exploitation and bastions of sweatshop working conditions. Some critics assert that exploitation is an explicit, if unadvertised, policy of multinationals. Others allege that governments of developing countries in effect encourage exploitation by offering multinationals cheap, compliant labor and minimal regulation of labor conditions.

This chapter confronts these concerns with analyses of how multinationals *might* influence the labor markets in which they operate and evidence on how they *do* influence working conditions and labor standards in host countries. A picture of the role of multinationals emerges by answering the following questions: How much host-country employment occurs in multinationals? In what circumstances could multinationals degrade labor conditions in a host country? How do multinationals treat their host-country employees? Do the policies and practices of multinationals spread beyond organizational boundaries to influence labor conditions in the broader host-country labor market?

This chapter also evaluates the argument that low wages and poor working conditions attract foreign direct investment and reviews efforts of international and nongovernmental organizations to use corporate codes of conduct to influence the human resource management policies of multinationals in host countries.

The Sphere of Influence of Multinationals

Nineteenth-century globalization included significant capital flows as well as the trade flows and mass migrations discussed in earlier chapters. But most direct investment flowed from capital-rich countries in Europe to less-developed countries, where capital was scarce and its marginal value was accordingly high. Along with trade and migration, international capital flows also declined dramatically during the interwar retreat from globalization. With the return to flexible exchange rates following the demise of the system of fixed exchange rates established by the Bretton Woods agreement and the subsequent relaxation of capital controls, however, international capital flows regained their earlier peaks during the 1990s. Post–World War II globalization brought a distinctive change in the destination of most international capital flows, however. Capital-poor developing countries, which had received disproportionately large shares of global investment flows at the beginning of the twentieth century, now receive disproportionately small shares. Most capital no longer flows toward the least developed nations where capital is scarce. Instead, as Obstfeld and Taylor note, "capital transactions seem to be mostly a rich-rich affair, a process of 'diversification finance' rather than 'development finance' " (Obstfeld and Taylor 2003, p. 175).

By the beginning of the twenty-first century, multinationals were a highly visible aspect of global capital movements. In 2001, some 850,000 foreign affiliates of about 65,000 multinational companies accounted for about 10 percent of world GDP (up from 5 percent in 1985). Employment in the foreign affiliates of multinationals grew from 24 million to 54 million workers between 1990 and 2001 (UNCTAD 2002b, p. xv). Notwithstanding the visibility of many multinationals, their economic power is easily exaggerated. By comparing the *sales* of multinationals with the *GDP* of countries, for example, one might conclude that half of the 100 largest "economies" in the world are multinationals. Every new student of economics is alerted to the mistake that produces this erroneous conclusion. GDP, the flow of new production in a country, counts the value *added* at each stage of the production process—a procedure that avoids counting purchased inputs (i.e., inputs that have already been counted as new production in other industries) several times. In contrast, sales include the value of purchased inputs—other industries' GDP—plus the value added. The overstatement from using sales is large: the value added of automobile manufacturers and oil companies is only 25–30 percent of sales, and the value added in service companies is about 35–37 percent of sales (De Grauwe and Camerman 2003; UNCTAD 2002a).

A proper comparison shows a rather different picture of multinationals and countries. When compared on the basis of value added, there are two companies among the largest 50 "economies." As the forty-fifth largest "economy" in 2000, Exxon Mobil ranked between Chile and Pakistan; at forty-seventh, General Motors ranked between Pakistan and Peru. There are many more corporations represented in the next 50 "economies," but the worldwide economic scope of multinationals is perhaps best described by the following facts: In 2000, the 10 largest multinationals produced .9 percent of the world GDP; the 100 largest multinationals produced 4.3 percent of world GDP.[1] Viewed by country, value added of foreign affiliates relative to national GDP ranged from 0.4 percent in Japan to a little more than 40 percent for Belgium/Luxembourg and Ireland among developed economies in 1999. For developing countries, multinationals' "presence" seems huge in three countries: Hong Kong (98.5 percent of GDP), Nigeria (86.8 percent), and Honduras (70.7 percent). These countries are outliers, however. At the other end of the scale, the value added of foreign affiliates represents less than 1 percent of the GDP of India and Panama. The median economic presence of multinationals among developing countries is about 9 percent (UNCTAD 2002b, p. 275).

Whether the economic power of multinationals is great or small, a key concern is that they seek cheap labor and weak labor standards when they choose their production locations. Modern patterns of foreign direct investment (FDI) undermine this view.[2] Most FDI now flows between the most industrialized nations, which offer superior labor conditions. The developing world, where working conditions are poorest, receives less than a third of the world's direct investment flows (table 6.1). Moreover, these investment flows remain very unevenly distributed within developing countries. According to the United Nations, in 2001 "the five largest host countries in the developing world [Hong Kong/China, Brazil, Mexico, Argentina, and Bermuda] received 62 percent of total inflows" and "the level of concentration of FDI in developing countries has in fact risen in recent years" (UNCTAD 2002b, p. 9). The entire continent of Africa receives less than 3 percent of world inflows. Clearly, efforts to find cheap labor and poor labor standards cannot be the primary factor motivating the international distribution of foreign direct investment, since most of it flows to countries with superior labor conditions.

Table 6.1
Foreign Direct Investment Inflows, 1982–99 (Percentage)

Countries	Share of World FDI Inflows		
	1982–87	1995–99	2001
World	100.0	100.0	100.0
Developed	74.6	67.5	68.4
Developing	25.3	29.3	27.9
Central/East Europe	0.03	3.2	3.7

Sources: UNCTAD 1993, Annex Table B; UNCTAD 2003, Annex Table A.I.1

Globalization skeptics also worry that multinationals may degrade labor conditions in host countries. The potential for such an impact should be related to the share of world employment opportunities offered by multinationals. Foreign affiliates' share of world employment is less than their 10 percent share of world output because they are more productive than host-country companies. Official statistics also overstate multinational company employment shares because they do not capture employment in the informal sector, which is unlikely to include multinationals. The recorded employment effect of foreign affiliates on host countries varies widely in both industrialized and developing countries (table 6.2). In the vast majority of developing countries where concerns about labor conditions are greatest, the foreign affiliate share of total employment is in the single digits.

The structure of economic activity in developing countries provides limited scope for direct foreign affiliate influence on employment conditions. Because more than half the employment in developing countries is concentrated in agriculture and small-scale family enterprises, relatively few workers experience labor conditions in the manufacturing and extractive activities in which most multinationals are found. Absent significant spillovers into the broader labor market, including sectors where multinationals have no presence, the labor policies of multinationals clearly apply to a distinct minority of the world's host-country workers.

This brief review establishes that (1) overseas subsidiaries of multinationals directly influence the working conditions of a small number of the world's workers—substantially less than 10 percent; (2) multinationals' influence on labor conditions in the poorest countries is even smaller, since most FDI flows occur between rich countries; and (3) with most FDI flowing to the most advanced countries, the notion that foreign investment seeks poor labor conditions seems unconvincing. But if their overall influence on countries has been overstated, how do multinationals influence labor conditions within their limited sphere of influence?

Can Multinationals Degrade Labor Conditions?

Whether or not a multinational company can degrade working conditions in a host country has nothing to do with the fact that its headquarters is in another country and everything to do with the extent to which it must compete with other multinationals or host-country companies for its workers. Consider the two methods by which foreign companies may enter a host country. Foreign direct investment may take the form of "greenfield" investments in newly constructed establishments or acquisition of existing companies in host countries. Greenfield investments are most common in developing countries, although mergers and acquisitions increased from 15 to 30 percent between 1993 and 1999 (Kucera 2002). If multinationals establish inferior conditions in greenfield plants, they expose themselves to

Table 6.2
Multinational Employment Shares in Selected
Host Countries, 1999

	Total employment share
Developed economies	
Belgium/Luxembourg	24.6
Denmark	16.3
New Zealand	15.8
United Kingdom	3.0
Norway	2.0
Japan	0.5
Developing countries	
South Africa	23.0
Malaysia	16.6
Singapore	10.4
China	9.5
Mexico	7.0
India	4.1
Korea	2.2
Jamaica	0.6
Panama	0.4
Barbados	0.2
Central/East Europe	
Hungary	27.4
Latvia	10.4
Estonia	9.4
Ukraine	0.7
Belarus	0.3
Bosnia/Herzegovina	0.2

Source: UNCTAD 2002b, Annex Table A.I.6

recruiting and retention difficulties when competing for labor with local companies. Any worsening of conditions in host-country acquisitions would expose the company to a higher quit rate as workers leave to join locally owned companies offering superior conditions. The overall level of working conditions will reflect the balance between the supply of and demand for labor in the host-country labor market.

Whether the arrival of multinationals can improve working conditions depends on labor supply conditions and the company's human resource management policies. In markets with a limitless supply of labor available at the current wage, increased labor demand from multinationals or native companies will raise employment but not wages. Many observers argue that such "infinitely elastic" labor supply characterizes labor markets with vast reserves of rural labor awaiting superior employment opportunities in a "modern" sector. In other countries, workers may require stronger inducements to overcome the costs of changing jobs. In these markets, labor supply is less elastic, and increases in labor demand from multinationals or native companies will raise both wages and employment. The main point is that when companies compete for labor, the effect on wages depends entirely on what workers are willing to accept—not on what companies may wish to pay. (A fall in wages is ruled out because if workers were willing to accept lower wages, competing employers would have forced wage cuts on them earlier.)

If multinationals do not compete with other companies for labor services, they may force labor conditions below competitive levels. Firms in isolated locations, such as some mining districts, may have such "monopsony" power, but situations in which labor has no option but to work for a multinational are not a general phenomenon. Indeed, by *adding* to the number of employers in a labor market, the arrival of multinationals may improve labor conditions by reducing monopsony power in host-country labor markets. This potential is particularly strong in countries with a history of state-owned enterprises with compensation and working conditions determined by central planning.

Some multinationals do not actually establish production plants in foreign countries. Nike, Reebok, Levi-Strauss, and other companies in the athletic footwear and clothing industries design and market their products but contract out production activities to companies in low-wage foreign countries. Technically, the headquarters company has no legal status in host countries and hence does not set working conditions at contractors' manufacturing sites. Many of these "design and marketing" companies have been severely criticized for alleged "sweatshop labor" conditions at their contractors' plants. How might such "indirect" presence of multinationals influence host-country labor conditions? Does competition for the business of "design and marketing" firms degrade local labor conditions? In principle, the answer should be the same as for the direct influence of multinationals discussed above: the effect that the additional jobs have on wages will depend on labor supply conditions, with the most likely outcomes being an improvement or no change. Ultimately, the question of whether multinationals bring inferior labor conditions can be settled only by empirical evidence, which we now consider.

Do Multinationals Degrade Labor Conditions?

Economic growth in less developed countries increasingly moves employment from the farm and the home to the factory. Throughout history, sweatshops have emerged with this shift in the locus of employment, even in countries that remained insulated from international commerce. Indeed, the spread of factory employment is possible only because factories, notwithstanding their shortcomings, provide a comparatively productive work environment that supports higher wages and offers a route to improved living standards. Economic growth, not multinational corporations, transforms work environments. When foreign direct investment accompanies economic growth, however, the question of whether the presence of multinationals worsens the consequences of the economic transition becomes relevant.

There is an extraordinary difference between the conclusions of the research community and the views of globalization skeptics about working conditions in multinationals. To some extent the difference in views reflects a tension between anecdotes and evidence. Evidence regarding multinationals' effects on labor conditions in both industrialized and developing countries is remarkably clear: on average, multinationals improve labor conditions in host countries.

Underlying the tension between anecdote and evidence are two different views of why companies locate production abroad. One view holds that multinationals seek specific locational advantages, such as mineral deposits or cheap labor. It is easy to see how the race-to-the-bottom hypothesis would emerge from the view that access to cheap labor is the dominant reason for producing abroad. Indeed, representatives of organized labor often characterize multinationals as global runaway shops—companies that abandon locations with superior labor conditions (and often unionized labor) to move to locations where labor is cheaper (and not unionized).

An alternative view that has dominated economic thinking about multinationals since the 1970s holds that they transfer important productive inputs that host countries lack: unique technology, managerial skills, and superior knowledge of organizational design and production methods (Hymer 1960; Caves 1996; Markusen 2002). Multinationals need such company-specific "knowledge capital" if they are to overcome their lack of familiarity with local regulations, marketing practices, human resource management policies and other aspects of management that are sensitive to differences in local cultures. So according to this view, production abroad is driven by company-specific assets that can profitably be combined with local inputs, rather than by an effort to exploit local inputs. Combining such firm-specific assets with local inputs should raise, not lower, the productivity of the latter. The knowledge-capital scenario is a recipe for higher, not lower, wages for host-country labor. In fact, prevailing evidence indicates that foreign affiliates have superior labor productivity (measured by value added per employee) in developed and developing countries (table 6.3).

The opening sentences of a recent study nicely summarize the conclusions of the research community on multinationals' effects on wages and other working conditions: "It seems to be a universal rule that, in every country,

Table 6.3
Manufacturing Labor Productivity, Foreign Affiliates'
Relative to Domestic Firms

Host country	Year	Relative labor productivity[a]
Finland	1998	1.04
France	1996	0.75
Ireland	1998	10.90
Japan	1998	1.29
Netherlands	1996	1.52
Norway	1992	1.09
Portugal	1998	1.71
Sweden	1999	0.89
United Kingdom	1997	1.53
United States	1999	1.46
China	1997	2.73
Hong Kong	1994	1.37
Malaysia	1995	1.65
Taiwan	1994	4.73

[a] Value added per employee in foreign affiliates divided by value
added per employee in domestic firms.

Source: UNCTAD 2002b, Annex Table A.1.5

foreign owned firms and plants pay higher wages, on average, than domestically owned ones. That is true not only in developing countries, but also
in high income countries, such as Canada, the United States and the United
Kingdom" (Lipsey and Sjoholm 2001). Simple comparisons of the compensation of workers by foreign-owned and by locally owned companies reveal
that foreign owners pay premiums that in some cases reach triple digits (table
6.4). Among OECD countries in 1998, the foreign-affiliate compensation
premium over host country firms in manufacturing ranged from 5 to 6 percent in France and the United States to 207 percent in Turkey (OECD 2002,
pp. 24–25).

Studies of wages in less developed countries in Latin America, Africa,
and Asia also find large foreign-ownership wage premiums (Aitken and Harrison 1999; Gorg Strobl, and Walsh 2002; Lipsey and Sjoholm 2001; Te Velde
and Morrissey 2001).[3] In China, a country that has had huge reserves of low-
wage labor, multinationals also pay wages well above the going rate: the
average annual wage per worker in multinationals is 150 percent of that paid
by state-owned enterprises and is more than double that paid by collectively
owned enterprises. The wage premiums paid by American and European
multinationals were even higher (Liu, Xu, and Liu 2003). Data from the
Vietnam Living-Standards Survey confirm that multinationals offer superior

Table 6.4
Relative Compensation of Workers in
Foreign-Owned Companies (Host-
country firms = 100)

Czech Republic[a]	126
Finland[a]	108
France	107
Hungary[a]	175
Ireland	133
Japan[b]	126
Netherlands	110
Norway	140
Sweden	107
United Kingdom	118
China: Rel. to state-owned	150
Rel. to collective	204
Turkey	219
Vietnam	150

[a] 1999
[b] 1996

Sources: OECD 2002, Liu et al 2003, Glewwe
2000.

compensation in less developed countries. Workers in multinationals operating in Vietnam earn twice as much as workers in household enterprises and
more than 1.5 times what they would earn in state-owned companies. A
similar picture emerges if one looks instead at per capita consumption expenditures. Even in the most labor-intensive multinationals, whose working
conditions are routinely targeted for sharp criticism, incomes exceed those
offered by alternative opportunities. Consumption by workers in foreign-
owned firms in the leather goods and the textile industries exceeds consumption in the general population by 81 and 48 percent, respectively
(Glewwe 2000). In short, foreign affiliates pay significantly more than locally
owned companies in host countries.

Why do profit-maximizing multinationals pay such huge premiums for
labor? Economists find corporate altruism as illogical as corporate malevo-
lence. What accounts for the sizeable foreign ownership wage premium? In
particular, do the premiums signify that multinationals improve wages in host
country labor markets? Although dramatic, the wage differentials reported in
table 6.4 do not reflect the "pure" effect of foreign ownership on wages, for
foreign companies provide an atypical picture of output and employment in
a host country. In country after country, the foreign affiliates of multinationals
are concentrated in high-wage industries, such as mining and manufacturing,
rather than low-wage industries such as services, agriculture, and wholesale

trade. Foreign affiliates of multinationals also operate larger establishments than do local companies and may enjoy greater economies of scale as a result. In industry after industry, foreign affiliates also employ more educated employees than do local companies. In short, part of the foreign affiliate wage differences in table 6.4 reflects differences in the workplaces, workforces, and industries of multinational enterprises (Flanagan 2001; Feliciano and Lipsey 1999; Lipsey and Sjoholm 2001; Te Velde and Morrissey 2001). Put differently, higher wages in foreign-owned firms reflect the higher productivity of foreign owned companies first noted in table 6.3. The close relationship between the relative wages and relative productivity in labor markets applies to wage differences between foreign affiliates and host-country companies.

Are the higher relative wages of foreign firms *entirely* a result of their high-productivity, high-wage characteristics? As it happens, controlling for skill mix, firm size, and industry greatly diminishes but does not eliminate the foreign-ownership compensation premium. A smaller foreign ownership premium still remains. The most convincing analyses on this point emerge from surveys that interview individual workers at their place of work and thus are able to relate the wage of individual workers to both their personal characteristics and the characteristics of their workplace (Flanagan 2001; Te Velde and Morrissey 2001). These "net" foreign-ownership premiums are on the order of 3–5 percent. Foreign owned firms still appear to pay *higher* wages for the human capital that they employ.

What accounts for the smaller premium remains a matter of debate. It may reflect unobserved quality differentials between the employees in foreign-owned and host-country companies. If host-country workers view employment in foreign firms as riskier or less certain, multinationals have to pay a compensating differential. Foreign firms may provide more firm-specific training to provide the skills needed to work with the knowledge assets that they bring from headquarters countries. One study finds evidence consistent with this hypothesis in 1998 data for manufacturing enterprises in Ghana. The foreign-ownership premium in starting wages was zero, but it grew over time for workers who received on-the-job training (Gorg et al. 2002). Union bargaining power or local regulations might also force foreign companies to pay higher wages, although a study of Australian data did not find support for the union-pressure hypothesis (Flanagan 2001). Foreign companies may also be more inclined to pay wage premiums to create incentives for employees to work harder. This "efficiency wage" hypothesis is difficult to test, however.

Oddly enough, the foreign-ownership pay premium that emerges in comparisons across companies does not by itself prove that multinationals actually improve host-country wages. Net foreign-ownership pay premiums may reflect the effect of employee or workplace characteristics that are not captured by national statistical systems. *Unobserved* workforce or management quality differences between foreign and domestic firms rather than foreign ownership itself may explain the differential. For example, if foreign-owned companies cherry-pick high-performance local companies through acquisitions, and some aspects of performance are unobservable, the foreign-ownership wage premium will simply reflect a change of ownership rather than a change in host-country wages. Such "selection effects" will mask the fact that foreign ownership produced no change in wages. Assessing whether multinationals have more than a selection effect requires analyses of how working conditions change after acquisition. Rather than studying how foreign-owned and host-country companies differ at a particular time, one analyzes how the performance and pay of a "panel" of companies changes over time when some companies switch from local to foreign ownership.

Recent panel studies for both developed and developing countries confirm that foreign acquisition improves wages in acquired companies. A study of acquisitions in the United Kingdom by both foreign-owned and domestic businesses found that during the first three post-acquisition years, wages increased in domestic plants acquired by foreign companies but declined in foreign-owned plants acquired by domestic firms (Conyon et al. 1999). A second study of U.K. plants revealed more heterogeneity and sensitivity to the nationality of the acquiring company (Girma and Görg 2003). Panel studies of Indonesian and Portuguese plants report similar findings. Two years after acquisition, wages in Indonesian plants acquired by foreign companies increased significantly relative to wages in plants that retained domestic ownership (Lipsey and Sjoholm 2002). Although selection effects are present in a Portuguese sample, the relative wage also increased over time in plants acquired by foreign owners (Almeida 2003). In short, unobserved selection effects may account for some of the cross-section foreign ownership performance and wage premiums, but most of the premium reflects the changes brought by foreign ownership. The findings are consistent with the idea that foreign ownership leads to performance improvements that permit payment of higher wages and are inconsistent with the notion that foreign firms degrade labor conditions at the firms that they acquire.

The hypothesis that multinationals establish overseas production facilities mainly to exploit particular geographic advantages, like low wages, does not survive this analysis of the wage practices of foreign-owned companies. Multinationals pay higher wages in their greenfield establishments, and they raise, not lower, wages in the plants that they acquire in host countries. Ruling out corporate benevolence (voluntary rent-sharing), productivity differences between foreign-owned and host-country companies must sustain the foreign-ownership wage premium. This interpretation fits well with the "knowledge capital" explanation of multinational activity. The evidence reviewed above confirms that foreign owned firms pay relatively higher wages because they perform better.

Their ability to transfer managerial expertise and technology that the host country lacks accounts for at least some of the superior performance. Empirical research on the exact technological and organizational sources of multinationals' competitive advantage is in its infancy, but there is evidence

that innovations in technology, products, and production processes all contribute to global competitive advantage. As discussed in chapter 4, multinationals and export firms invest more in research and development and learn
more from their global supply chains than do companies that are not globally
engaged.

Foreign-owned businesses also tend to adopt more advanced human resource management policies. A study of Australian data shows that foreign-
owned establishments are more likely to use practices such as performance
appraisal, bonuses and incentives, total quality management, skills audits, and
quality circles. The Australian data also indicate that the higher wages and
high-performance human resource policies adopted by multinationals are associated with lower quit rates. Lower turnover costs reward employers offering superior working conditions (Flanagan 2001). The presence of
multinationals may have stimulated an increased use of profit-sharing, employee stock-ownership plans, and other schemes relating employee pay to
organizational performance (Kurdelbusch 2002).

Studies of data for Australia and the United States reveal a seldom-noted
feature of the foreign-ownership wage premium: it is almost entirely a consequence of the wage difference between foreign-owned establishments and
host-country establishments with exclusively domestic operations (Flanagan
2001; Doms and Jensen 1998). That is, there is no significant difference
between wages paid by foreign-owned companies and host-country multinational companies. No matter where their headquarters are located, multinational companies adopt more advanced, high-performance human resource
policies and pay higher wages.

Missing from these analyses are studies of the effect that "design and
marketing" multinationals have on local labor conditions, since host-country
contractors are not identified as foreign owned. Although the "design and
marketing" sector constitutes a distinct minority of the multinational activity
reviewed early in the chapter, studies of how working conditions at contractors' facilities compare with conditions in other host-country facilities
would be helpful in assessing some concerns of globalization skeptics. Systematic data for such comparisons are scarce, but the earlier discussion in
chapter 4 of working conditions in export processing zones is probative, since
production for "design and marketing" multinationals is exported. The evidence reviewed in that discussion indicated that workers producing for export generally earn more than other host country workers. Research by national and international governmental organizations also contradicts the
claims that contractors degrade local labor conditions: "In Nike subcontractor
factories in June/July 2000, annual wages were $670 compared with an av-
erage minimum wage of $134. In Indonesia, annual wages were $720 compared with an average annual minimum of $241" (Lim 2001).

To summarize: global companies do not typically adapt completely to
local human resource management practices, nor do they pay lower wages
than host-country businesses. Instead, they follow distinctly different policies

than local companies; they employ relatively skilled workers, provide them with firm-specific training to complement the knowledge assets brought by many foreign owned firms, and adopt high-performance methods of work organization. Foreign-owned establishments are also larger and are in industries that pay relatively high wages. These practices are a recipe for relatively high wages, exactly as analysts have discovered in countries at all stages of development. The foreign-ownership wage premium undermines the hypothesis that multinationals generally exert monopsonistic power in host country labor markets. Global companies appear to gain some advantages from their distinctive policies in the form of lower turnover costs.

Pay Spillovers to Host-Country Businesses

Foreign-owned companies may pay higher wages and implement more advanced human resource management policies, but how do they affect the *average* wage level in host countries? The answer to this question rests on how multinationals influence the wages paid by locally owned firms. Spillovers between foreign-owned and local companies may be either positive or negative. Multinationals may improve pay in local businesses through knowledge spillovers or by reducing monopsony power in local labor markets. Productivity spillovers to domestic businesses may occur as workers who acquire company-specific human capital while employed at foreign owned companies later move to domestic companies. Alternatively, domestic companies may observe the more efficient methods of multinationals or may be driven to find more efficient production methods in order to survive in competition with multinationals that produce for local sale. Multinationals may produce negative spillovers, however. Competition from foreign-owned companies may reduce the market share of local companies, forcing them to higher average cost levels, for example (Aitkin and Harrison 1999).

Summarizing some two dozen efforts to measure the net effect of multinationals on the productivity of host-country companies in both developed and developing countries mimics the legendary two-handed economist. On the one hand, analyses of wage or productivity differences between companies or industries at a particular time find a positive productivity spillover from foreign-owned to local businesses. A study of manufacturing firms in Ghana finds that domestic companies that are owned or chaired by individuals with prior work experience at foreign-owned companies in the same industry are relatively productive (Görg and Strobl 2005). At least in Ghana, labor mobility from multinationals produces positive spillovers for domestic firms. On the other hand, studies that use company or industry panel data to study productivity changes over time find either no relationship or a negative effect of multinationals' presence on productivity in local companies. Controlling for numerous differences in the way the studies were conducted fails to explain the rather dramatic difference in results (Görg and Strobl 2001). Positive wage spillovers from foreign-owned to local businesses are more likely in industrialized than in developing countries. In short, research studies do not find consistent patterns of either positive or negative productivity and wage spillovers from multinational to local companies. Whatever one's priors, this empirical question must be listed in the unresolved column for now.

Research on the Chinese labor market indicates that the spillover effects of multinationals extend far beyond wages. Until recently, the Chinese labor market was segmented between rural and urban areas, and further among regions. Urban residents were accorded urban residency status, which included assignment to a (lifetime) job at a state-owned enterprise in their city. The only way for rural individuals to acquire urban residency status and state employment was by obtaining a college degree. In addition,

> each worker also had a work-related personal file (dang'an). When one was allocated a job her personal file would be placed with the labor office of the local government bureau responsible for the enterprise. Should she seek a job transfer to another unit, she must obtain the consent of both her existing work unit and her new work unit. Job transfers between units subordinate to the same local government bureau would already be hard; job transfers between work units of different government bureaus would be even harder, as . . . this would disrupt the state's manpower allocation plan. . . . [J]ob transfers between two cities would be still harder, as . . . restrictions were placed limiting the influx of immigrant manpower from other cities (and, of course, from the rural areas). (Liu et al. 2003, p. 203)

Two developments stimulated the salutary effects of multinationals on the Chinese labor market. During a period of reforms that gave state-owned enterprises more authority over personnel decisions, multinationals provided a badly needed human resource management model for organizations that had no experience with this function. Through joint ventures and labor market competition, the state-owned businesses learned and began to emulate multinationals' practices. That the emulation was not complete is clear in the size of the multinational companies' wage premiums that remained as the century closed (Liu et al. 2003). Nevertheless, multinationals did have a positive influence on labor conditions at the state-owned enterprises. Indeed, a 1995 revision of Chinese labor laws was widely interpreted as raising the labor practice requirements at these businesses to the legal standards for multinationals (Markel 1994).

Efforts to attract foreign investment also led the Chinese government to relax the geographic restrictions on multinationals' labor recruitment. Multinationals gradually were permitted to recruit based on merit rather than location. Both rural and urban workers flocked to the multinationals, and by 1997, almost half of the employees of multinationals in Guangdong province, a major location of foreign companies, had migrated from other provinces.

Headquarters-Subsidiary Differentials

If the evidence overwhelmingly rejects the proposition that multinationals degrade wage and nonwage working conditions, why do critics of globalization inevitably tie multinationals to inferior labor conditions? Critics often seem to frame their expectations of appropriate conditions from working conditions in a company's headquarters country. "Wages are a mere ten percent of what the company's U.S. workers earn!" Such rhetoric ignores the fact that all wages in the host country—wages paid by domestic businesses and foreign affiliates alike—are a fraction of wages paid in the headquarters country. Indeed, evidence reviewed earlier in this chapter shows that locally owned companies pay even less than foreign affiliates.

Workplaces in host and headquarters countries vary along dimensions other than wages. International organizations tabulate huge differences in literacy, education, and health and communications infrastructure between industrialized and developing countries. From the perspective of a headquarters country, all of these factors lower the relative productivity of foreign workers and hence lower their relative compensation. We saw in chapter 3 how the vast compensation differences between countries closely reflect productivity differences. Differences in the compensation paid by the majority-owned, nonbank foreign affiliates of U.S. multinationals in 2002 show a similar relationship. Compensation per worker in the affiliates tracks the differences in productivity very closely (fig. 6.1), with international differences in the labor productivity of foreign affiliates accounting for almost half of their international differences in compensation.[4] Each point in the figure reflects the pay and productivity of U.S. affiliates in a different country. As one looks across countries, workers in the more productive affiliates receive higher compensation. With the headquarters of most major multinationals located in the most productive countries in the world, the pay difference between headquarters personnel and workers in foreign affiliates reflects productivity differentials.

Labor market alternatives available to workers in host countries usually differ from the alternatives available in home countries. Framing is crucial. Working conditions that appear inferior from the perspective of the headquarters country may be superior from the perspective of a host country whose workers have limited skills and few job alternatives.

Do Multinationals Provoke a Race to the Bottom?

The analysis in chapter 4 established that countries with poor labor conditions do not obtain superior export performance. Low wages reflect low productivity, so that countries with low wages do not necessarily have low labor costs per unit of output. We now consider a related question: Do countries with poor labor conditions gain larger shares of world foreign direct

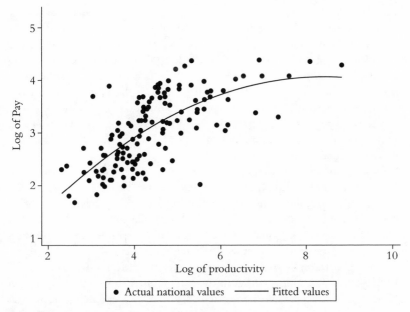

Figure 6.1. Pay and Productivity of Multinational Affiliates

investment? Data reported earlier in this chapter support a negative response: most FDI flows now occur between industrialized countries, which normally have superior labor conditions. Clearly, efforts to locate facilities where labor conditions are poorest cannot be the primary factor governing the destination of foreign direct investment.

The fact that poor labor conditions signal low skills may discourage investment in some areas. Technologies and production processes originally developed for use in the high-skilled labor markets of industrialized countries may not thrive in a low-skill environment. Foreign investors' interest in the health of a potential host country's workforce signals their concern with labor quality. According to a recent report, "health is a positive and statistically significant determinant of FDI inflows to low and middle income countries" (Alsen, Bloom, and Canning 2004). The decline in foreign investment in China following the outbreak of Severe Auto-Respiratory Syndrome (SARS) in 2003 is a notable example.

Many other factors are likely to influence FDI decisions more powerfully than do labor conditions. Most important is the expected return on capital. Capital scarcity in most developing countries implies a high marginal productivity of capital, but many institutional factors also influence the "expected" return. Prominent among these are risk factors associated with the political and social climate. Risks of expropriation, repudiation of contracts, and corruption all tend to discourage foreign investment by reducing its expected return, as does extensive government intervention in the economy.

Risk of expropriation is highest in a few African countries with unusually troubled histories (Liberia, Somalia, Sudan, Uganda, and Zaire) and lowest in most OECD countries. The share of government consumption in the economy, a rough indication of the extent of public intervention into markets, ranges from the single digits in Argentina, Japan, Korea, Luxembourg, Mexico, and Singapore to as high as 50 percent in the Congo.[5] To further muddy the waters, countries with poor labor conditions tend to be countries in which direct risks to investment are high. (Risks of expropriation and repudiation of contracts are highest in countries with few civil liberties and considerable child labor, for example.)

In some instances, risks may be countered by potential market size, measured by the number of consumers, or their wealth or potential purchasing power. Trade costs, including those stemming from trade policies, also influence investment flows, but they influence horizontal and vertical investment in different ways. Horizontal foreign investment—more or less replicating headquarters production activities in a foreign country—becomes more attractive when transportation costs or barriers to trade with a country are relatively high. Locating facilities in the foreign market is then cheaper than trading with it. In contrast, trade costs and barriers that encourage horizontal investment tend to discourage vertical investment (extracting or producing inputs that will be used in a later stage of production in another country) by raising the costs of moving items between different stages of the global production chain.

The likely importance of investment risks, market size, and trade costs for foreign direct investment does not rule out labor conditions' influence. Local institutions may raise or lower wages relative to productivity. Job safety regulation may be more or less costly. The presence of child labor and forced labor can provide a cheaper but less skilled workforce. Freedom of association rights that promote union organization may produce upward wage pressure (again, relative to productivity). And so forth. The key questions are (1) Do relationships between FDI and labor conditions exist? (2) If so, how important is their influence on FDI relative to investment risks, market size, and trade costs?

A regression analysis of how the share of world foreign direct investment inflows varied across more than 75 countries during 1991–96 illuminates these issues. The analysis includes measures of the risk of expropriation and the government's share of economic activity to capture risks to investment, population, and per capita GDP for the size and wealth of the market, measures of trade volumes and policy, and measures of land area and skill—possible complements to foreign investment.[6] These factors provide a baseline explanation of investment shares to which measures of working conditions, labor rights, and labor regulations may be added.

The baseline analysis, reported fully in the appendix to this chapter, confirms that other things equal, laws and practices that put property at risk discourage foreign investment. Weak property rights as signaled by a high risk of expropriation discourage investment. A substantial government regulatory presence also discourages investment inflows. Large markets attract foreign direct investment, with population size more important than income per capita.

Investment shares are larger in countries with relatively high educational attainment. Human capital and foreign investment shares are always positively correlated—suggesting complementarities between skill and investment—but the precision of the result varies with the exact specification of a country's openness to international trade in the regression analysis. The tendency for foreign investment shares to be higher in countries with a more highly educated population is measured most precisely where open trade policy measures openness; the relationship remains positive but not statistically significant when trade volumes measure openness. There is no evidence consistent with the view that countries with less skilled labor attract more FDI.

With regard to international trade itself, countries with large trade volumes and/or more open trade policies have larger foreign investment shares. Free trade and foreign investment are clearly complementary. All told, the factors in the baseline model account for slightly more than 90 percent of the variation in FDI shares among 78 countries in the early 1990s.

Adding measures of working conditions and labor rights to this baseline empirical model of how world FDI shares vary among countries produces a surprisingly simple conclusion: with one exception, labor conditions in a country are not significantly correlated with the country's share of investment inflows. The exception is job safety: other things equal, investment shares are *lower* in countries with relatively high fatal job accident rates. That is, where there is a significant relationship between a labor condition and FDI share, the correlation is again the *opposite* of that predicted by the race-to-the-bottom hypothesis that countries with poor labor conditions attract more foreign investment. The signs on most other measures of labor conditions are also consistent with the view that investment is attracted to superior working conditions, but the results are measured too imprecisely to place great weight on them.

The analysis also does not find significant links between FDI shares and labor rights. The influence of de jure and de facto freedom of association rights in a country receives particular attention, given allegations that multinationals frequently try to suppress these rights. The former consist of legal rights to freedom of association and to form collective organizations at the workplace. The latter consist of actual collective workplace activity as indicated by the extent of unionization, the dominant collective bargaining structure, and the level of strike activity. The labor relations setting may influence the costs of doing business in a country, and it is natural to ask whether multinationals systematically locate in countries with accommodating industrial relations environments—that is, those with restrictions on freedom of association, low unionization, low bargaining costs, and few strikes. Again the story is quite simple: the cross-country econometric analysis uncovers no significant connection between the characteristics of a country's industrial relations system and inflows of FDI. In no case is there evidence of a significant correlation between foreign direct investment inflow shares and freedom of association or collective bargaining characteristics. The same may be said of efforts to find a significant statistical relationship between FDI and child labor, forced labor, and gender discrimination.

To summarize, the evidence does not support the view that poor working conditions or weak labor rights attract foreign direct investment. This conclusion holds as strongly for an analysis of poorer, non-OECD countries (also reported in the appendix to this chapter) as it does for the analysis of the larger sample of countries at all levels of economic development. In fact, the positive association between skill (education) and FDI shares is more powerful and significant in the analysis of low-income countries.

Foreign investment inflows may also vary with the strength of national labor market regulations. Indices of the strength of national labor regulations in the mid-1990s help evaluate whether investment is attracted to countries with weak labor regulations, for example. These include measures of the strength of employment laws (pertaining particularly to job security arrangements), industrial relations laws (addressing collective bargaining rights and procedures), social security laws (providing benefits for unemployment, injured workers, etc.), and civil rights laws.[7] Adding these variables to the baseline model of FDI shares tests whether foreign investment is significantly influenced by the strength of national labor regulations in potential host countries. The analysis finds that countries with relatively strong employment and social security legislation had relatively high shares of investment inflows in the early 1990s, with other influences held equal. Somewhat surprisingly, this finding holds for countries with relatively high costs of firing workers or lengthening the workweek. No significant relationship between FDI shares and collective action or civil rights regulations emerges. The results as a whole give no indication that countries with weak labor regulations attract more foreign direct investment. These conclusions are also supported in analyses restricted to non-OECD countries.

Other cross-country analyses also find no tendency for countries with poor labor conditions or weak labor regulations to attract more investment. Several studies find relatively low FDI in countries with relatively high child labor force participation rates, other things equal (Busse and Braun 2003a; Flanagan 2003; Kucera 2002). Likewise, foreign investors do not appear to be attracted to countries known for the use of forced labor. A recent cross-country study finds an *inverse* relationship between the varieties of forced labor in a country and investment inflows (Busse and Braun 2003b).

Do politically repressive countries offer cost advantages that attract multinationals? After all, wages may be lower in societies in which workers lack freedom of association rights. As one would predict from the fact that most

FDI flows occur between industrialized countries, the raw data do not support the hypothesis that investment is systematically attracted to repressive regimes. Formal statistical analyses confirm this intuition. Cross-country and fixed-effect country panel regression analyses of the determinants of per capita FDI during the 1990s conclude that societies that repress political rights and curtail worker representation do not attract international investors (Harms and Ursprung 2002). The analysis is based on a sample of 62 developing and emerging economies, thereby excluding industrialized countries that are both less repressive and the sources and destinations of most investment flows. A study of a more limited sample of countries also finds that a country's degree of unionization and strike activity do not significantly influence the share of U.S. multinational capital or employment in the country (Bognanno, Keane, and Yang 2005).

Cross-country statistical analyses support four general conclusions: (1) Working conditions, labor rights, and domestic labor regulations have a relatively minor influence on foreign direct investment flows. Potential risks to investments and the product market size usually trump labor market considerations in choosing destinations for FDI. (2) In instances in which labor conditions have a significant influence, countries with superior conditions or stronger labor regulations attract more FDI. (3) The results are consistent with the hypothesis that foreign investment is complementary with high-productivity *skilled* labor, not the unskilled labor associated with substandard labor conditions. (4) The truly powerful influences on the location of multinational activity are the scope of national markets and legal institutions that govern the security of foreign investments. Countries that wish to attract FDI have powerful alternatives to substandard labor conditions. Government actions to reduce risks associated with expropriation and uncertain contract status and to reduce its own presence in the economy appear to be particularly productive strategies for increasing a country's share of world FDI. These findings emerge from analyses of countries at all levels of economic development as well as analyses restricted to poorer, non-OECD countries.

Codes of Conduct

Notwithstanding evidence that the foreign affiliates of multinationals generally provide better working conditions than host country companies, international organizations, nongovernmental organizations, and multinational companies themselves have developed wide-ranging corporate codes of conduct in recent years. As voluntary standards of conduct, the codes represent efforts to develop norms of behavior for multinationals. This section reviews the content of such codes and assesses their potential for influencing labor conditions in host countries.

International Codes of Conduct

Early statements of labor rights may be found in human rights declarations by international organizations. The original purpose of the statements was to provide goals for national policies in member countries. The UN Universal Declaration of Human Rights (United Nations, 1948) asserts general rights "to work, to free choice of employment, to just and favorable conditions of work and to protection against unemployment," to equal pay for equal work, "to form and to join trade unions," and to remuneration ensuring "an existence worthy of human dignity" (Article 23). The declaration also supports "reasonable limitations of working hours and periodic holidays with pay" (Article 24) and "a standard of living adequate for the health and well-being of himself and of his family" (Article 25).[8]

More recently, the International Labor Organization (ILO), the UN agency responsible for establishing international labor standards, and other international organizations have incorporated the four "core" areas of labor standards into "codes of conduct" explicitly directed at multinationals.[9] The ILO's Tripartite Declaration of Principles concerning Multinational Enterprises and Social Policy emerged in 1977 (and was revised in 2000 to take account of the Declaration on Fundamental Principles and Rights at Work), following extensive consultations and negotiation between employer, labor, and government organizations.[10] The ILO Declaration states a number of principles for multinational enterprises while simultaneously stating that it does not aim to establish "inequalities of treatment between multinational and national enterprises." In addition to emphasizing the importance of respecting the core labor standards, the declaration urges multinationals to promote stable employment opportunities on a nondiscriminatory basis, preferably with significant training opportunities.

Remuneration, nonmonetary working conditions, and standards of industrial relations offered by multinational enterprises "should be not less favorable to the workers than those offered by comparable employers in the country concerned" (paragraphs 33 and 41). "Wages should be related to the economic position of the enterprise, but should be at least adequate to satisfy basic needs of the workers and their families" (paragraph 34). Recent proposals to impose living wage requirements on multinationals may be rooted in this statement and the earlier Universal Declaration of Human Rights. The ILO declaration urges all companies to respect the minimum age of employment, without specifying what the age should be. "Multinational enterprises should maintain the highest standards of safety and health, in conformity with national requirements, bearing in mind their relevant experience within the enterprise as a whole, including any knowledge of special hazards" and should apprise workers' representatives of significant risks (paragraph 38).

The OECD has developed *Guidelines for Multinational Enterprises* for its

30 mainly industrialized member countries and 7 nonmember countries (Argentina, Brazil, Chile, Estonia, Israel, Lithuania, and Slovenia). Most of the world's FDI flows between OECD countries, which are also the home to most major multinational enterprises. The nonbinding OECD guidelines mainly restate the four core labor standards. They also call for companies to "observe standards of employment and industrial relations not less favorable than those observed by comparable employers in the host country" (OECD 2000). By 2000, the OECD had 246 corporate codes in its inventory.

Three features of the codes developed by international organizations are quite striking. One is the contrast between brief, general statements that multinationals should not be held to a *higher* standard than local businesses and the lengthy specifications of how specific conditions should never be *less* than those at local businesses. As we have seen throughout this chapter, wages paid by multinationals consistently exceed the wages paid by host country companies. Schizophrenia over the appropriate criteria for compensation in multinationals constitutes the next notable feature. The implication that labor conditions in multinationals should be similar to those in local companies implies acquiescence in labor market outcomes. In other clauses, the emphasis on family need over productivity in determining compensation encourages multinationals to override market criteria, even if local companies do not. Need-based standards contrast with the economic principles of wage determination in ways that could reduce the employment of low-skill workers. They imply that multinationals should adopt the "living wage" criteria used in a few U.S. cities to determine the wage of employees of public-sector contractors. Such policies can have unintended consequences: if need dictates paying more than the market wage, companies may shift production to countries where higher wages are already supported by higher productivity. The final notable feature is the voluntary, nonbinding character of all these codes. International organizations lack the powers to enforce their guidelines.

Corporate Codes of Conduct

Notwithstanding the initiatives of international organizations, many countries in the world do not pass domestic legislation supporting all core labor standards or do not enforce the labor laws that are on their own books (chapter 7 will explore this topic). Corporate codes of conduct can provide support for basic labor rights and standards where national governments have failed to adopt the standards suggested by international organizations. Like the principles developed in the UN, ILO, and OECD statements, corporate commitments are not legally enforceable. Unlike the statements of international organizations, however, corporate commitments may be backed by the reputation of the company. In some instances, markets may discipline companies that fail to honor the commitments in their corporate codes if consumers are willing to punish bad behavior through their purchasing decisions (Elliot and Freeman 2003). In short, the goal of corporate codes is to establish a mechanism of global accountability for working conditions and labor rights.

Many large multinational enterprises now have such codes of conduct, but they come in many varieties (Posner and Nolan 2003). Two fundamental design issues are the scope of the codes and their provisions for monitoring compliance. The stronger codes commit the company to follow certain absolute standards, while weaker codes indicate that the company's policy is to comply with local legislation, which may be weak. A second consideration is whether the code covers the multinationals' contractors and subcontractors, an issue of particular importance for design-and-marketing multinationals. There are also several monitoring options. Self-monitoring probably has the least credibility. Professional auditors, including major accounting firms, provide an alternative, but they do not necessarily have the institutional competence to assess compliance with labor standards regulations. Professional auditors also may lack credibility if their fees are paid by the multinational that they are auditing. Nongovernmental organizations provide another independent alternative.

Voluntary corporate codes of conduct face inherent limitations on the scope of their influence. Multinationals typically operate in the "formal" sector of developing countries, where employment relationships are subject to labor market regulations or collective bargaining contracts. They are rarely found in agriculture or the informal sectors, which provide much of the employment in most developing countries (chapter 2). In short, most employment in developing countries may be beyond the reach of corporate codes of conduct.

Even for jobs within the formal sector, two factors may limit the changes in practice induced by voluntary corporate codes of conduct. First, companies selling products with widely known brand names have the strongest incentives to commit to such codes. These are the companies that are most vulnerable to retaliation by consumers who are disaffected with a company's actual or reported labor conditions. Companies producing generic products, for which brand attachment is slight, have little need to fear such retaliation. Preservation of corporate reputation mainly stimulates the adoption of corporate codes for companies with branded products. Even among branded companies, there will be an effort to limit codes to descriptions of existing practice, so that the existence of the code does not induce changes in the company's labor practices abroad.

Although there is little research on the effect that international and corporate codes of conduct have on multinationals' labor practices, one can provide best-case estimates of their effect on world labor conditions. The overseas affiliates of multinationals provide less than 10 percent of the world's employment. Only companies with strong brands operating in less developed countries are sufficiently concerned about reputation to develop and enforce a code of conduct. As a rough guess, less than 5 percent of the world's employees will work in companies with a code of conduct. Many of the codes are likely to describe rather than change existing practice. Finally, if implementation of the codes is costly—if they are more than a statement of existing practice—the employment of some host-country workers may be jeopardized. This seems like a weak, uncertain method for improving world labor conditions relative to other methods discussed in this book.

Given the evidence and analysis, the following appraisal of the potential for multinationals' codes of conduct seems on the mark:

> There is a real danger therefore that well intentioned efforts to raise the wages and working conditions of workers in developing countries may work to the detriment of these workers and their families. Instead of focusing on codes of conduct, monitoring, and compliance, society would be better served if efforts were directed by activist groups and universities/colleges to the reduction or removal of existing trade barriers and domestic impediments to economic efficiency in both developed and developing countries. (Brown et al. 2004, p. 21)

Legal Action over Labor Practices

A more adversarial and decidedly nonvoluntary approach to influencing the labor practices of multinationals is through litigation mounted in the headquarters country of the offending company. Even in U.S. courts, where the main litigation efforts have occurred, the viability of this approach is not yet fully established.

The key question is whether foreign workers can sue multinationals in their home country for human rights abuses, such as the use of forced labor or the suppression of unions, in foreign countries. The situation is further complicated when the abuses may be related to the activities of a foreign government. A government's conscription of labor for a foreign investment project provides an example. Can the conscripted workers seek redress from the multinational company in its home country?

Conventions of legal jurisdiction limit litigation options. Courts in the United States cannot hear claims against foreign governments. Conscripted workers cannot sue the conscripting government in a U.S. court. Moreover, in most instances the foreign employees of multinationals based in the United States cannot use U.S. law; the law of the country in which they work covers them. In recent decades, human rights organizations have found a possible exception to this rule for instances in which internationally recognized human rights are violated by U.S. companies. The legal vehicle is the Alien Torts Claims Act (ATCA), passed in 1798 to combat piracy on the high seas. The law gives federal district courts jurisdiction over any civil action by a foreigner against any other person on U.S. territory for acts committed abroad "in violation of the law of nations or a treaty of the United States." The law lay dormant for some 190 years before human-rights attorneys began using it on behalf of victims of abuses committed overseas.[11]

The most prominent case involving workers' rights grew out of the involvement of four Western oil companies in a project in Myanmar to develop a pipeline to supply natural gas to Thailand. The pipeline went through regions dominated by ethnic minorities opposed to the government, and the government used violent means to suppress resistance and then conscripted labor to construct a path for the pipeline. Unocal, an American oil company with headquarters in California, participated in the project even after being informed by a consultant of the government's practices. In due course, 14 villagers from the area filed suits against Unocal in U.S. federal court and California state court. The U.S. district court hearing *Doe v. Unocal* concluded in 2000 that Unocal *knew of* human rights violations, but nevertheless was *"not legally responsible"* because there was no evidence that Unocal had participated in or influenced the military's unlawful conduct. There also was no evidence of an overt conspiracy between Unocal and the military. A three-judge panel of the U.S. Ninth Circuit Court of Appeals reversed the district court in 2002, stating that the appropriate legal standard was whether Unocal "knowingly assisted the military in perpetuating abuses" during the project. This decision was in turn vacated in 2003 when the Ninth Circuit decided to hear the appeal before a larger panel of judges.

In the meantime, the California courts ruled that the case against Unocal should go to trial because there were material issues of fact about whether Unocal is responsible for human rights violations. On a motion for summary judgment, the California court ruled in 2004 that there was sufficient evidence to permit a jury to find that Unocal's joint venture hired the military, making Unocal vicariously liable for the military's human rights abuses. If the allegations were proven, Unocal would have breached the California constitution as well as tort and unfair business practice statutes. This was the first time any court had ordered a U.S. multinational to stand trial for its alleged complicity in human rights violations committed abroad.

A few months later, in December 2004, Unocal settled with the legal organizations representing the plaintiffs. Unocal agreed to pay villagers and fund improvements to living conditions, health, and education along the project route. The monetary commitment and other terms of the settlement were confidential. As a result, the issues never received a full hearing in either the state or federal courts, and the legal standards applicable to actions under ATCA or state actions remain undetermined.[12]

Although the exact legal issues remain unresolved, the threat of trials that might reveal unsavory facts about labor conditions tolerated in their foreign operations clearly provides a powerful incentive to settle litigation over alleged human rights abuses. Yet litigation has distinct limitations as a strategy for improving labor conditions abroad. It is an expensive and time-consuming method of addressing individual situations. As such, it may be suited for addressing atypical worst cases, but it ranks well behind expanded trade, international migration, and foreign investment as a strategy for general improvements in working conditions and labor rights around the world.

Summing Up

The second wave of globalization produced understandable concerns and conjectures about multinational companies' influence on working conditions and labor rights around the world. Fueling the concerns is the view that a quest for maximum profits would lead multinationals to seek the lowest possible labor costs. (Curiously, the fact that profit-seeking, host-country companies would share this objective receives less attention.)

The evidence reviewed in this chapter finds few grounds for such concerns. The presence of multinationals in world markets tends to be exaggerated. Accounting for less than 10 percent of world output and an even smaller fraction of employment in most developing countries, multinationals cannot have a major influence on world labor conditions. Moreover, multinational and domestic companies alike must accommodate themselves to the realities of the labor markets in which they hire workers. No company can force down wages or degrade nonwage working conditions when workers have the option of working for other employers. When such a choice exists, only increased labor supply or decreased labor demand weakens working conditions. In contrast, increased production by multinationals raises labor demand—a recipe for higher employment and either improvement or (when there is considerable unemployment) no change in wages and nonwage conditions.

Multinationals themselves pay higher wages than host-country companies for a given skill of labor in both industrialized and developing countries. When multinationals acquire host country businesses, they institute changes in production methods and human resource management practices that raise productivity sufficiently to support higher wages. In most developing countries, however, multinationals account for too little employment to raise the general wage level, unless their wage practices lead local employers to raise wages to retain workers who might otherwise move to multinationals. The research evidence is ambiguous on this point. Some multinationals import technology and production processes that require skilled labor that is relatively abundant in industrialized headquarters countries. To the extent that this occurs, multinationals may increase the wage differential between skilled and unskilled workers in the host country. A wider spread between skilled and unskilled wages provides a stronger incentive to acquire more education—a process that will eventually narrow the skill differential as the supply of skilled workers increases. Whether the differential provokes more educational investment depends on the cost of acquiring more education in developing countries. Policies that reduce such costs in the face of larger skill differentials could very effectively raise the overall educational attainment and skill of the population.

The view that poor labor conditions attract multinational companies also receives no support. The fact that most flows of foreign direct investment occur between advanced countries with high labor standards signals the low weight accorded labor considerations in locating multinationals. Factors such as market size and the risk of the investment climate are far more influential. So are the presence of trade barriers that influence the cost of exports and other alternatives to direct investment. Statistical analyses confirm that after holding the effects of these influences constant, countries with poor labor conditions or weak labor regulations do not attract more FDI than countries with superior labor conditions. The view that countries might compete for FDI by degrading their labor conditions is thus doubly wrong. Most important, it overlooks the interest of producers in minimizing costs *per unit of output*. Poor labor conditions signal low productivity, so that low wages per worker tend to be offset by low output per worker. The evidence is more consistent with a view that multinationals are not attracted to low-productivity workforces, which usually are also low-wage workforces. The second error is more subtle. Given the role of labor markets in establishing labor conditions, it is unclear how a country would degrade its conditions as a matter of policy, other than neglecting labor rights that are granted through a political process. Evidence presented in this chapter shows that such a strategy may backfire: other things equal, a country's share of world FDI in fact improves with job safety, for example. Other studies also show that countries with high child labor force participation are less likely to attract FDI.

The discussion in this chapter casts reasonable doubt on the efficacy of corporate codes of conduct for advancing labor conditions in developing countries. Such codes target firms that on average offer superior labor conditions. The codes at most are likely to influence the policies of only a fraction of multinationals, which themselves account for a small fraction of employment in developing countries. At best, such policies may eliminate a few worst cases. At worst, they may redirect the location choices of multinationals to wealthier countries where the productivity of the workforce supports the codes' higher standards. As mechanisms for advancing general labor conditions in developing countries, such codes have less scope than other policies discussed in this book.

The fact that multinationals have a salutary effect on host country labor conditions does not absolve them of all adverse effects in the global economy. It just turns out that their less admirable policies usually occur outside labor markets. In some cases, multinationals have diverted the institutions of international trade policy from their focus on international trade policy (Bhagwati 2004, chap. 12). In others, multinationals have either remained neutral or participated in corrupt ethical practices. Data from one survey of 4,000 companies doing business in the transition economies of eastern and central Europe provided information on the frequency of bribes to government officials to obtain favorable legal or regulatory treatment and illicit payments to obtain public contracts. An analysis of the data concluded: "The results are sobering. Corruption not only reduces FDI inflows [as many researchers have found] but attracts lower quality investment in terms of governance standards . . . [R]ather than importing higher standards of governance, FDI firms would appear to magnify the problems of state capture and procurement kickbacks, while paying a lower overall bribe burden than domestic firms" (Hellman, Jones, and Kaufmann 2002, p. 21). Yet some multinationals have turned a blind eye toward significant violations of human rights in host countries. The violations and their tolerance present very difficult problems to the international community: the abuses cannot be addressed by legal actions in the host country that is responsible, and the legal actions against multinationals in their headquarters countries remain experimental and uncertain.

CHAPTER 7

National and International Labor Regulation

The three preceding chapters documented the role of market forces—international product markets, international labor markets, and international capital markets—in advancing labor conditions around the world. This evidence is largely consistent with the predictions of economic theory and provides an important counterweight to the doubts of globalization skeptics summarized in chapter 1. Global market forces provide a powerful mechanism for advancing labor conditions, albeit with important effects on income distributions that have motivated inhibiting political responses.

Globalization skeptics offer more than a suspicion of market forces. They propose an alternative, in their view superior, mechanism for advancing labor conditions: international labor standards regulation. The idea is to bring national labor regulations into conformance with an international standard. Some suggest that conforming national labor regulations to international labor standards should be a requirement for receiving trade preferences—a clear prejudgment that regulation trumps market forces as a mechanism for improving worldwide labor conditions. This chapter addresses the effect of national and international labor standards regulation in an effort to assess the efficacy of regulation in advancing worldwide labor conditions.

This agenda raises several interesting questions of political economy. In country after country, the employment relationship is perhaps the most regulated of economic exchanges. Yet national labor regulations vary widely around the world. Why do countries differ in the labor regulations that they choose for themselves? Does globalization influence the level and pattern of national labor regulations? What claim to superiority do the standards determined by international organizations have over standards determined by national governments? Are the mechanisms of globalization and international labor standards complements in the improvement of labor conditions?

This chapter first examines the great diversity of national labor regulations found around the world. All countries regulate some aspects of the employment relationship, but the scope and methods of regulation vary enormously. We then consider how well the diverse international patterns of labor regulation accord with alternative explanations of why nations regulate the employment relationship. The discussion includes new evidence on relationships between globalization and the scope of national labor regulation. International labor standards work by inducing governments to alter national labor regulations, a mechanism that presumes that national labor regulations effectively advance labor conditions. A review of the evidence on the effectiveness of national labor regulation in developed and developing countries assesses the validity of this presumption.

The chapter then examines both the rationale for international regulation of labor standards and the past effects of the system administered by the International Labor Organization for over 85 years. The data show that countries that adopt more international labor standards have superior working conditions and labor rights. The central question is whether this correlation supports a conclusion that international labor standards improve national labor conditions or reflects a tendency for countries with superior labor conditions to adopt more international labor standards. The discussion also includes a brief appraisal of the role of labor clauses recently included in some regional free trade agreements.

National Regulation of Labor Conditions

In all countries of the world, irrespective of stage of development or ideological orientation, collective actions via legislatures or private institutions, such as labor unions, regulate important aspects of the employment relationship. Though the extent and substance of labor regulation vary widely, no country has been willing to permit market forces to be the sole arbiter of national employment conditions.

National political processes produce a striking variety of labor regulations, setting standards for wages, work hours, workplace health and safety, collective bargaining, and nondiscrimination and mitigating some of the risks encountered in labor markets. The numerous statutory regulations that support each of these objectives are not easily summarized. The most comprehensive effort to provide comparative information on labor regulation assesses the legal protection of a standard worker or employer in 85 countries in 1997 (Botero et al. 2004). This remarkable project records details on statutory provisions addressing dozens of aspects of the employment relationship for each country. In some cases, the information is simply whether or not statutory protection exists (e.g., is there a nondiscrimination law?). In others, there is an effort to assess the costs of certain personnel actions, such as increasing work hours (in the face of overtime requirements) or dismissing workers (in the face of requirements for advance notice and dismissal pay). In what follows, we examine the costs of expanding work hours and dismissals and aggregated indices of employment laws, collective relations laws, civil rights (reflecting nondiscrimination and maternity rights), and social security laws.[1]

Employment laws include limits on the attractiveness of temporary or part-time employment, regulation of wages and work hours, and statutory job security (restrictions on dismissals). According to the measure developed by Botero et al. (2004), in the late 1990s New Zealand had the least regulation of the employment relationship, and the Russian Federation had the most. *Collective relations laws* regulate the formation of labor unions, collective bargaining, and collective disputes, such as strikes and lockouts. Peru offered the strongest protection for collective relations, and Malaysia and the United Kingdom offered the weakest protections. Statutes in Slovenia provided the strongest civil rights protection, and statutes in Singapore provided the weakest. *Social security laws* determine the eligibility requirements and most generous benefits for unemployment, sickness, health, old age, disability and death. Denmark, other Scandinavian countries, and the Russian Federation offered the most comprehensive benefit levels. At the other extreme, Malawi offered none. Countries clearly make diverse choices in their approach to regulating the employment relationship.

Although labor regulations emerged in a slow historical evolution in many of the most industrialized countries, there is no longer a significant association between level of development and most labor regulations. In contrast, the findings in chapter 3 show that actual labor conditions are highly correlated with the level of development. Clearly, per capita GDP and other indicators of development are not simply proxies for a country's level of regulation. Only the social security laws, which can require substantial government budget outlays, are significantly and positively correlated with per capita GDP (Botero et al. 2004). Yet many countries that cannot afford generous social security systems do not appear to rely instead on extensive (but budget-friendly) regulations to protect labor. If they did, the different varieties of national labor regulation would be negatively correlated, reflecting political tradeoffs. Instead, the different indices employment laws are positively and significantly correlated with one another. No evidence that countries systematically trade off between the different varieties of labor regulations emerges in the cross-country data.

Why Regulate National Labor Markets?

The underlying distrust of labor market forces reflected in labor regulations has several roots. The widely (if uncritically) accepted assumption of unequal bargaining power between employers and workers provides the most common basis for labor regulations. Collective action by legislatures or labor unions counters what is seen as an inherent ability of employers to impose working conditions on employees. This motivation for labor regulations is accepted far too uncritically. Inequalities of bargaining power are possible in labor markets, but they are not inherent. Nor do markets always accord employers the upper hand. True, many employers may announce conditions of employment on a take-it-or-leave-it basis. But if workers leave it, choosing to work for another employer instead, the power to announce the conditions amounts to little practical economic power.

Bargaining power in fact depends on the degree of choice available to employers and workers respectively. In announcing working conditions, any employer is constrained by the conditions available at other employers in the labor market, just as in demanding superior conditions, each worker is constrained by the conditions that other workers in the market are willing to accept. Inequalities in bargaining power emerge when the choice available to either side of the labor market diminishes. When workers have no choice of employers, an employer can force wages and other working conditions below competitive market norms. Similarly, when a labor union diminishes employer choice by establishing a single labor agreement for all workers or when regulations establish minimum conditions for all workers, workers have superior bargaining power. In short, most employment regulation rests on the assumption that employers have more choices than do workers in labor markets. This may be true in some markets, but is hardly a convincing general model of labor markets. Relative bargaining power surely varies with occupation and geography, for example, and in the face of such variation it is difficult to maintain the view that regulation corrects inequalities in bargaining power in general. When regulation is not accompanied by inequalities of bargaining power, regulatory interventions into labor markets may produce economic costs, worsening the employment prospects of some workers.

Perceived inequalities in bargaining power do not provide the only rationale for employment regulation. Though some working conditions, such as wages and work hours, are personal and may vary by individual, others by their very nature jointly affect most or all employees. Job safety provides an example of such "workplace public goods." It is difficult to provide a safe or healthy workplace for one worker without simultaneously providing it for all workers. No one worker is likely to lobby hard for the optimal level of job safety, because that worker receives only a fraction of the benefits. Collective action is more likely to reflect the total benefit of a safer, healthier job environment to the entire workforce.

Other regulations seek to insure against the risks of the employment environment in situations in which private insurance arrangements are unlikely to emerge because of concerns over moral hazard or adverse selection. Regulations providing for unemployment insurance, workers compensation, and health and retirement benefits provide common examples.

In short, societies may regulate the employment relationship to counter market failures (i.e., to increase the efficiency of labor markets) and to alter the distribution of economic opportunities in favor of labor. Cross-country variations in regulation may reflect differences in the benefits and costs of establishing regulatory statutes (North 1991). Such benefits and costs can be difficult to observe, however, making the economic efficiency theory difficult to test. But if economic efficiency provides the dominant motivation for regulation, net economic benefits should follow. Evidence that national employment regulations increase unemployment or produce other costs casts doubt on the *economic efficiency* rationale for regulation (Botero et al. 2004).

Efforts to establish greater labor market efficiency may not be the only or even primary rationale for employment regulation. *Political theories* emphasize that pro-labor regulations reflect efforts by left-of-center governments to redistribute resources to their political supporters. International differences in regulation reflect differences in the historical influence of left-of-center governments, as well as variations in the constitutional checks and balances on their power.

A country's *legal traditions* may also influence the extent of its employment regulation. Botero et al. (2004) emphasize the distinction between common law and civil law systems: "Common law emerged in England and is characterized by the importance of decision making by juries, independent judges, and the emphasis on judicial discretion as opposed to codes" (pp. 1344–1345). Common law systems place dominant emphasis on the private rights of individuals and take a more skeptical stance toward the role of the state. In respecting the private rights of individuals, common law systems place a relatively large weight on private ownership rights and resist government intervention favoring labor standards.[2] "Civil law is characterized by less independent judiciaries, the relative unimportance of juries, and a greater role of both substantive and procedural codes as opposed to judicial discretion." (pp. 1344–45) Countries with civil law traditions develop more extensive domestic labor regulations than countries with common law traditions. Civil law systems emerged in France, Germany, and Scandinavia. Both common and civil law systems were extended to other parts of the world through patterns of colonization and conquest. Socialist systems accord the state a dominant role in the ownership of property and control of resource allocation. To maintain the support of the working class, socialist systems should produce considerable regulation of labor relative to other legal systems. Botero et al. (2004) provide evidence for the primary importance of legal tradition and secondary impact of political orientation in explaining variations in employment regulations across countries.

Globalization and National Labor Regulation

Globalization skeptics advance a fourth influence on national regulations—*international competition*. In this view, countries with weak domestic employment regulations have the lowest production costs and hence enjoy superior export opportunities. Indeed, some critics assert that global competition pressures national governments to weaken labor regulations and reduce social benefits. Missing from such assertions is a discussion of how national political systems reach a consensus to diminish a country's labor regulations. Political actions that weaken national labor regulations worsen the protections of *all* workers in an effort to provide new trade-related job opportunities for *some* workers. If all workers vote, such actions do not survive a simple political calculus. Convincing political analyses in which trade produces a general weakening of national labor regulations seem elusive. More plausible is the possibility that regulations may be selectively relaxed (e.g., in some export processing zones). We shall test the general version of the hypothesis that countries that are open to international trade will have weaker employment regulations. The selective version cannot be tested because the data do not capture exemptions from basic national labor regulations.

Simple comparisons of the strength of labor regulations do not find weaker regulations in countries with open trade policies. Economies that are open to international trade offer significantly greater protection of labor than closed economies in the areas of employment, collective relations, and social security (table 7.1). (Higher scores on the indices of labor protection devised by Botero et al. (2004) denote greater labor protection.)[3] Open and closed economies do not differ significantly in their protections of civil rights or their cost of dismissals or expanding work hours. The margin of superiority for open-economy countries is largest for social security laws.

For most countries, national labor regulations are determined at the country level, which accounts for the use of unweighted data in table 7.1. If the analysis takes account of the *coverage* of national regulations by weighting estimates by national labor force size, some of the results must be qualified. China and India are two of the economies with closed trade policies in the late 1990s. Both have huge labor forces, and China scores particularly high on the indices of social security and dismissal protections. When weighted by labor force size, the estimates no longer show a significant difference in social security laws between open and closed economies, and dismissal protection is significantly greater in closed economies. The weighted results should not be overinterpreted, since they reflect the size of one or two countries.

Appearances can be deceiving, however. After all, many factors influence the labor regulations that countries choose for themselves and must be taken into consideration before determining whether globalization adds to our understanding of why national labor regulations vary around the world. Previous research shows the influence of a country's legal traditions, political orientation, and, for social security regulations, level of development on the extent of labor regulation (Botero et al. 2004). Given these influences, is a country's trade volume or its trade policy stance also related to its level of labor regulation? Adding measures of trade volumes and trade policies to the

Table 7.1.
Domestic Labor Regulation and Trade Policy

	Mean	St. dev.	Min	Max	n
Employment regulations					
All countries	1.58	0.41	0.76	2.4	85
Open	1.52	0.46	0.76	2.38	45
Closed	1.52	0.33	0.87	2.4	21
Industrial relations regulations					
All countries	1.24	0.49	0.25	2.29	85
Open	1.28	0.55	0.25	2.29	45
Closed	1.08	0.39	0.47	1.86	21
Social Security regulations					
All countries	1.67	0.70	0	2.7	85
Open	1.85	0.61	0.47	2.70	45
Closed	1.03	0.67	0	2.24	21

Sources: Botero et al (2004).

analysis of Botero et al. can address this question. But if countries with weak labor regulations have more trade, how should one interpret the correlation? Countries that have less labor regulation to begin with may be more likely to adopt open trade policies or have larger trade shares. Alternatively, exposure to international markets may lead governments to weaken labor regulations in an effort to gain international competitive advantage. The statistical approach to sorting out the direction of influence between openness and national labor regulations relies only on variations in openness that cannot reasonably be attributed to national labor policies. (See the appendix to this chapter.)

These analyses show that for all but one variety of labor regulation, neither open trade policies nor the share of trade in GDP are significantly related to the strength of a country's statutory protection of labor. The exception: there is some weak evidence that open economies have weaker social insurance systems. Otherwise, there is no reliable evidence that regulations provide less protection for workers in open economies. The analysis indicates that the apparent superiority of labor regulations in open economies in table 7.1 reflects higher per capita income and institutional features of those countries rather than openness per se. After adjusting for these factors, however, there is no support for the hypothesis that globalization undermines national labor regulations, except in the case of social security, and there the evidence is not strong. A country's dominant political orientation and legal tradition appear to be more powerful influences on the strength of its national labor regulations than does its openness to international competition.

Do National Labor Regulations Improve Labor Conditions?

To alter national labor conditions, international labor standards must induce changes in national labor regulations. But what is the evidence that national labor regulations themselves advance labor conditions? Who benefits from labor regulations? Who incurs the costs? Research into the effects of national labor regulations supports the economic adage that there is no such thing as a free lunch. Most regulations are more likely to change the *distribution* of well-being among workers than to produce a general improvement in labor conditions.[4] There is growing evidence in many countries that labor regulations often produce efficiency losses—a net deterioration in a country's labor conditions.

How can regulations intended to improve a country's labor conditions backfire? Most unintended consequences of regulations flow from efforts to escape regulatory costs, much like the adjustments that individuals and organizations make to avoid taxes. Regulations that raise wages or other variable employment costs create incentives to reduce employment. Payroll taxes levied to finance social benefits and (for low-skill workers) minimum wage legislation constitute the most common examples. Employment reductions are reflected as increased unemployment, increased employment in the (unregulated) informal sector, or withdrawal from the labor force (lower labor force participation rates). Each of these outcomes is inferior to employment. Even transfers from employment in the formal sector to employment in the informal sector carry with them a significant deterioration of working conditions and labor rights (chapter 2). Informal employment exists beyond the reach of regulations and involves lower wages, longer hours, and less certain employment than jobs in the formal sector.

The ability of employers to adjust employment in the face of regulatory costs will generally vary by industry and occupation. The availability of substitutes for labor and the ability to pass increased regulatory costs into prices without extensive sales losses are important determinants of the scale of employment adjustments. The elasticity of labor demand—the percentage change in employment in response to a 1 percent increase in labor costs—summarizes the degree to which employers are able to decrease employment in response to cost increases. Estimates for industrialized countries suggest an average labor demand elasticity of about −1, with a wide variety around the average for individual industries (Hamermesh 1993). On average, a 10 percent employment loss follows a 10 percent increase in labor costs. Labor demand appears to be more responsive to labor cost changes in less developed countries (Heckman and Pages 2004).

Employers may try to mitigate employment losses by shifting at least some of the regulatory costs onto workers. If a country imposes a 10 percent tax on wages to fund social insurance, for example, employers may attempt over time to reduce wages by 10 percent. That is, they may seek to mitigate the employment costs by restoring total compensation to its original level but with a different mix of wages and social insurance. To the extent that the costs of social benefits and employment regulations are shifted to workers, countries with comparatively high social benefits or extensive labor regulation can remain competitive in international markets.

To what extent do efforts to shift the costs of social benefits to workers mitigate potential employment losses from social insurance taxes? For many years, studies of this issue were confined to advanced economies. These studies indicate that the payroll taxes that fund social benefits eventually are shifted to workers, leaving no long-term employment effects (Hamermesh 1993). Recent studies of microdata in several Latin American countries now provide some of the most convincing evidence on the extent of shifting in less developed countries. For much of the post–World War II period, Latin American economies followed highly protectionist, import-substitution development strategies, a sharp contrast and less successful approach than the open–economy, export-led growth strategies followed by several Southeast Asian countries. Most Latin American countries also initiated and extended pro-labor regulations much earlier in the development process than did OECD countries. Particularly in closed economies, regulations effectively redistributed some of the rents in highly protected product markets to labor. At least in Latin America, labor regulations may have been a cheaper alternative to social insurance. "The weak fiscal systems in place in the region together with the low level of income and a tradition of tax evasion, corruption and noncompliance made the social insurance schemes used in more developed countries prohibitively costly" (Heckman and Pages 2004, p. 7). In the face of the superior performance of economies that remained open to international trade, many Latin American countries lowered tariffs and initiated other trade reforms during the 1990s, making the costs of the earlier policies more transparent.

The study of the Latin American experience finds considerable evidence of *partial* shifting of the costs of social benefits and regulations onto workers. In other words, the net effects of regulation in these countries was reduced but not eliminated by the lower wages paid to covered workers. Partial shifting effectively reduced the differences in the total compensation of workers covered by the regulations and uncovered workers and mitigated but did not eliminate employment losses. A review of estimates for several Latin American countries concluded that on average, "a 10 percent increase in non-wage labor costs can lead to a decline in employment rates ranging between .6 and 4.8 percent with most of the evidence shaded toward the high end of this spectrum. . . . However, we find robust evidence that social security contributions are not fully shifted to workers. Payroll taxation tends to reduce employment and increase unemployment rates across samples and specifications" (Heckman and Pages 2004, p. 43). In comparing estimates for Latin America with those for OECD countries, the authors conclude that "increasing social security contributions by 10 percent will lower employment by 7 percent in the overall sample, 10 percent in the OECD and 4.5 percent in Latin America. . . . All in all . . . increasing social security taxes leads to substantial costs in terms of reductions in employment and increases in unemployment" (pp. 77–78).

Employers may also try to mitigate the consequences of minimum wage laws on their labor costs—particularly the costs of employing low-skill workers. In principle, carefully designed minimum wages can counter instances of employer monopsony power. In practice, minimum wage statutes apply broadly, not merely to labor markets in which power resides with employers. In markets where the statutory wage floor exceeds the market wage, those who retain their jobs will be better off, while those who lose their jobs or cannot obtain a job must settle for less favorable alternatives—unemployment, employment in jobs not covered by minimum wage legislation, or withdrawal from the labor force. Evaluations of minimum wage legislation have a long history in economics. After more than 60 years of research on the consequences of the policies, debates continue on the exact extent of the employment losses that they induce. A broad evaluation of minimum wage legislation in OECD countries concludes: "Both theory and empirical evidence are inconclusive about the precise employment effects of minimum wages over some range relative to average wages. However, at high levels, there is general agreement that a statutory minimum wage will reduce employment. While sometimes conflicting, there is evidence that young workers may be most vulnerable to job losses" (OECD 1998, p. 57).

Studies of the effects of minimum wage laws in Latin American countries confirm significant employment losses, particularly for young, unskilled workers. Two factors magnify the losses. First, increases in the wage floor "ripple" up through the wage structure to preserve wage incentives between different job levels. There is some evidence that the ripple effect is much stronger in Latin American countries than in the United States. Second, when minimum wages rise in covered or regulated employment, wages do not fall in the unregulated, informal sector. Most economists would expect workers who lose their jobs when minimum wages rise in the covered sector to seek work in the unregulated, informal sector, where wages could adjust downward to accommodate increased labor supply. But downward wage flexibility is not observed in the informal sectors in Latin American countries (Maloney and Nunez Mendez 2004; Montenegro and Pages 2004).

Other regulations exempt certain categories of workers, such as temporary and part-time employees, creating an incentive for employers to give preference to exempted workers over covered workers. Such regulations effectively redistribute job opportunities from covered to uncovered workers. A more subtle example of such redistribution occurs when regulations raise fixed rather than variable hiring costs. With higher costs per employee, employers are likely to adjust to fluctuations in product demand by altering their employees' hours worked rather than the number of employees.

Patterns of gainers and losers also emerge in countries with strong employment protection legislation that is designed to discourage the dismissal of employed workers. Requirements for advance notice and severance payments raise the cost of dismissing workers and achieve their objective of reducing layoffs. Realizing that these protections raise the cost of varying employment to adjust to business fluctuations, employers become more reluctant to hire. Both dismissals and hires decline, leaving little change in employment at existing firms. A study of employment protection legislation (EPL) in OECD countries concludes: "Stricter EPL appears to expand the number of stable jobs, as intended by its supporters. However, unemployment spells also tend to last longer. With stricter EPL, fewer individuals become unemployed but those who become unemployed are at a greater risk of remaining unemployed for a year or more" (OECD 1999a, p. 88). On this point, the differences in unemployment durations between North America (where statutory dismissal regulation is limited) and Europe (where statutory dismissal costs can be quite high) are revealing. Over the past 20 years, some 45 to 50 percent of unemployed in the European Union (but only 5 to 7 percent of unemployed in the United States) have been out of work for more than a year (OECD 2003, p. 327). Negative relationships between job protection and employment levels emerge in analyses of Latin American labor markets. Heckman and Pages write, "Most of the individual country studies demonstrate that regulations promoting job security reduce covered worker exit rates out of employment and out of unemployment, and on net reduce employment" (2004, p. 2).

Collective representation regulations can also have costly effects. A recent study examines how changes in Indian industrial relations laws have influenced growth, poverty, and broad labor market outcomes (Besley and Burgess 2004). The study exploits the fact that Indian states are subject to common industrial laws except in the area of industrial relations; the Indian constitution grants state governments the right to amend the national Industrial Disputes Act of 1947. Over the years, the states have amended the law, so that regulations are distinctly more pro-labor in some states than in others. More work time is lost to strikes in states with pro-labor regulation, and other labor costs may be higher. The law applies only to "registered" manufacturing firms, however, so that the higher costs do not apply to unregistered or informal firms. The study offers convincing evidence that states with more pro-labor regulations have slower growth of output and employment in manufacturing, lower productivity (which implies diminished working conditions), higher unemployment, and a growing informal sector. These states also had more urban poverty. The authors find little evidence "that pro-worker labor market regulations have actually promoted the interests of labor." On the contrary, they found that these regulations "have been a constraint on growth and poverty alleviation" (Besley and Burgess 2004, p. 124). Clearly, government regulation of labor markets can influence labor conditions, but the influence need not be positive.

Overall assessments of the effects of national employment regulations remain quite dour. After reviewing the studies of Latin American countries, Heckman and Pages (2004) conclude:

> The evidence assembled in this volume suggests that labor market regulations are an inequality-increasing mechanism, because some workers benefit while many others are hurt. . . . Insiders and entrenched workers gain from regulation, but outsiders suffer. As a consequence, job security regulations promote inequality among demographic groups. . . . The benefits of programs funded with mandatory payroll contributions should be weighed against their costs in terms of employment. . . . Regulation acts unevenly across different groups in society. Young, uneducated, and rural workers are much less likely to enjoy coverage than older, skilled and urban workers. (pp. 2, 85)

A broader study of labor regulations around the world reaches similarly pessimistic conclusions about the effects of domestic labor regulations on workers. After controlling for level of development (per capita GDP), Botero et al. (2004) find that their indices of employment laws, collective relations laws and social security laws (summarized in table 7.1) are significantly correlated with several adverse macroeconomic outcomes. On average, countries with greater legal protection of labor have more output and employment in the informal sector (which operates beyond the reach of regulations and does not incur regulatory costs), lower male labor force participation rates, higher youth unemployment rates, and a higher overall unemployment rate. These studies are consistent in showing that national labor regulations produce highly selective improvements in labor conditions, leaving many segments of the labor force with fewer and inferior employment opportunities than they would have had with less regulation.

One may acknowledge these effects on broad labor opportunities and still ask whether national labor regulations produce countervailing gains in wages, nonmonetary working conditions, and labor rights. Extending the approach adopted in the study of labor regulation by Botero et al. (2004) provides a straightforward check for links between national labor regulations and the labor conditions analyzed in this book. The basic approach is to regress the measure of each labor condition on the log of GDP (shown to be an important determinant of labor conditions in chapter 3) and indices of national employment regulations, considered one at a time. These indices may play two roles. There may be a direct link between regulatory content and a labor condition. (The collective relations index reflects laws that cover freedom of association, the formation of unions and collective bargaining, for example, and the civil rights index reflects statutes that should promote gender equality.) Alternatively, each index may provide some information on a country's general regulatory climate for labor.

An important concern is whether causality runs from regulation to labor conditions, as when a country passes legislation to alter labor conditions, or the other way around, as when a country only legislates regulations that codify existing practice. In principle, causality could run in either direction. The statistical approach to sorting out the direction of influence between national labor regulation and actual labor conditions relies only on variations in regulation that are believed to be independent of labor conditions. (See the appendix to this chapter for details.)

The results of the analysis are easily summarized. After accounting for the effect of a country's level of development, the indices of national labor regulations are not significantly related to any of the measures of labor conditions analyzed in this book. Information on the strength of national labor regulations does not improve our understanding of why labor conditions vary among countries. Countries with relatively strong pro-labor regulations on average have no better labor rights and working conditions than countries with weaker regulations.

That national employment regulations improve the working conditions of *some* workers is beyond dispute. The question is whether those benefits outweigh the costs incurred by *other* workers, whose employment opportunities are diminished as a result of the regulation. The cumulative evidence that national labor regulations diminish opportunities, without improving labor conditions in a statistically discernable way for the workers that they benefit, indicates that they produce net costs for the labor force.

Labor Unions

Much the same may be said about the effect of labor unions. Labor unions are one of the institutional constants of economic life, signaling the widespread interest of workers in collective representation at the workplace. One might presume that this interest in collective representation rested on evidence that labor unions unquestionably advance working conditions and labor rights, but their actual effect is much more complicated and mixed.

Consider the following case history, reported in the *New York Times* and *International Herald Tribune*. The Indonesian government suppressed labor unions for more than 30 years in an effort to expand exports and attract foreign investors with cheap labor. The suppression ended in 1998, when the International Monetary Fund made a $14.1 billion economic rescue package contingent on the adoption of labor rights. This was part of a general effort by international aid organizations to assist in the spread of freedom of association rights and other "core" labor standards. Over 70 national unions and 10,000 local unions formed. Wages subsequently rose by 60 percent in three years in Jakarta, but productivity did not increase accordingly. (Productivity in Indonesia is lower than in China and India, two of its major low-wage competitors in international markets.) In response, many Indonesian companies replaced employees "with contract laborers who cannot bargain, or are moving their jobs to nonunion countries." The World Bank estimated that "every 10 percent gain in minimum wages has been accompanied by a drop of 0.6 percent in declared employment . . . pushing more workers into the sector of the economy operating outside a regulatory framework" (Arnold 2004). Ironically, unions have also resisted several attempts at a corporate restructuring that was also sought by the IMF and (in a country without unemployment insurance) have bargained hard over dismissal pay.

This scenario illustrates many of the conflicts inherent in assessing unions' effects on labor conditions. Working conditions improved for those workers who received 60 percent pay increases *and* retained their jobs; but conditions deteriorated drastically for the workers who lost their jobs in the face of the large pay increases. Bargaining hard over dismissal pay may delay or prevent firings, but employers who face higher dismissal costs become more reluctant to hire workers, and it becomes harder for unemployed workers to find a job. When pay increases are not matched by productivity increases, employment shifts to countries with lower labor costs per unit of output. These countries may not be lower wage countries; labor productivity may be higher. Efforts to block industrial restructuring and other activities that raise national productivity may save the jobs of some union members, but they also retard the general advance of real wages. Workers who are not in the protected jobs bear the costs of the union action.

In short, labor unions cannot improve working conditions for *all* workers without improving labor productivity. When union actions do not improve productivity, the relevant questions become: *For whom* are labor conditions being improved? Which workers will gain, and which workers will lose from the union actions? What happens to working conditions in the sectors that are not covered by union contracts? Workers who lose their jobs in the unionized sector seek work in nonunion employment—effectively increasing the labor supply to nonunion firms. The increasing labor supply diminishes wages and other working conditions in the nonunion sector—or the informal sector in less developed countries. Whether by statute or by collective bargaining, efforts to establish minimum employment standards tend to benefit some workers at the expense of others.

Unions are not monolithic, and the influence of any particular union cannot be taken for granted. The actual outcome of bargaining between unions and employers depends importantly on details of the collective bargaining system and the economic and political environment in which bargaining occurs (Flanagan 1999, 2003a). Moreover, many labor unions pursue important objectives beyond their immediate workplace goals. One can point to the role of the Solidarity labor union movement in Poland and trade union activism in other countries in effecting the spread of political democracy, for example.

International Regulation of Labor Conditions

The evidence on the variety and effects of national labor regulations informs and prejudices a discussion of international labor standards. Why should diverse national regulations give way to uniform international regulations? Why should uniform international regulation be standardized on the most costly domestic regulations, given evidence that stronger regulations produce adverse consequences for some workers? Finally, and fundamentally, why seek to equalize labor standards when theory as well as the evidence in chapters 4 through 6 shows that countries improve their labor conditions by exploiting their *differences* in international markets? These crucial questions receive little attention in discussions of international labor standards policy. This section examines the uneasy case for some system of international labor standards and reports on the effects of the current system of international labor standards administered through the ILO.

A Case for International Regulation?

Why should international labor standards override the labor regulations chosen through national political processes? The strongest economic argument for international regulation is to correct negative externalities produced by national regulatory policies. But just how applicable is the externalities argument? Do one country's low labor standards impose costs on other countries? Do another country's high labor standards place it at a disadvantage in international competition? The key externality argument advanced by globalization skeptics is that countries with poor labor conditions have an unfair international competitive advantage over countries with (costly) superior conditions. (The 1919 preamble of the ILO anticipates this argument when it states, "The failure of any nation to adopt humane conditions of labor is an obstacle in the way of other nations which desire to improve the conditions in their own countries." The ILO and many globalization skeptics believe that a system of international labor standards will remove that obstacle.)[5] Most developing countries contend instead that the implementation of international labor standards would rob them of their comparative advantage in low-skill labor.[6]

Evidence discussed in earlier chapters refutes this rationale for international labor standards regulation. Countries with poor labor conditions do not gain competitive advantages in international markets. In particular, poor labor conditions are not associated with superior export performance (chapter 4) or larger inflows of foreign direct investment (chapter 6). Because poor labor conditions signal low labor productivity as well as low wages, they cannot reliably provide international competitive advantage. Trade and investment flows instead depend mainly on a variety of nonlabor benefits and costs associated with international transactions. Moreover, countries with an open trade policy or a large trade sector do not have inferior labor conditions, given their stage of development. In short, the evidence does not support the view that international competition produces externalities that might be addressed by a regime of international labor standards.

Nor can a case for international labor standards regulation be based on the effectiveness of national regulations in improving labor conditions. On balance, national labor regulations have produced net costs with selective income redistribution. Developing countries clearly and sensibly worry that the main achievement of uniform international labor standards, as with national labor regulations, will be redistribution from weaker participants in international labor markets to the stronger, rather than an improvement in overall labor conditions.

In short, the economic argument for international labor standards seems weak. We are left with the question of whether past achievements provide a pragmatic empirical case for international labor standards. Have more than 85 years of international labor standards had a positive effect on actual labor conditions around the world?

Current System of International Labor Standards

Since 1919, proposals for labor standards have emerged from tripartite discussions between representatives of labor, management, and governments in the ILO. Founded in 1919, the ILO is the only surviving major creation of the Treaty of Versailles, which established the League of Nations. In 1946, it became the first specialized agency of the United Nations, and it remains the only UN agency in which worker and employer representatives participate as equal partners with governments. The ILO pursues its mandate to promote "internationally recognized human and labor rights" by formulating "international labor standards in the form of Conventions and Recommendations setting minimum standards of basic labor rights."

The ILO labor standards emerge from a slow, bureaucratic process. Labor is the source of many proposals for new or revised labor standards, but governments, employers, ILO industrial committees, and the UN itself also propose standards.[7] For proposals approved for further consideration, the ILO prepares a comparative study of the relevant laws and national practices and asks member countries to comment on the study after conferring with national labor and employer organizations. Final consideration occurs at annual ILO Labor Conferences. Prior to the conference, a tripartite committee examines the proposals. The employers' and workers' groups of the committee meet separately in order to discuss the draft texts and develop a unified viewpoint, if possible. Sometimes, groups of governments also develop a common position. Votes in the conference committees preserve equality between representatives of labor, employers, and governments. The tripartite committee submits a report and the proposed text of a labor standard to the full conference. The report typically contains an indication as to what kind of instrument(s) should be envisaged for adoption.

Conventions are international treaties that create no legal obligation after they are adopted by the conference until member countries ratify them.[8] (Subsequent references to labor standards will pertain to ILO conventions.) Successful standards are normally discussed and voted at two successive annual labor conferences. To be adopted, a proposed standard must receive two-thirds of the votes cast. Each clause must be voted separately. In rare instances, a proposed standard may be discussed at only one conference and requires a majority of three-fifths of the votes cast.

Both the structure of the deliberations and the voting requirements enhance the tripartite aspects of the deliberations. No interest group has sufficient votes to carry the day. For a proposed convention to survive this process, its language must be modified sufficiently to gain acceptance by at least two of the three interest groups. Conventions bind only member countries that ratify them, and even these countries may denounce previously ratified conventions after 10 years from the date on which the Convention first takes effect. The process provides many opportunities for employer groups to object to wording or proposals viewed as too costly and for labor representatives to object to conventions viewed as insufficiently responsive to workers' interests.

By May 2004, the ILO had formulated 185 conventions pertaining to labor conditions, ranging from the very general to the very particular.[9] With 175 member countries, the number of ratifications of operative conventions (existing at least 10 years) ranges from a high of 163 (forced labor convention) to a low of one (conventions on wages, hours of work and manning at sea, and seafarers' identity documents). The most widely ratified conventions address basic rights such as equal remuneration, the right to organize and bargain collectively, and nondiscrimination in employment, while the least frequently adopted address labor conditions for narrowly defined worker groups. Most conventions state policy objectives rather than specific outcomes. (The ILO has never issued a convention stating an international minimum wage, for example, although it has issued standards [conventions] urging member countries to adopt minimum wage policies.)

Eight of the 185 conventions support the four "core" labor rights now emphasized by several international and nongovernmental organizations: forced labor (conventions on forced labor [1930] and the abolition of forced labor [1957]), freedom of association (conventions on freedom of association and protection of right to organize [1948] and the right to organize and bargain collectively [1948]), discrimination (conventions on equal remuneration [1951] and discrimination in employment and occupation [1958]), and child labor (conventions on minimum age [1973] and worst forms of child labor [1999]). On their face, the eight ILO "core" labor standards also seek to establish basic worker rights rather than economic outcomes. (For example, the minimum age of employment convention leaves the determination of a specific minimum age to each country within parameters set by the convention.) That said, ratification of most core conventions would influence labor market outcomes, if ratification altered labor market arrangements in member countries. By reducing labor supply, for example, abolition of forced labor and minimum age requirements should raise wages of some jobs. Similarly, legislation promoting collective bargaining is likely to produce changes in pay and working conditions in at least some sectors. Whether these impacts are appropriate at all stages of development has been part of the ongoing debate over labor standards and trade policy.

Even with a focus on four core labor rights (supported by the eight labor standards noted above), the tripartite, political setting of the ILO limits its ability to specify compliance obligations and assess the compliance of member countries. An expert group noted, "Difficulties in deciding what the core labor standards mean in practice, . . . in identifying operational indicators of compliance with core labor standards so that an observer easily recognizes compliance or noncompliance, . . . with separating intention from capability in government performance in implementing compliance, . . . with finding accurate, representative, comparable sources of information about compliance or noncompliance, . . . [and] in drawing valid inferences from the information sources that are available" (National Academy of Sciences 2004, pp. 18–19).

Assessing violations of freedom of association illustrates some of the difficulties. Freedom of association and a right to collective bargaining seem to imply that employers cannot punish workers for exercising their rights, but the ILO has never concluded that hiring permanent replacements for striking workers, as permitted by legislation in the United States and several African nations, violates this core standard. "Closed shop" requirements, which require employers to hire only members of a particular labor union, deny freedom of association to nonmembers, but the ILO remains silent on how this and other practices are to be harmonized with the basic core standards. Similarly, nondiscrimination would appear to rule out employment quotas for specific groups, but as Moran notes, the ILO permits "their use to achieve numerical targets" (2004, p. 5). Finally, the abolition of forced labor seems incompatible with work by prison inmates at below-market wage rates or as a condition of parole. Moran writes that "ILO jurisprudence considers employment of prison labor by private contractors to be impermissible, but many governments, including New Zealand, the United Kingdom, and the United States consider private contractors to be an integral part of the modern management of penal institutions" (p. 3). Prison labor under government supervision and control is exempt from the ILO's definition of forced labor.

Even when noncompliance is clear, ILO enforcement resources consist of carrots, not sticks, and the costs incurred by countries that fail to ratify conventions seem low. The ILO can ask member countries to explain why they have not ratified particular conventions (Article 19 of ILO constitution), to report on the implementation of conventions that they have ratified (Article 22), and (since 1998) to report on efforts to address the principles of core labor standards that have not been ratified. Compliance with reporting requirements is low. The ILO also provides technical and financial assistance to countries seeking to improve enforcement of conventions.

Article 26 empowers the ILO to investigate noncompliance complaints. After an investigation and report of findings by a Commission of Inquiry, the ILO may only recommend changes in a member country's laws and practices. The ILO website observation that "the complaints procedure has not been used often" seems well supported by the fact that there have been only 25 Article 26 complaints since 1960 (6 during the 1990s). If countries ignore ILO recommendations, the ILO cannot impose direct sanctions, but Article 33 permits it to recommend that member countries take appropriate action.[10] These features of ILO activities condition the empirical analysis of the effects of international labor standards.

Political Economy of International Labor Standards

Ratification of both core and noncore conventions varies widely among member countries. As of May 2004, about 102 member countries had ratified all eight core conventions, with considerable ratification activity since 1998. This group includes several eastern and western European countries as well as Botswana, the Central African Republic, Indonesia, Senegal, and Yemen. Ratifications notwithstanding, some of these countries are frequently criticized for the absence or lack of enforcement of basic labor rights addressed by the core standards. At the other end of the distribution, only two countries (Democratic Republic of Timor-Leste and Vanuatu) had not ratified any core standards. The United States is one of four countries that had ratified only two fundamental conventions.[11] Interestingly, although the United States has ratified conventions addressing child labor and forced labor, it has not ratified the four conventions addressing freedom of association and discrimination—two areas of human rights in which the country has significant domestic legislation.[12] Ratification activity is clearly a noisy indicator of effective labor standards in member countries.

Although the number of ILO conventions ratified by a country may overstate or understate its effective labor standards, ratifications do seem to be positively correlated with the extent of national labor regulation and actual labor conditions across countries. Three of the four indices of national labor regulation in 1997 discussed in the first part of this chapter are positively and significantly correlated with the number of ILO labor standards ratified by a country (fig. 7.1). Only the index of civil rights regulation shows little substantive or statistical relationship with ratifications. Countries that have ratified the most international labor standards have the strongest national labor regulations on average. The qualification is important: in each of the figures, the national observations are widely dispersed around the regression line that describes the average relationship. For any particular level of ratifications, countries differ widely in the strength of their national labor regulations.

Countries that ratify more international labor standards also tend to have

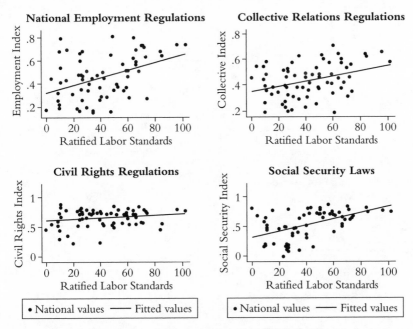

Figure 7.1. Labor Standards and National Labor Regulations, 1997

superior working conditions (fig. 7.2) and labor rights (fig. 7.3). On average, the countries that have ratified more international labor standards have higher wages, lower numbers of work hours, and fewer fatal accidents, although the relationship with accidents is not statistically significant. They also have lower child labor force participation rates, smaller gender wage differentials, fewer people in forced labor, and stronger freedom of association rights. Three separate indicators of freedom of association show consistent relationship to ratifications: the countries that subscribe to the most international labor standards score highest on indexes of civil liberties, statutory rights, and the extent of union membership. Two cautions accompany these correlations, however. The dispersion of national observations around the average relationship is even more pronounced in the case of labor conditions. Moreover, the substantive association between country-specific labor conditions and international labor standards is not strong in most cases. For example, figure 7.2 shows that on average, weekly work hours are lower in countries that have ratified many ILO labor standards. But the relationship is so slight that a one-hour reduction in the workweek is associated on average with ratification of 11 ILO standards. Four ratifications are associated with a 1 percentage point reduction in the child labor force participation rate.

Comparisons of national labor regulations and labor conditions with the ratification of core labor standards—the current international political emphasis—yields similar but less precise results. With only seven core labor

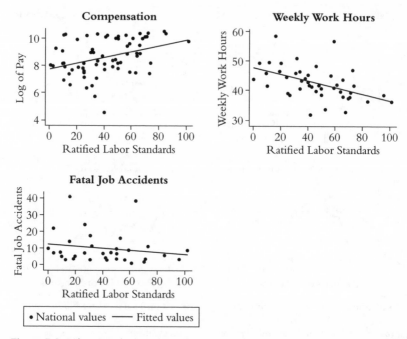

Figure 7.2. Labor Standards and Working Conditions, 1995

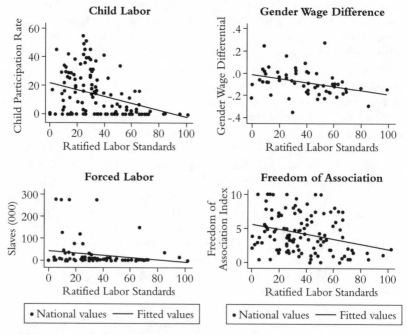

Figure 7.3. Labor Standards and Labor Rights

standards in 1995, statistical tests rest on very limited international variation, and statistical significance is lower. (In 1999, the ILO issued an eighth core standard, forbidding the worst forms of child labor.) The dispersion of national values around the average correlation becomes even more dramatic.

The correlations nonetheless raise a provocative interpretive question: Does the adoption of international labor standards lead to improved labor conditions? Along with the designers of the international labor standards system, contemporary globalization skeptics provide an affirmative answer. In their view, a country's ratification of ILO conventions will lead to the passage and enforcement of national legislation that improves working conditions and labor rights. In this scenario, international labor standards would counter any tendency for international competition to degrade labor conditions.

The main difficulty with this view is that it ignores the costs of political action. Under current arrangements, non-ratification of ILO labor standards is virtually costless. In contrast, the ratification of international labor standards that require the passage and implementation of new domestic legislation to alter labor conditions can impose significant domestic economic and political costs on a country. Why would countries commit to potentially costly domestic actions by ratifying ILO conventions when the costs of non-ratification are so low? Introducing this political calculus implies that countries that ratify the standards are likely to be the countries for which ratification is least costly in terms of adjusting national legislation and institutions. Countries whose labor conditions and/or national legislation *already* provide protections that are at least as strong as those proposed in the ILO convention have the lowest ratification costs. In this scenario, the causality imagined by labor standards proponents is reversed, with improvements in national labor conditions leading to the ratification of international labor standards. A country's ratification of international labor standards is "endogenous"—determined by domestic labor conditions. In short, the ratification of international labor standards is a purely symbolic act; it produces no change in national labor regulations or labor conditions.

Which scenario is correct? The answer to this question has enormous consequences for the role of a system of international labor standards. According to the traditional exogenous labor standards view, labor standards are one of several factors determining labor conditions. Per capita GDP and openness to international competition are among the other factors discussed in this book. According to the endogenous labor standards view, existing national labor conditions and regulations are a key determinant of the number of labor standards that a country ratifies.

Working with these ideas, one study analyzed the joint determination of both core and noncore ratifications and labor conditions (child labor, civil liberties, and workforce health [life expectancy]) using data for about 100 countries in 1980 and 1990. The results of the analysis support the view that countries ratify standards that they have already attained. That is, measures of labor conditions are significant in the ratifications equations, but measures of ratifications are not significant in the various labor conditions equations (Flanagan 2003b). This support for the endogenous labor standards analysis of the political economy of ratifications undermines the view that the adoption of international labor standards is a catalyst for improving national labor conditions.

Ratification and the Race to the Bottom

If national ratifications of ILO labor standards are largely symbolic acts, it is difficult to see how countries that fail to ratify many international labor standards gain international competitive advantage. The view that countries that eschew costly labor standards find it easier to sell their exports and attract foreign direct investment is undermined by evidence that countries ratify standards that they have already achieved. The act of ratification does not alter labor conditions. If this implication is accurate, the number of ILO labor standards ratified by a country should not be a significant determinant of its labor costs, exports, or foreign direct investment inflows.

Do countries that ratify key ILO conventions incur higher labor costs? The analysis of labor costs in chapter 3 finds that international differences in productivity and prices accounted for about 90 percent of the international differences in manufacturing pay in both the early 1980s and the late 1990s. Does information on countries' ratification of international labor standards help explain the remaining international wage variation?

Cross-country regression analyses find no significant correlation between pay and ratification of specific core standards in either time period, and they find no evidence that ratifications of these core labor standards gradually influence compensation over time (Flanagan 2003b). For the late 1990s only, there is a weak positive correlation between pay and the total number of core labor standards ratified by a country. This result, which places labor standards addressing issues as varied as collective bargaining, discrimination, forced labor, and child labor on an equal statistical footing, is difficult to interpret given the lack of statistically significant correlations with measures of individual core standards.

There are also solid statistical grounds for being skeptical of the cross-country estimates. If unobserved country-specific factors are correlated with both wages and ratifications, the cross-section estimates of the relationship between ratifications and wages will be biased. The presence of unions or extensive domestic labor market regulation might produce both more ratifications and higher labor cost, for example. Fixed-effects estimation on panel data, which eliminates country-specific effects on pay that do not change over time, confirms that there is no significant relationship between country-specific *changes* in the ratification of core or total labor standards and *changes* in compensation between the early 1980s and the late 1990s (Flanagan 2003b).

If ratifications do not have a significant influence on labor costs, the argument that ratifications provoke competitive disadvantage would seem to collapse. Nevertheless, a test for direct links between ratifications, export performance, and FDI inflows provides the last step in assessing the role of international labor standards regulation on labor conditions. The method is the same: Measures of ratification activity are added to baseline models of a country's export-to-GDP ratio and a country's share of world FDI inflows, first discussed in chapters 4 and 6 (and explained more fully in the appendices to those chapters). The results of such analyses confirm and reinforce the labor cost findings. There is no statistically significant relationship between a country's export share of GDP and the number of ILO labor standards that it has ratified. Likewise, no significant relationship between a country's share of world FDI inflows and its ratification emerges from the analysis (Flanagan 2003b). Countries do not incur higher labor costs and suffer international competitive disadvantage when they ratify ILO conventions. But this is because ratification does not produce advances in national labor conditions.

To summarize, this section addressed the question of whether adoption of ILO labor standards produces improvements in labor conditions, or whether labor conditions instead influence the ratification of political labor standards. Ratifications of ILO labor standards appear to be largely symbolic, reflecting previously attained labor conditions. As such, they cannot increase labor costs. Statistical analyses of ratifications and labor conditions find little evidence that a country's effective number of core or noncore labor standards is associated with improvements in labor conditions. On the other hand, there is strong evidence that countries with open trade policies have superior working conditions and labor rights (chapter 4). Those who propose imposing trade sanctions in an effort to induce adherence to ILO labor standards appear to be proposing a policy (trade sanctions) that is likely to diminish labor conditions to induce compliance with labor standards that are not demonstrably effective in improving labor conditions.

Monitoring Compliance with International Labor Standards

The evidence reviewed in this chapter indicates that voluntary international labor standards have had little or no effect on labor conditions to date. Indeed, of all the mechanisms for advancing labor conditions considered in this book, the ILO system of labor standards appears to be last in effectiveness. Perhaps one should expect no more from a policy of voluntary compliance. Policy proposals to punish noncompliance follow from such a conclusion. Such proposals raise two key questions: (1) How costly is it to identify noncompliance? and (2) What is an appropriate punishment, given the objective of improving working conditions?

Monitoring compliance with core labor standards to judge the need for trade sanctions or other punishments presents significant challenges. Assessments of noncompliance must first confront the broad statements of principle presented by core labor standards. No single indicator is likely to summarize compliance adequately, and many measures may provide ambiguous signals. One expert committee, after delineating the challenges and ambiguities that could arise in trying to assess noncompliance with each core labor standard, recommended a daunting list of 114 (!) indicators for assessing compliance (National Academy of Sciences 2004). The indicators cover a country's legal framework, government performance, and overall outcomes. For assessing compliance with the freedom of association labor standard, for example, the committee recommends no fewer than 21 indicators of a country's legal framework, 13 indicators of its government's performance in implementing the legal framework, and 4 indicators of outcomes.[13] How this remarkable array of information is to be synthesized or aggregated into a judgment on compliance remains undefined. Not all the indicators can be equally important, but no weighting scheme is advanced. Nor are data currently available on all items. (A purpose of the expert report was to delineate the requirements for a compliance assessment system.) The overwhelming impression is that such a system would be very costly and eminently challengeable.

Labor Standards Requirements in Regional Trade Agreements

The ILO administers the most comprehensive and broadly applicable system of international labor standards. Since the 1990s, however, some regional free trade agreements have included language pertaining to labor standards in signatory countries. Such labor chapters first appeared in the North American Free Trade Act and later in trade agreements negotiated by the United States with Jordan, Chile, Singapore, and five Central American countries.[14] In each instance, U.S. political concerns that trading partners might seek competitive advantage by degrading domestic labor conditions motivated the negotiations of labor standards provisions in the final agreements.

The regional labor provisions do not seek to replace ILO standards. Indeed, in almost identical language the last three agreements confirm each signatory's commitment to the ILO standards: "Each party shall strive to ensure that such labor principles and the internationally recognized labor rights . . . are recognized and protected by its domestic law." The agreements also do not seek uniform labor standards among signatories, but recognize "the right of each Party to establish its own domestic labor standards, and to adopt or modify accordingly its labor laws," while striving for "labor standards consistent with the internationally recognized labor rights." Reflecting the influence of race-to-the-bottom thinking, the labor provisions instead commit each country to enforcing its national labor laws and to avoid changing the laws to obtain trade advantage: "The Parties recognize that it is inappropriate to encourage trade or investment by weakening or reducing the protections afforded in domestic labor laws."[15] The regional free trade agreements also establish bureaucratic mechanisms for reviewing and assessing alleged violations of the labor provisions.

The history of these agreements is too short for a convincing assessment of the effects of the labor provisions of regional trade pacts. On their face, neither the commitments nor the enforcement mechanisms appear strong—hardly surprising given the compromises of an international negotiation process. The complaints of labor rights organizations and labor unions about the limitations of the provisions support this impression. The labor clauses may have provided political cover needed to pass free trade legislation, but one must conclude provisionally that the labor standards clauses are unlikely to have an important direct effect on labor conditions in signatory countries. On the other hand, evidence presented earlier in this book indicates that they may have an important indirect impact by promoting freer trade between the countries.

Conclusions

One of this book's goals is to illuminate the respective roles of international markets and regulation in advancing worldwide labor conditions. Chapters 4 through 6 discussed international markets' effect on labor conditions. This chapter addressed the influence of national and international labor standards regulation.

Countries have many reasons for regulating the employment relationship, including increasing economic efficiency, correcting perceived inequalities of bargaining power, and insulating workers from labor market risks. The manner and extent to which countries address these concerns varies widely, however. Though virtually all countries have some laws that define basic worker rights, regulate individual employment contracts, establish bounds for collective action, and provide social benefits to workers, they differ in the specific rights, rules, and benefits provided to workers. Countries choose these different labor regulations on the basis of prevailing national norms and values. The values themselves are reflected in the characteristics of a country's legal traditions, the teachings of its dominant religions, as well as its general political orientation. These institutions and their underlying values are likely to change slowly, if at all. In short, there is little basis for predicting a convergence in national employment regulations in the near future.

Neither the size of a country's trade sector nor its trade policy stance appears to influence the extent of labor protection afforded by national labor legislation, ceteris paribus. This important finding undermines the key rationale for a system of international labor standards—that unregulated countries will degrade (costly) national labor protections in order to gain international competitive advantage. Analyses of data from a large sample of countries at various levels of economic and political development showed no evidence of weaker labor protections in countries that are open to international competition.

The absence of a deregulatory race to the bottom cannot be traced to the strength of the current system of international labor standards. Though the level of national labor regulation is positively, albeit loosely, correlated with ratification of ILO labor standards, the causality runs from national regulation to adoption of ILO standards. That is, countries tend to ratify international standards that their domestic regulations already satisfy, rather than incurring the political costs of introducing or altering national legislation to meet a higher standard. The ratification of ILO labor standards appears to be a symbolic act, signaling a country's existing levels of labor conditions.

Reinforcing the evidence that ratification of ILO labor standards is a symbolic act are findings that the number of standards ratified have no influence on a country's labor costs, export performance, or ability to attract foreign direct investment. Efforts to attach labor standards clauses to regional free trade agreements are based less on the efficacy of the current system of ILO standards than the need to provide political cover against charges that free trade agreements initiate a race to the bottom in national labor regulations and labor conditions.

Modern proposals for international labor standards envisage a system with stronger enforcement powers, including the use of trade sanctions to punish noncompliance. The trade sanctions proposal is doubly misconceived. It proposes cutting off a mechanism, international trade, that demonstrably improves labor conditions in order to encourage the adoption of another mechanism, international labor standards, that has not demonstrably improved labor conditions in the past. Even those who believe that a system of enforceable international labor standards can advance labor conditions should oppose enforcement tools that directly counter their basic objective of improving worldwide labor conditions.

All the evidence presented on the ineffectiveness of the current system of international labor standards emerges from a system of voluntary compliance. Proposals for an enforceable system of international standards envisage a mandatory compliance regime that would differ from both the ILO system and the labor clauses in recent free trade agreements, raising the question of how probative the evidence presented in this chapter is for current proposals. The most pertinent evidence for such proposals pertains to the effect of domestic regulations on labor conditions. Unlike international labor standards, domestic regulations are not benign; they seem to have real effects on efficiency and distribution. But as we have seen, these effects rarely benefit workers generally. Though specific groups of workers may gain, they do so at the expense of other workers. The regulations create groups of "haves" and "have-nots" by raising the extent and duration of unemployment, shifting remaining employment from the covered (regulated) to the uncovered (unregulated) sectors, and reducing labor force participation. A system of mandatory international labor standards raises parallel concerns. In a world in which it is difficult to improve labor conditions generally without first raising labor's productivity, there is a danger than politically driven methods of setting standards and assessing compliance by countries will produce patterns of international gainers and losers rather than a general improvement in labor conditions.

CHAPTER 8

Taking Stock and Looking Ahead

This book began by reporting a widely held indictment of "globalization" for its detrimental effects on labor conditions around the world. Globalization skeptics assert a two-count indictment: Globalization degrades labor by (1) increasing worldwide inequality and (2) increasing sweatshop working conditions. The underlying theme is that the spread of economic integration undermines the labor conditions of the weakest workers as a consequence of an international "race to the bottom." Arrayed against this indictment is the very different view of globalization and labor conditions presented by economic analysis, which views international economic integration as a strategy for improving world labor conditions and reducing international inequality. The objective of this book has been to evaluate these contending views by examining how three specific mechanisms of globalization—international trade, international migration, and the activities of multinational companies—influence labor conditions. For each of these mechanisms, the book has presented conceptual arguments about their likely effects and empirical evidence about their actual effects on labor conditions.

This book examined the evolution of two broad aspects of labor conditions: actual working conditions and a set of basic labor rights that cut across workplaces. The analysis of working conditions focuses on wages, hours of work, and on-the-job health and safety, and the analysis of labor rights addresses freedom of association, nondiscrimination, elimination of child labor, and abolition of forced labor. Measures of each of these working conditions and labor rights have been developed for a large sample of countries at various stages of economic and political development. For most measures, data are available for several decades in the late twentieth century. Where possible, the narrative supplemented the modern record with information from the first wave of globalization a century earlier. This is the place to take stock of what has been found, beginning with the questions raised in the introduction.

Have labor conditions improved or deteriorated over time? Quite simply, the review of working conditions and labor rights in chapter 2 shows that no measure of labor conditions deteriorated during the late-twentieth-century wave of globalization. One can go further: focusing on the trade mechanism of globalization, countries with open trade policies during the last third of the twentieth century had labor conditions that were, on average, superior to those of countries with closed trade policies. One cannot indict international trade by a simple comparison of labor conditions in countries with open and closed trade policies. One also cannot prove that free trade improves labor conditions with the comparison; sorting out the probable role of trade, migration, and multinationals occupied most of the book.

The data also are not kind to the second count in the indictment. The large literature on worldwide inequality finds a continuing decline in the world poverty rate during the second wave of globalization and an apparent decline in the number of poor in the world by the end of the twentieth century. Some readers may find this surprising in the face of widespread evidence of increased wage and income inequality within countries in the late twentieth century. The two facts are easily reconciled: though poverty declined as incomes grew at the bottom of the income distribution, incomes grew even more at the top of the distribution.

This book's focus on labor conditions emphasizes a much broader notion of compensation than one finds in computations of how wages or incomes are distributed among individuals or families. Work includes both monetary and nonmonetary benefits and costs, but tabulations of wage and income distributions capture only monetary returns. During the late twentieth century, the international distributions of various labor conditions evolved differently. Consistent with reported changes in income distributions and national growth rates of per capita income, wage rates diverged—growing most rapidly in high-wage countries. The same is true of fatal job injury rates and measures of work hours, albeit for a much smaller sample of countries. On the other hand, life expectancy and civil liberties converged—advancing most rapidly in the countries with relatively poor initial conditions.

Clearly, standard income distributions provide an important but decidedly incomplete picture of how labor conditions change around the world. In the late twentieth century, a convergence in some nonmonetary conditions to some extent countered the divergence in wages. Wage developments alone do not fully describe the evolution of labor conditions for most workers during a period of growing economic integration. A comprehensive assessment of globalization's effects on labor must more beyond income distributions and poverty counts.

Labor Conditions under Autarky

To place globalization's role in perspective, it is helpful to ask how labor conditions would evolve in the other extreme—a world of autarky or complete national economic self-sufficiency. Of the many potential influences on labor conditions in such a world, two seem paramount: the level of economic development and national labor regulations. Chapter 3 reviewed the conceptual bases for expecting higher per capita income to produce superior working conditions and labor rights, then turned to an empirical analysis of the relationship. Both cross-country and panel analyses in chapter 3 confirm the powerful influence of higher per capita income on labor conditions. This finding alone offers a powerful policy implication: any policy or institution that advances growth of per capita income improves virtually all labor conditions (and, conversely, policies that retard growth degrade labor conditions). At the same time, labor conditions vary in their sensitivity to per capita income. Moreover, taking account of the effect of level of development still leaves considerable unexplained variation in most labor conditions.

Some of this variation can be traced to a country's political and economic institutions. At any level of development, countries that protect property rights have superior labor conditions. So do countries with democratic political processes and broad civil liberties. Labor conditions also reflect a country's social diversity. Countries with substantial ethnic diversity record poorer working conditions and labor rights than ethnically homogenous countries. Religious diversity is associated with superior labor conditions, however. Some national social and institutional features mirror past acts of globalization. Ethnic diversity in some countries reflects colonial boundaries and the era of the slave trade. Historical immigration policies influence current ethnic and religious diversity in other countries. But the diversity of modern labor conditions that is traceable to institutional factors is unlikely to be altered materially by the currently viable array of globalization policies.

All countries, including those that remain closed to international trade, regulate aspects of the employment relationship. Statutory law and private institutions, such as labor unions, influence most aspects of the employment relationship and hence the level and structure of labor costs. In all cases, the objective is to improve labor conditions for at least some members of the labor force. The exact regulations vary widely around the world, reflecting the different legal and religions traditions and political orientations of countries. The variance itself provides an opportunity to study whether countries with more protective labor regulations have superior labor conditions. A review of microstudies of industrialized and developing countries supplemented by new econometric analyses in chapter 7 concludes that national labor regulations are not a reliable way to produce *general* improvements in national labor conditions. Though some groups of workers usually gain from labor regulations, the gains come at the expense of other workers who are relegated to inferior working conditions as a result of the regulations.

Globalization's Effects on Labor Conditions

How does globalization alter the labor conditions that a country would experience under autarky? Globalization skeptics effectively claim that countries that open their borders to trade, to investments by multinational companies, and to immigration risk forcing their labor conditions below the baseline established by their level of development, national institutions, and domestic labor regulations. Evaluating these concerns requires answers to two central questions: Do mechanisms of globalization degrade a country's labor conditions? Do poor labor conditions enhance a country's export performance?

Trade, Working Conditions, and Labor Regulations

Liberalizing trade induces changes in the structure of production as countries begin to export more of products that they produce relatively efficiently in world markets. In evaluating free trade's effects on working conditions, one should first ask whether the changes in the structure of production are likely to improve or degrade employment conditions. Concentrating a nation's labor (and other) resources in industries in which a country enjoys a comparative advantage or economies of scale is a recipe for raising labor's productivity, and higher productivity supports higher wages and more favorable, albeit costly, nonmonetary working conditions. The changes in the structure of production that accompany liberalized trade should therefore improve, not degrade, working conditions. This linkage between freer trade and improved working conditions is indirect, however. Improved efficiency in resource use raises a country's real per capita income above its level under autarky. Free trade's effects on working conditions should be captured through improvements in per capita income. The empirical analysis reported in chapter 4 confirms this theoretical prediction. Liberalized trade mainly improves working conditions through its effects on a country's level of development, although countries that are open to trade also seem to have somewhat better job safety records, other factors held constant.

Much the same conclusion emerges from studies of labor conditions in export processing zones. While working conditions in the zones often fall well short of conditions in most OECD countries, they are superior to the conditions that accompany alternative jobs in many exporting countries. That is why the zones are able to attract workers. Subjecting the zones to the working conditions typical in advanced Western countries would raise labor costs sufficiently to jeopardize employment opportunities. A more convincing approach to improving labor conditions is to improve productivity, as higher productivity supports higher wages and/or superior nonmonetary working conditions.

The resistance to these benefits of free trade comes largely from those resources that would have to adjust in the short run (particularly workers in industries in which a country lacks a comparative advantage) and their political allies. As discussed in chapter 4, spending some of the net gains from shifting to a regime of superior labor conditions on easing the short-run adjustment to the new regime constitutes a productive approach to addressing the opposition. The "art" of policy design is to formulate compensatory policies that actually encourage the desired adjustment.

Few aspects of economic activity are regulated more heavily than the employment relationship. Indeed, to a large extent a country's employment regulations are independent of its level of development. Employment regulations address a variety of concerns over labor market failures and inequalities of bargaining power between employers and their employees, and some regulations may raise the costs of doing business in a country. Avoiding regulatory costs may give businesses a competitive edge in international competition. Following this thought, some globalization skeptics argue that some national governments may limit the extent or enforcement of their labor market regulation in order to improve their export performance. In this view, governments would enhance the competitive prospects of their export industries by reducing labor protections. As discussed in chapter 7, the assertion that governments degrade national working conditions bypasses a discussion of how they achieve this result. Actions by governments occur through a political process, and a convincing argument must demonstrate why that process would regularly produce outcomes unfavorable to workers. No such argument has yet been advanced. On the other hand, the evidence is quite clear: The extent of most national labor regulation is not significantly correlated with a country's openness to international trade (chapter 7).

Of course, this analysis takes each country's laws as written, not as they are enforced. Even in countries in which the political process provides significant labor protections, administrative decisions may undermine the legislative results by not enforcing the laws. Moreover, nonenforcement could be used selectively to favor companies or industries competing in international markets. The research community has found it easier to describe de jure than de facto labor regulations. There is no direct measure that permits a ranking of countries by the quality of enforcement of labor regulations. Yet, persistent nonenforcement should show up in the bottom line: countries with poor enforcement should have weaker labor rights. Here again, the evidence is not kind to race-to-the-bottom views of the effects of international competition. Openness to international competition strengthens most labor rights both indirectly (by raising real per capita income, which is associated with stronger rights) and directly, through mechanisms that are not associated with raising the level of development. (Recall that trade has only an indirect effect on most working conditions.) Acts of nonenforcement may occur, but the bottom line is that countries that are open to trade enjoy superior labor rights.

International Migration

The principle behind international labor migration is simple: workers improve their working conditions and labor rights by moving from countries with poor labor conditions to countries with superior labor conditions. In many respects, this simple principle describes a process that reduced transatlantic wage inequality during the nineteenth-century wave of globalization. That experience is testimony to migration's power as a force for worldwide equalization of labor conditions, just as subsequent immigration restrictions are testimony to the power of forces in destination countries whose working conditions may be threatened by the presence of immigrants in the labor market.

International migration will not replicate that role during the current globalization. Although the incentives for migration between many countries are now even larger than in the nineteenth century, destination countries are awash in immigration restrictions and there is no current international forum or procedure for negotiating a reduction in restrictions. No international organizations—least of all those that seek free trade, that claim responsibility for reducing world poverty, or that develop standards for improved labor conditions—are willing to propose reductions in international barriers to labor migration. Nor is the issue on the agenda of the nongovernmental organizations that claim to be most concerned about the plight of workers in a world of global competition. Acquiescence in suppressing this mechanism for improving the condition of labor and reducing international inequalities in labor conditions seems to be the only common ground of an enormous collection of international and nongovernmental organizations that otherwise have a wide variety of views on globalization.

Postwar progress in reducing barriers to international trade cannot justify neglect of the migration mechanism. Although international trade and migration are substitutes to some extent, they are not complete substitutes. Various costs to conducting trade and migration prevent either mechanism from providing all the gains of the other. The current regime of immigration restrictions effectively truncates important complementarities between trade and migration. When selectively formulated with a pro-skill bias in admissions, these restrictions may thwart efforts of poor workers to improve their labor conditions and may effect a brain drain from some of the world's poorer countries. Moreover, the demand to circumvent the barriers creates a new illegal industry of trafficking in humans, which frequently gives rise to new varieties of forced labor. Ironically, the silence of so many parties on a fundamental mechanism of globalization furthers an activity, forced labor, that virtually all parties oppose.

Multinational Companies and Labor

To some observers, large multinational companies appear to be bastions of power with limitless discretion in the treatment of their employees. It is a short step to claim that such companies exploit foreign workers and degrade host-country working conditions. In fact, the sphere of economic influence of multinationals is often overstated, and they employ less that 10 percent of the world's workers (chapter 6). But their size or level of employment is not the key to their effect on working conditions. Ultimately, conditions in the labor markets in which they operate govern the working conditions that they offer. The labor market power of multinationals is also constrained by the amount of choice available to workers. Multinational (or national) companies can provide substandard employment conditions if workers have a limited choice of employers. With reasonably competitive labor markets, such monopsonistic employer power disappears, and inferior working conditions reduce the supply of workers willing to accept employment.

There is no need to debate or conjecture about the degree of monopsony power in foreign labor markets, as there is now ample evidence on the multinationals' wage practices in many industrialized and developing countries. The unanimous verdict is that multinationals pay higher wages, even after adjustment for differences in industries, quality of workforce, size of the company, and other factors. The higher wage policies of multinationals appear to rest on technology and human resource management practices that raise their relative productivity (chapter 6). In contrast, there is little evidence one way or the other about comparative nonwage employment conditions at plants run by multinationals. Information on their work hours, job safety, and the like must await the development of new databases. Arguments concerning the consequences of offering substandard working conditions apply symmetrically to wage and nonwage conditions alike, however.

We also lack general studies of the relationship between multinationals and labor rights at the company level. There are no general studies of whether multinational companies are more likely to grant freedom of association rights, less likely to employ child or forced labor, or less likely to discriminate. There are anecdotes of multinationals turning a blind eye toward human rights violations by governments in some host countries. The discussion of Unocal in Myanmar (formerly Burma) in chapter 6 provides an example. Other anecdotes illustrate principled stands by major multinationals against such violations. In a *Wall Street Journal* article, the chairman and chief executive officer of Reebok International discusses the "appalling [human-rights] record" of the government of Myanmar and observes: "It's impossible to conduct business in Burma without supporting this regime. In fact, the junta's core funding derives from foreign investment and trade. But foreign investment and aid yield little benefit to the nearly 50 million citizens who live under the military's ruthless campaign of intimidation." The article goes on to observe that although several major multinationals withdrew from the country, "some of the regime's principle business partners continue to be multinationals, many based in Europe. Those lifelines must be cut to weaken the regime's hold on the people of Burma" (Fireman 2005). Other business leaders have taken steps toward greater transparency in revealing the fees that they must pay to operate in some host countries, thus encouraging inquiries to the host country governments about why more of the fees do not emerge in public projects to improve life in those countries.

Which anecdotes are typical? Where does the balance lie? Though it is difficult to get beyond anecdotes at the company level, there is general evidence of the role of multinationals at the country level. Quite simply, foreign direct investment does not flow disproportionately to countries with poor labor rights (chapter 6). This may reflect the fact that poor labor conditions signal a low-productivity workforce, and FDI is complementary with skilled labor. It also may reflect the fact that many countries with poor labor rights also offer other significant risks to investment. It seems that with regard to labor rights, one can identify instances of both good and bad behavior among multinationals. Perhaps the lack of a relationship in the FDI data reflects a rough cancellation of these two forces. In principle, a potential role for some multinational codes of conduct is to limit the instances in which individual companies turn a blind eye to bad practices.

Policies and Policy Principles

Few people actively support poor labor conditions; many advance proposals for improving them. How should one sort through the flow of proposals to decide which ideas deserve serious attention? A very useful first principle of policy choice is to favor policies that expand, rather than contract, opportunities for target groups. The mechanisms of globalization fare very well by this criterion. The evidence developed and presented in this book and reviewed in the early part of this chapter shows how international trade, international migration, and multinational companies contribute to improved working conditions and labor rights. Contrary to the indictment of globalization outlined in the first chapter, the world's workers would gain from *fewer* restrictions on these mechanisms of globalization. This conclusion applies most strongly to the world's poorest workers. Relaxing barriers to international migration offers the most promising opportunity for expanding the positive impact of globalization on labor conditions, but prospects for international action to promote the international movement of labor seem dim at the beginning of the twenty-first century. In the meantime, further reductions in trade barriers can continue to produce broad improvements in worldwide labor conditions.

This is the place to ask why skepticism about globalization's effects on labor conditions survives in the face of evidence on how trade, migration, and multinational companies expand opportunities for labor. The short-term distributional consequences of global flows of goods, labor, and capital probably motivate the strongest resistance to globalization, although the motivation is often artfully camouflaged. The fact that globalization improves opportunities for most workers does not prevent those subjected to the costs of adjustment from trying to avoid those costs. Globalization skeptics could be more candid about the fact that their real concerns are not with the world's most destitute workers, but rather with unskilled workers in rich countries who bear the brunt of adjustment to trade or migration from low-wage countries. The policy conflicts of globalization are inherent. Economics is about getting the long-run incentives right, but politicians must address short-run complaints if they are to have a long run.

Policy support for workers who must adjust the most to globalization should meet the same criterion: favor policies that expand opportunities. Efforts to restrict globalization in an effort to freeze current employment structures fail by this criterion. So do policies that provide lump-sum transfer payments to workers who claim to have lost their jobs to globalization. (Admittedly, the case for such transfers may be stronger for older worker cohorts with limited prospects for transfer to new types of employment.) Much better are policies that provide incentives for workers to make transitions and ensure them against the major wage losses those transitions may produce.

Distrust of labor market outcomes constitutes a second source of skepticism about the consequences of globalization for workers. Much distrust of markets rests on uncritical allegiance to the view that workers always have inferior bargaining power in labor markets. But this view rests on a misunderstanding of the source of labor's bargaining power. Ultimately, bargaining power rests on the scope of one's opportunities. Providing more employment opportunities—for example, more companies producing for export or more multinational companies competing for workers' services—raises worker bargaining power. Reducing opportunities diminishes bargaining power. Policies that expand labor market opportunities raise workers' relative bargaining power; policies that restrict these opportunities reduce it.

A tendency to calibrate labor conditions in developing countries against conditions in OECD countries also feeds skepticism about globalization's effects on workers. This is a disingenuous and ultimately dangerous frame for policy action. We have seen how the superior conditions in industrialized countries rest on the superior productivity of their workforces. Without the human and physical capital investments that produce high productivity in rich countries, the poor countries will be unable to match their labor conditions. First-best policies for improving working conditions in poor countries will raise the productivity of the labor force, not impose conditions that labor's productivity will not support.

International Labor Standards

International labor standards stack up poorly against the criterion that one should favor policies that expand opportunities for workers. Regulating labor standards does not by itself create superior opportunities. Chapter 7 reviewed the limitations of the current voluntary system of standards administered by the ILO. Though countries that ratify (officially subscribe to) more labor standards have superior labor conditions, the correlation appears to result from a process of symbolic ratification—countries tend to ratify standards that they have already met.

Faced with an ineffective voluntary system of standards, many globalization skeptics propose adding elements of compulsion to international labor standards, notably using trade sanctions against countries that do not subscribe to core labor standards. This proposal fares even worse by the criterion of expanding workers' opportunities. Trade sanctions prevent or limit a process (free trade) that demonstrably advances working conditions and labor rights around the world. How can one justify a policy that freezes and may even degrade labor conditions in some of the world's poorest countries? One cannot justify it on the grounds that the cost must be borne to promote a more powerful force for improving labor conditions. Evidence of past performance does not support such a claim. Looking backward, using trade sanctions to encourage adoption of international labor standards deploys a policy that limits labor's opportunities to obtain compliance with policies that do not demonstrably expand opportunities.

Looking forward, one should evaluate the prospects for different results— an expansion of workers' opportunities—from a policy regime in which countries incurred real costs by not ratifying international labor standards. Would such a system be more likely to advance labor conditions around the world? To answer the question, one must imagine how the system might work. The implementation issues are clear. First, the standards must be chosen. Chapter 7 reviews the current ILO process for formulating labor standards, emphasizing the fact that in most cases the tripartite process produces rather broadly worded statements of principle rather than specific requirements. If a mandatory labor standard regime tilted toward standards with specific requirements, the key question would be "Whose standards would be adopted?" The possibility that labor conditions in advanced countries would frame the choice of standards remains a key concern of many developing countries, which worry that a labor standards regime could become disguised trade protection. Once standards have been chosen, compliance must be evaluated to determine whether countries should be sanctioned. Chapter 7 reviews the difficulties in assessing compliance with key labor standards.

The most important question of all is whether compliance in a mandatory labor standards regime would improve labor conditions. Evidence from the current regime of voluntary international labor standards does not help with this question. One must look instead to experience with national labor regulations. Chapter 7 reviews evidence on this question from various parts of the world, finding that national labor regulation benefits some workers and harms others. Consistent with this appraisal, this study did not find significant links between the strength of national labor regulations and the general level of national labor conditions.

Finally, no system of international labor standards is likely to reach workers in the informal sector, where much of the employment in developing countries occurs (chapter 2). Employment in the informal sector has little contact with national and international labor regulations. Developing countries can be pardoned for suspecting that proponents of labor standards are far more interested in raising labor costs in the export sectors of low-wage countries than in improving labor conditions for the much larger number of workers employed in the informal sector. Improving employment conditions of workers in the informal sector requires offering more opportunities for employment in the formal sector, an objective that is satisfied by expanding, not contracting, economic growth and export production.

Targeted Incentive Policies

Not all policies pertaining to labor conditions emerge from national and international governmental organizations. Some private, nongovernmental organizations target specific working conditions or labor rights for action. Carefully designed targeted policies could complement the positive effects of globalization in advancing labor conditions. After all, economic growth and the mechanisms of globalization account for only a portion of the international variance in labor conditions. Policies that target specific labor conditions should fulfill the same criterion as policies for improving labor conditions in general; above all, they should expand the opportunities of the targeted group. Two examples, child labor and forced labor, illustrate the potential complementarities between globalization and well-designed targeted policies, as well as the pitfalls of policies that do not satisfy the "expand opportunities" criterion.

CHILD LABOR. Child labor is ultimately linked to family poverty—either chronically low incomes or income variability that produces periods of poverty that families cannot counter because they lack personal savings or access to credit institutions. Looking across countries, child labor diminishes as the level of development rises. Looking within countries over time, researchers have found that child labor falls with advances in real per capita income. A growing body of country case studies clarifies that when income improves, families move their children from employment to superior alternatives, such as schooling.

Liberalized trade addresses the underlying cause of child labor. The export expansion that accompanies international economic integration is unlikely to influence child labor directly, because most child labor does not occur in manufacturing or other export industries. (The dramatic exceptions, such as carpet weavers in Nepal, constitute a very small fraction of worldwide child employment.) By increasing adult incomes, however, export expansion enables families to move their children out of employment. The presence of multinational companies in a country should also tend to reduce the national incidence of child labor, given that they typically pay higher wages. We find no evidence, however, that countries with extensive child labor attract disproportionately high amounts of foreign investment, presumably because direct foreign investment is complementary to skilled labor.

Child labor also varies widely among countries at the same level of development and openness, raising the question of how targeted policies might reduce the variance. One must remember the role of poverty: policies that address symptoms rather than the root cause of child labor are likely to worsen the problem by limiting even further the alternatives available to poor families. Policy responses may again be separated between those that increase the opportunities available to children and those that diminish those opportunities or have unintended, undesirable consequences.

Whether administered by the WTO or national legislatures, trade sanctions against countries with extensive child labor provide an example of measures that diminish opportunities. Effective trade sanctions limit output, employment, and income in at least some export industries. Though few children are employed in the export sector, the declines in adult incomes induced by sanctions pressure families to have their children work more. Trade sanctions are also poorly targeted. Trade agreements specify tariffs and other trade policies by country and industry. Sanctions make no distinction between companies that do and do not employ children. If sanctions work as they have in a few highly publicized cases, they further impoverish poor families and leave children with fewer, less attractive opportunities than they had before sanctions were imposed.

Consumer labeling provides a frequently suggested response to child (and forced) labor. The purpose is to provide consumers with information on a product's conditions of production so that they can choose to purchase only from manufacturers who certify that they have not used child (or forced) labor. Certification occurs on the basis of inspections by nongovernmental organizations. The process tests consumers' "willingness to pay" for labor rights, since certified products normally cost more to produce and hence carry a higher price. A majority of consumers express such willingness in surveys of intentions. If consumers in fact will pay for superior labor rights, a consumer labeling policy raises the demand for products of companies that do not use child (or forced) labor and lowers demand for the products of companies that refuse certification. The policy may have similar effects on patronage at retailers who respectively agree or refuse to agree to sell labeled products. Implementation details again become important; the process must be monitored to avoid counterfeiting of certification labels, for example.

Such consumer labeling policies would seem to reach a minority of child labor. As we have seen (chapter 2), most child labor occurs in agriculture and informal services that do not reach export markets. When labeling policies do reach their target, however, they reduce the opportunities available for children. If consumers respond by purchasing fewer items involving child labor, child employment will surely decline *in that industry*, but what alternatives do the displaced children from impoverished families face? If the job that they lose was their best alternative prior to the labeling policy, a successful policy drives them to a poorer alternative. On the other hand, if labeling policies raise the demand for products made by adult labor, they may indirectly reduce child labor by relieving the family poverty that is its root cause. Labeling policies would be more convincing mechanisms for improving child welfare if there were a mechanism to redistribute the additional money that consumers pay for "certified" products to the victims of the policy.

More attractive, because they create better opportunities, are school attendance subsidies for children and rural credit institutions that permit families to borrow in the face of a bad harvest or other unexpected income loss rather than put children to work to make up the shortfall. Whether paid in cash or in a basic staple such as rice, the subsidy addresses the source of the problem rather than the symptom. The results of several subsidy experiments in increasing and lengthening school attendance are quite encouraging (chapter 7).

FORCED LABOR. Policy proposals to eliminate forced labor must confront two salient facts regarding modern slavery. The first is the sheer variety of forced labor arrangements in the world. Chapter 2 provides a brief review. A minority of modern slavery corresponds to mental images developed from histories of pre–Civil War plantation life in the American South or the overseas practices of colonial countries. Chattel slavery, locally important in Mauritania and a few other countries, corresponds most closely to the traditional image of forced labor but is a small part of the current worldwide problem. The variety of motivations underlying modern forced labor arrangements should encourage a variety of policy responses. With possibly one exception—economic growth—no single policy response is likely to address all forced labor situations effectively.

Recognition of the changed economics of forced labor, in all its varieties, must also inform policy responses. In earlier times, slaves were sufficiently expensive, that purchasers faced incentives to assert ownership and to provide for at least basic maintenance of slaves to realize returns on their investment. One study of the pre–Civil War labor force in the southern United States observed: "It was not unusual for well-trained mechanics to sell for two-thousand dollars, while able bodied field hands brought eight hundred to one thousand dollars" (Spero and Harris 1931, p. 5). Self-interested slave owners therefore faced strong incentives to provide some level of food, clothing, and shelter to their slaves. Modern forced labor often does not require such investments. Even in an era in which forced labor is illegal and widely condemned, rapid population growth and limited opportunities have reduced the price of slaves to levels that encourage neither private ownership nor private maintenance. Turnover of forced labor is very cheap, and slave "holding" has replace slave ownership (Bales 2004).

In the face of these facts, this book has established two broad findings. First, both the variety and scope of forced labor arrangements diminish with economic development. Policies that accelerate economic growth will erode forced labor by providing more alternatives to the victims. Some argue sensibly that growth policies will have an even more powerful effect if accompanied by reduced government corruption and improved education. Reduced corruption, because modern forced labor is rarely legal, and government corruption is required to prevent the enforcement of laws that forbid it. Education, because it is the main mechanism for making people aware of their rights and alternatives (Bales 2004). Second, and more surprising for some readers, globalization does not seem to aggravate the forced labor problem. By raising per capita income, free trade contributes to eliminating conditions that support forced labor. Also, in a world of unencumbered international migration—the world of the nineteenth-century wave of globalization—few incentives would exist for trafficking in humans. Barriers to globalization, not globalization itself, tend to support this variety of forced labor. These broad influences suggest necessary conditions for eliminating forced labor; the variety of forced labor arrangements argues for a variety of policy responses to complement growth and economic integration.

Policy responses may again be grouped into those that increase the alternatives and opportunities available to those in forced labor and those that diminish those opportunities or have unintended, undesirable consequences. For trafficking in humans, reducing the barriers to legal migration would diminish the demand for trafficking and the debts and bondage that flow from this demand. Some migrants lack the resources to fully pay trafficking fees in advance. Fulfilling the debt obligation in the destination country frequently leads to forced labor of indefinite duration.

In contrast, some observers propose tightening border controls to combat trafficking—exactly the opposite approach. There are at least two notable consequences of this proposal. It may convert some temporary international migration into permanent migration, as migrants decide that they may not be able to leave again if they return home. By raising the risks of apprehension, the policy would also produce increased smuggling fees. Though increased trafficking charges should reduce the flow of illegal migration, it will also raise the indebtedness of those workers who still use the services of traffickers, making them even more vulnerable to lengthy forced labor arrangements in destination countries.

Debt bondage arrangements may be countered with government reha-
bilitation programs in which the government (or judiciary) (a) cancels out-
standing "debts," (b) liberates bonded workers, and (c) provides them with
resources, such as money and land, to make an economic start. The idea is
attractive, but experience with such programs suggests that the devil is in the
implementation details. In India, a government program was subject to significant administrative corruption (Bales 2004). Properly administered, however, this approach not only eliminates the immediate problem but also provides victims with potentially superior alternatives. The development of
simple credit union arrangements goes further, by providing options for credit
that may eliminate the need to accept bondage arrangements in the first place.

Proposals to impose trade sanctions against *countries* using forced labor
emerge from many national and international legislative bodies. Higher tariffs
reduce exports of all goods and slow a country's rate of economic growth.
Trade sanctions limit the alternatives not only of enslaved workers but of all
workers. Nor can the sanctions target offending companies, such as a
consumer-labeling program might. Trade policies are national policies that at
most can target by industry. But a policy that punishes an entire industry for
the behavior of some companies does not solve the problem. It makes it
worse by reducing the workers' opportunities and leaving them more vulnerable to forced labor arrangements. The fundamental problem with using
trade sanctions to enforce basic labor rights is the failure of such policies to
provide superior opportunities to victims. Imposing market-driven sanctions
on products produced with forced labor through consumer labeling policies
has already been covered in the earlier discussion of policies to reduce child
labor.

Slave redemption programs, well-motivated humanitarian efforts to buy
back slaves from slaveholders, fall in the unintended consequence category.
These programs raise the demand for slaves. By rewarding the slave trade,
they create incentives for the continuation of the trade and, at worst, its
expansion.

Final Remarks

This book has reviewed evidence that has emerged in the work of academic scholars, international organizations, and national governments
in an effort to trace the links between labor conditions and three major
mechanisms of globalization. Confronted with evidence, the indictment of
globalization outlined in chapter 1 fails. Each of the globalization mechanisms
works to advance working conditions and labor rights. Barriers to globalization retard the advance of labor conditions. The book has also been clear
that globalization is only one of the factors influencing labor conditions in
most countries. It is of great importance, however, rivaled only by the role
played by advances in per capita income. Other influences, not always iden-

tified in this book, also account for the huge dispersion in labor conditions around the world. Not surprisingly, there is room for thoughtfully designed and targeted policies to supplement the role of global forces. At the beginning of the twenty-first century, the challenge is to devise a focus on the policies that expand opportunities and to resist seduction by punitive policies that limit the opportunities of those whose labor conditions cry out for improvement.

APPENDIX A

Measurement of Labor Conditions

Chapter 2 introduces the measures of labor conditions used in this book. This appendix provides further information on the issues raised and choices made in developing the cross-country data set used in the analyses reported in this book. The analyses consider three dimensions of working conditions (pay, hours of work, and job safety) and four dimensions of labor rights (child labor, freedom of association, forced labor, and employment discrimination).

Pay

This book measures pay with five-year averages (1980–84 and 1995–99) of annual compensation per worker in manufacturing developed by the United Nations Industrial Development Organization and reported by the World Bank (2001a). This measure of pay "includes all payments in cash or in kind made to 'employees' during the reference year in relations to work done for the establishment. Payments include: (a) direct wages and salaries; (b) remuneration for time not worked; (c) bonuses and gratuities; (d) housing allowances and family allowances paid directly by the employer; and (e) payments in kind"; plus all contributions by employers to social security programs on behalf of their employees (UNIDO 2002, p. 10). The measure is available for a wider range of countries than alternative measures. The compensation data are from surveys of relatively large establishments in the formal sector and "are converted into U.S. dollars using the average exchange rate for each year" (World Bank 2001a, table 2.4). The effectiveness in capturing some elements of compensation may vary from country to country. Fixed-effects estimates of compensation relationships are included to check for biases which measurement error that persists over time might introduce into cross-section analyses. (As reported in the text, such biases appear to be absent from the compensation relationships.) The same measure is used in the analysis of pay in the apparel and footwear industries. The pay data (and related productivity data) for these low-wage industries were obtained directly from UNIDO (2001 and earlier issues).

Hours of Work

Efforts to develop consistent hours of work data for a large sample of countries encounter significant international differences in reporting practice, driven in part by whether statistical agencies collect work hours information from households, business establishments, or social insurance records. Countries variously report measures of actual hours worked, usual hours of work (which includes normal scheduled hours and any regular overtime, but excludes irregular overtime or unusual absence), hours at the work site, or hours paid for. The ILO (2003, chap. 6) defines *hours actually worked* as "time spent at the workplace on productive activities and on other activities that are part of the tasks and duties of the job concerned (for example, cleaning and preparing working tools)." *Usual hours of week* "identifies the most common weekly working schedule of a person in employment over a selected period . . . the modal value of the workers' 'hours actually worked' per week over a long period." This measure is derived from household surveys and is least likely to suffer significantly from different conceptual approaches by national statistical agencies, according to the ILO. The percentage of employees working more than 40 hours a week, one of the measures of work hours used in this study, is derived by the ILO from national measures of usual hours of work (ILO 2003).

Measures of annual hours of work are typically derived from a combination of household and establishment surveys (ILO 2003). At times, legislative or collective bargaining provisions for standard hours schedules may influence computations. Given the number of sources and variety of data adjustments required to prepare these estimates, the international comparability of annual work hours estimates is less certain than for measures based on usual hours of work. Fixed-effects estimates can control for ongoing differences in the measurement of this variable by national statistical systems.

A third measure, the weekly hours of work in manufacturing, has the virtue of focusing on the industry that is the main source of exports for many countries. Business establishments are the typical source of weekly hours data, and national statistical systems vary in the work hour concept that they report. Although an hours worked concept is preferable for the subject of this book, some countries publish data only on weekly hours paid for. In cross-section statistical work, this difficulty is addressed by including dummy variables for the hours concept adopted by each country. In panel analyses, fixed-effect regressions pick up constant differences attributable to different national measurement practices. The weekly hours of work in manufacturing data are from the ILO website (http://laborsta.ilo.org/).

Job Safety

Injury frequency rates record the number of new cases of injury during a calendar year as a fraction of employment, but both the numerator and the denominator present choices. Countries may tabulate either the number of "reported" or "compensated" new cases of injury. Rates are therefore sensitive to national rules governing qualification for injury compensation. The base may be the number of employees, insured employees, hours worked, or employees exposed to risk. Variations in definition and measurement clearly will bedevil cross-country comparisons. In the face of such variations in measurement procedures, not to mention standard measurement errors, panel (fixed-effect) estimation seems more promising than cross-section estimation, but the ILO (2001, p. 1139) notes that changes "in the number of cases of occupational injury over . . . time may reflect not only change in conditions of work and the work environment, but also modifications in reporting procedures or data collection methods, or revisions to laws or regulation governing the reporting or compensation of occupation injuries." Data on injury rates are available at http://laborsta.ilo.org/

Freedom of Association

This study analyzes two measures of freedom of association. Chapter 2 includes a discussion of the Freedom House index of civil liberties, which is available from 1972. See the Freedom House website (http://www.freedomhouse.org/ratings/index.htm) for additional details. The index of freedom of association and collective bargaining rights (FACB) is available only for the mid-1990s (Kucera 2002). This index is based on an evaluation of 37 potential interferences with rights to form and operate unions, bargain collectively, and strike. Interferences include violence, arrest or imprisonment of union members or organizers, exclusion of sectors or worker groups from union membership, restrictions on scope of collective bargaining, strike prohibitions, and restricted rights in EPZs. For a country, each interference receives a score of 1 if present and 0 otherwise. Each interference also receives a subjective importance weight (1, 1.25, 1.5, 1.75, or 2), and the weighted scores are summed to a raw score for the country. After rescaling, each country's FACB index number ranges from 0 to 10, with low numbers reflecting superior workplace freedom of association rights. The FACB index therefore reflects both the number of rights restricted in the country and the subjective weighting of each right. Removing the subjective weights has little effect on the ranking of countries, however; the correlation between the weighted and unweighted indices is .99. Information on restrictions on these rights comes from three sources: the International Confederation of Free Trade Unions' *Annual Survey of Violations of Trade Union Rights*, the U.S. State Department's *Country Reports on Human Rights Practices,* and the ILO's *Reports of the Committee on Freedom of Association.* The correlation between this workplace-oriented index and the broader FH index of civil liberties is .56 in the mid-1990s for the 104 countries with data on each index. Since each country receives similar treatment in the construction of measurements, these data are well suited for comparative analyses.

Forced Labor and Employment Discrimination

This study analyzes two measures of forced labor and one measure of employment discrimination (by gender). Chapter 2 includes a discussion of the measurements and data sources for these labor rights. In each case, the independent scholars who developed the measures applied consistent standards to all countries. As noted in chapter 2, one cross-section is available for each measure.

Child Labor

This study uses ILO data on the labor force participation rate of 10- to 14-year-old children as the indicator of child labor in a country. These data generally come from national household surveys, but the quality and consistency of the data surely vary between countries. Chapters 2 and 3 cite some potential concerns with the data. Fixed-effects estimates control for the effects of measurement errors that are fixed over time.

International Comparisons

Cross-country comparisons are riskiest for data series in which statistical production is decentralized to national statistical offices, and international organizations are unable to adjust the resulting statistical series to a common definition. This problem is most likely to arise for nonmonetary working conditions. Industrial accidents (job safety) and hours of work provide the most difficult areas of comparable documentation faced in the present study. In each difficult case, the study tries to mitigate the potential for erroneous comparisons by (a) using multiple indicators of a working condition or labor right and checking for consistency among the indicators, and

Table A.1
Variables, Sources, and Definitions

Variable	Source	Definition
Area	Encyclopedia Britannica	In millions of square kilometers
Child labor	ILO, LABORSTA website	Labor force participation rate of 10- to 14-year-old children
Civil liberties	Freedom House	Index of civil liberties
Civil rights	Botero et al. (2004)	Index of national civil rights regulations
Collective relations	Botero et al. (2004)	Index of workplace collective relations regulations
Democracy	(constructed)	(14—Civil liberties—Political rights)/12
Distance	World Bank (2001a)	Distance from capital city of major trading partner
Educ	World Bank (2001a)	Years of schooling, population over 25 years of age
Employment relations	Botero et al. (2004)	Index of workplace employment regulations
Ethnic	Alesina et al. (2002)	Ethnic diversity measure
Exprop	International Country Risk Guide (2005)	Index of expropriation risk
Fatal injuries	ILO, LABORSTA website	Fatal injuries per 100,000 manufacturing employees
FACB	Kucera (2002)	Index of workplace freedom of association and collective bargaining rights
Firing costs	Botero et al. (2004)	Index of firing costs
Forced labor	Busse and Braun (2003a)	Number of types of forced labor in country
GDPCAP	Heston et al. (2002)	Chain-linked real per capita GDP
Gender differential	Weichselbaumer and Winter-Ebner (2003)	Net gender differential
Govshare	Heston et al. (2002)	Share of government consumption in GDP
Hours cost	Botero et al. (2004)	Cost of increasing work hours
Annual hours	ILO (2003b)	Annual hours of work, all employees
Long hours	ILO (2003b)	Percent of employees working more than 40 hours per week
Weekly hours	ILO, LABORSTA website	Weekly hours of work in manufacturing
Island		Dummy variable taking value 1 if a country is an island
Labor costs	World Bank (2001a)	Labor costs per worker in manufacturing
Legal	Botero et al. (2004)	Dummy variables for origins of a country's legal system
Left	Botero et al. (2004)	Percentage of years between 1975 and 1995 in which a country's chief executive and legislature have a left or center orientation

(continued)

Table A.1 (*Continued*)

Variable	Source	Definition
Life expectancy	World Bank (2001a)	Years of life expectancy at birth
Open policy	Sachs-Warner (1995) Wacziarg-Welch (2003)	Dummy variable for open trade policy
Political rights	Freedom House	Index of political rights
Pop	Encyclopedia Britannica	Population
Productivity	World Bank (2001a)	Value added per worker in manufacturing
Religion	Alesina et al. (2002)	Religious diversity measure
Rule of law	International Country Risk Guide (2005)	Index of rule of law
Slavery	Bales (2004b)	Estimated number of slaves
Social Security	Botero et al. (2004)	Index of national social security regulations
Trade share	Heston and Summers (2002)	(exports + imports)/GDP

(b) using statistical techniques to adjust for national differences in definition and method, as indicated in the foregoing discussion.

When a single organization or researcher prepares comparative data, such as most of the labor rights measures used in this study, concerns with cross-country data comparability diminish. A summary of the variable names, data sources, and definitions is in table A.1.

APPENDIX B

Open and Closed Economies, Late Twentieth Century

Open economies	Closed economies
Australia	Algeria
Austria	Argentina
Barbados	Bangladesh
Belgium	Benin
Bolivia	Brazil
Botswana	Bulgaria
Canada	Burkina Faso
Chile	Burundi
Cyprus	Cameroon
Denmark	Cape Verde
Ecuador	Central African Republic
Finland	Chad
France	China
Greece	Colombia
Hong Kong	Congo, Republic of
Indonesia	Costa Rica
Ireland	Cote d'Ivoire
Italy	Dominican Republic
Japan	Egypt
Jordan	El Salvador
Korea, Rep. of	Ethiopia
Luxembourg	Gabon
Malaysia	Guatemala
Mauritius	Guinea

Open economies	Closed economies
Netherlands	Guinea-Bissau
Norway	Haiti
Portugal	Honduras
Singapore	Iceland
Spain	India
Sweden	Iran
Switzerland	Iraq
Taiwan	Kenya
Thailand	Lesotho
United Kingdom	Liberia
United States	Madagascar
Yemen	Malawi
	Mali
	Malta
	Mauritania
	Mexico
	Mozambique
	Nepal
	New Zealand
	Nicaragua
	Niger
	Nigeria
	Pakistan
	Panama
	Papua New Guinea
	Paraguay
	Peru
	Philippines
	Poland
	Romania
	Russia
	Rwanda
	Senegal
	Sierra Leone
	Somalia
	South Africa
	Swaziland
	Syria
	Tanzania
	Togo
	Trinidad & Tobago
	Tunisia
	Turkey
	Uganda
	Uruguay
	Venezuela

Open economies	Closed economies
	Yugoslavia
	Zaire (Congo, Dem. Rep.)
	Zambia
	Zimbabwe

Note: "Open" ("closed") economies were open (closed) by the Sachs-Warner criteria for at least three of the years 1970, 1980, 1990, 2000.

APPENDIX C

Chapter Appendices

Appendix to Chapter 3

The discussion in chapter 3 refers to the results from regression analyses of (1) the determinants of international differences in compensation (labor costs) and (2) the relationship between labor costs, level of development, economic and political characteristics, and social diversity. This appendix provides details about the underlying statistical analyses. Appendix A summarizes the definitions and data sources of all variables.

Analysis of Compensation (Labor Costs)

The discussion of links between compensation and productivity in chapter 3 refers to the regression analyses of international compensation differences for the manufacturing sector and for apparel and footwear—two low-wage manufacturing industries that play a significant role in discussions of globalization. For each industry, the analysis relates total compensation (labor costs) per worker to value added per worker and the average price level of consumption in purchasing power parity (PPP) terms to capture international cost-of-living differences not accounted for by the exchange rate conversion. All variables are in natural logarithms and are weighted by the size of the labor force in each country observation.

Total compensation "includes direct wages, salaries, and other remuneration paid directly by employers plus all contributions by employers to social security programs on behalf of their employees." As a broad measure of productivity, value added per worker captures the influence of capital, technology, education, training, experience, as well as unobservable influences on worker efficiency. Both the compensation and productivity data are from United Nations surveys of relatively large establishments in the formal sector, and "the data are converted into U.S. dollars using the average exchange rate for each year" (World Bank 2001a, table 2.5). The United Nations warns that the effectiveness in capturing some elements of compensation may vary from country to country. (The fixed-effects estimation discussed below removes constant country-specific anomalies in the measurement of compensation.)

For total manufacturing, apparel, and footwear industries, the cross-country analyses are conducted on 1995–99 averages for 58 countries (total manufacturing) or 28 countries (apparel and footwear industries). National differences in unobserved labor regulations, collective bargaining arrangements, or other institutions may be correlated with both compensation and productivity, however, producing biased cross-country estimates of the links between those variables. Therefore, fixed-effects estimates supplement the cross-country estimates for total manufacturing and apparel. Panels of 58 countries (manufacturing) and 28 countries (apparel) with 1980–84 and 1995–99 averages of the data provide the raw material for the fixed-effects estimation. (There are insufficient observations to conduct a fixed-effects analysis of compensation in the footwear industry.)

Cross-country variations in labor productivity and price levels account for more than 90 percent of the international variation in labor compensation for all three industries. Both the productivity and price variables are also economically and statistically significant in the fixed-effect results for manufacturing. Productivity is significant throughout the analyses of all industries (table A3.1). The international price level is significant only for total manufacturing and is somewhat weaker in the fixed-effects estimates.

To summarize, a strong positive correlation between international productivity and compensation differences emerges in both the cross-country and fixed-effects analyses for total manufacturing. Much the same may be said of the relationship between productivity and compensation in two low-wage industries, apparel and footwear, qualified slightly by the inability to conduct a fixed-effects analysis for footwear.

Analysis of Income Elasticities of Labor Conditions

Chapter 3 provides a discussion of the sensitivity of labor conditions to a country's level of development (real per capita income) and changes in the level development. The discussion is also based on cross-country and panel estimates of the income elasticities of labor conditions. The following regression equation (with all variables weighted by labor force size) provided cross-country estimates for 1995:

Table A3.1
Regression Analysis of Compensation (Labor Costs)

Estimation	Productivity	Price	Constant	R^2
A. Manufacturing				
1. Cross-country	0.712	0.731	−1.204	0.97
(1995–99)	(.063)★	(.132)★		
2. Fixed effects	0.909	0.453	−2.100	0.91
	(.036)★	(.070)		
B. Apparel				
1. Cross-country	0.985	−0.139	0.003	0.93
(1995–99)	(.111)★	(0.459)		
2. Fixed effects	0.942	−0.04	0.153	0.84
	(.173)★	(0.486)		
C. Footwear				
1. Cross-country	0.721	0.529	−0.582	0.92
(1995–99)	(0.129)	(0.318)		

Notes: Dependent Variable: Annual labor costs (compensation) per worker.
All variables in natural logarithms. All observations are weighted by labor force.
Robust standard errors in parentheses for cross-country estimates.
★ p-value < .01

Sources: UNIDO (2001); World Bank (2001a)

(3.1A) $\ln(LC)_i = a_0 + a_1 \ln(GDPCAP)_i + \varepsilon_i$

The dependent and independent variables are, respectively, the natural logs of a labor condition (LC) and real per capita income (GDPCAP) in country i, and ε_i is the country-specific error term. For each labor condition, table A3.2 reports the estimated income elasticity, a_1. Many countries report values of zero for two measures of labor rights—the child labor force participation rate and the number of varieties of forced labor. For these two measures, equation 3.1A is estimated using tobit analysis. For all other measures of labor conditions, the equation is estimated using ordinary least squares. The reported 1995 cross-country estimates are representative; unreported cross-country estimates for every 5 or 10 years (as data permitted) from 1970 to 2000 showed little difference in estimates of income elasticities.

For some measures of labor conditions, one may question whether causality runs from per capita GDP to the labor condition or the other way around. (Work hours, an input to production, may present the strongest case for reverse causality.) Taking the view that per capita GDP might influence

Table A3.2
Income Elasticities of Labor Conditions

Labor conditions	1995 Cross-country			Fixed effects,[a] 1970–2000	
	Coefficient	R^2	n	Coefficient	Period
Long hours	−0.015 (.10)	0	37	−0.005 (.024)	1990–2000
Annual hours	−0.06 (.04)	0.06	27	−0.05* (.006)	1990–2000
Weekly hours	−0.048* (.007)	0.40	43	−.033* (.005)	1980–2000
Fatal accidents	−0.23 (.23)	0.09	32	−0.47* (.07)	1970–2000
Life expectancy	0.10* (.014)	0.63	105	0.14* (.008)	1970–2000
Child labor	−7.62* (.60)	.15[b]	110	−5.42* (1.74)	1970–2000
Civil liberties	−0.46* (.09)	0.57	104	−0.21* (.04)	1972–2000
Freedom of association	−0.34** (.14)	0.21	92	n.a.	Late 1990s
Forced labor	−29.01* (10.05)	.08[b]	101	n.a.	Late 1990s
Slavery	−1.47** (.69)	0.23	69	n.a.	Late 1990s
Gender differential[c]	−0.006 (.031)	0	56	n.a.	About 1985

Notes: All variables in natural logarithms. All observations weighted by labor force. Robust standard errors in parentheses for cross-country estimates.
n = number of observations
[a] Random-effects estimates reported when a Hausman test finds no significant difference between fixed and random effects. Also, fixed effects not available for tobit estimator.
[b] Pseudo R^2 from tobit estimation.
[c] 1985 cross-section (see text)
n.a. not available
* p-value < .01
** p-value < .05

working conditions and labor rights with a lag, unreported regressions tested for the effects of 5- and 10-year lags in per capita GDP on labor conditions in the cross-country and panel analyses. In most cases, the lagged values of per capita GDP had similar coefficients and were statistically stronger. In no case did the reported elasticities and semi-elasticities change sign or lose statistical significance.

Table A3.2 also reports panel data estimates of income elasticities for the late twentieth century obtained from the following regression model:

(3.2A) $\ln(LC)_{it} = a_0 + a_1 \ln(GDPCAP)_{it} + \lambda_i + \varepsilon_{it}$

In this regression, t indexes the year, and λ_i represents the fixed effect for country i. The panel consists of country data for intervals during 1970–2000. (With complete data, the panel consists of (1) observations every five years during this period for civil liberties, the fatal job accident rate, life expectancy, and real per capita GDP, (2) observations for 1970, 1980, 1990, 1995, and 2000 for child labor and weekly hours of work in manufacturing, and (3) observations for 1990, 1995, and 2000 for annual work hours and long work-weeks.) Data limitations impose unbalanced panels for most measures. Sample sizes range from more than 100 countries (for life expectancy) to fewer than three dozen countries (for some measures of work hours).

Most panel results are fixed-effects estimates. Where a Hausman test rejects the hypothesis of no difference between fixed-effects and random-effects estimates (weekly work hours and fatal job injuries), random-effects estimates are reported. For variables with only one annual observation (both measures of forced labor [late 1990s], the measure of discrimination [roughly 1985], and the FACB index [mid-1990s]), only cross-country estimates of income elasticities are available.

Table A3.3 reports income semi-elasticities, also estimated by the ordinary least squares, tobit, and panel methods used for table A3.2. Each figure describes the absolute change in the measure of labor conditions to a 1 percent change in per capita GDP. For example, the fixed-effect estimates indicate that a 1 percent difference in per capita GDP between countries is associated with a difference of about five fatal on-the-job injuries per 100,000 employees, nine years life expectancy, and 1 point on the 7-point civil liberties scale. Where results are statistically significant, higher per capita income is associated with superior working conditions and labor rights, as discussed in chapter 3.

Table 3.1 in chapter 3 reports outliers—countries with unusually large positive or negative deviations from the value of a labor condition predicted by the cross-section semi-elasticity for their level of development in 1995. Each figure reported in table 3.1 is the ratio of the regression residual (actual minus predicted value of the labor conditions) for the country to the mean squared error for the cross-country regression for the labor condition. All figures are computed from the regressions reported in table A3.3.

Institutions, Social Diversity, and Labor Conditions

Chapter 3 also discusses the role of economic and political institutions and social diversity (measured by ethnic and religious diversity) on labor conditions around the world. To estimate their actual influence, measures of these factors are added as independent variables in equation 3.2A. Indices of the rule of law and risk of expropriation represent economic institutions. Each index is measured on a 10-point scale, with higher values indicating

Table A3.3
Income Semi-Elasticities of Labor Conditions, 1995

Labor conditions	1995 Cross-country			Fixed effects,[a] 1970 2000	
	Coefficient	R^2	n	Coefficient	Period
Long hours	−0.53	0	37	−2.20★	1990–2000
	(5.76)			(.84)	
Annual hours	−116.16	0.07	27	93.83★	1990–2000
	(73.60)			(10.40)	
Weekly hours	−2.08★	0.38	43	−1.37★	1980–2000
	(.32)			(.20)	
Fatal accidents	−2.36★★	0.16	32	−6.01★	1970–2000
	(.90)			(1.32)	
Life expectancy	6.71★	0.69	105	8.78★	1970–2000
	−0.44			(0.40)	
Child labor	−12.67★	0.18[b]	110		1970–2000
	(1.04)				
Civil liberties	−1.36★	0.43	104	−0.68★	1972–2000
	(.16)			(.13)	
Freedom of association	−1.26★★	0.17	95	n.a.	Late 1990s
	(.57)				
Forced labor	−2.68★	.12[b]	106	n.a.	Late 1990s
	(.85)				
Slavery	−3034030	0.14	69	n.a.	Late 1990s
	(2226022)				
Gender differential	−.004	0	56	n.a.	About 1985
	(.017)				

Notes: See notes to table A3.2.
[a] Random effects estimates reported where Hausman test finds no significant differences between fixed-effect and random-effect estimates.
[b] Pseudo R^2 from tobit estimation
★ p-value < .01
★★ p-value < .05

superior institutions (International Country Risk Guide). A broad measure of civil and political liberties is derived from the (highly correlated) Freedom House indicators of civil liberties (CIVIL) and political rights (POLITICAL). Following a procedure adopted by Rodrik (1999), DEMOCRACY is defined as (14-CIVIL-POLITICAL)/12. Thus defined, DEMOCRACY takes positive values between 0 and 1, with higher values indicating more democratic institutions. This measure, which captures a broader range of liberties than voting rights, is available annually from 1972 (Freedom House). The analyses in this book use data for every five years in the 1970–2000 period (after applying the 1972 value to 1970). Alesina et al. (2003) developed and reported the measures of ethnic and religious diversity. The measure, one minus the Herfindahl index of group shares in a country's population, reflects the probability that two randomly selected individuals from a country belong to different ethnic (or religious) groups. For country j: $DIVERSITY_j = 1 - \Sigma s^2_{ij}$, where s_{ij} is the share of group i in country j's population.

Estimates of the effects of institutions and social diversity on labor conditions are developed from country panels of data for 1980, 1985, and 1990—dates imposed by the availability of data on economic institutions. (Measures of social diversity exist only for the early to mid-1990s but are unlikely to change markedly over time.) Random effects estimation captures the effects of the latter variables from cross-country variation, and the effects of development and economic and political institutions from both the cross-section and overtime variation available in the panel. For the FACB index, gender pay differences, and both varieties of forced labor, the absence of panel data permits only a cross-section analysis. The measures of child labor and forced labor are truncated at zero—most developed countries report no child or forced labor. Tobit analysis is used to estimate these regressions, using panel data in the case of child labor and cross-country data in the case of forced labor.

The results indicate several links between a country's labor conditions and its economic, political, and social characteristics (table A3.4). Correlations between labor conditions and per capita income survive the addition of the new variables to the model. Most measures of labor conditions are significantly correlated with DEMOCRACY. Countries with democratic political institutions tend to have superior labor conditions. Institutions and social diversity variables are selectively influential on various labor conditions. (See discussion of these results in text of chapter 3.)

Appendix to Chapter 4

Chapter 4 discusses (1) how international trade theories imply that trade improves working conditions by increasing the efficiency of resource use, which should raise per capita income, and (2) how liberalized trade may have an additional direct influence on some labor rights. In contrast, the race-to-the-bottom hypothesis predicts that free trade degrades labor conditions. This appendix provides details of the econometric analyses of links between a country's openness to international trade and the labor conditions that are discussed in the chapter. The regression analyses reported below add measures of openness to the cross-country and panel regression models described and applied in the appendix to chapter 3. Appendix A summarizes the definitions and data sources of all variables.

Table A3.4
Labor Conditions, Institutions, and Social Divisions, 1980–95

	Weekly hours[a]	Fatal accidents[a]	Life expectancy[a]	Civil liberties[a]	Child labor[b]	Forced labor[c]	Gender differential[d]
Per capita GDP	-0.076	-0.138	0.082	-0.07	-3.219	-59.988	-0.077
	(.020)★	(-0.152)	(.009)★	(.024)★	(.154)★	(21.191)★	(0.048)
Rule of law	0.001	0.058	0.001	-0.056	-0.423	-13.186	0.016
	(0.009)	(0.092)	(0.004)	(.013)★	(.108)★	(10.214)	(0.031)
Expropriation	0.004	-0.017	0.014	0.01	0.132	31.236	0.057
	(0.005)	(0.049)	(.002)	(0.008)	(.072)★★★	(10.751)★	(.032)★★★
Democracy	-0.096	-1.01	0.019	-1.546	-1.473	-77.458	0.128
	(.042)★★	(.412)★★	(0.016)	(.058)★	(.406)★	(32.948)★★	(0.110)
Ethnic	0.042	1.085	-0.21	-0.002	9.630	-49.731	0.254
	(0.066)	(.503)★★	(.040)★	(0.079)	(.473)★	(21.174)★★	(0.169)
Religion	-0.004	-1.078	-0.013	-0.121	-12.689	-42.219	-0.153
	(0.064)	(.444)★★	(0.038)	(.073)★★★	(.570)★	(32.764)	(0.144)
Constant	4.453	4.106	3.427	2.747	26.467	303.171	-0.081
R^2	0.38	0.49	0.77	0.91	—	0.35	0.51
Countries	51	38	97	97	96	93	55
Observations	76	98	272	281	273	93	55

Notes: [a] Random-effects estimates.
[b] Random-effects tobit estimates.
[c] Tobit estimates.
[d] Ordinary least squares estimates.
★ p-value < .01
★★ p-value < .05
★★★ p-value < .10

Cross-Country Analysis

The cross-country analysis tests for the effect of a country's openness to trade on the measures of labor conditions using data for 1995, except in the case of discrimination, where data for 1985 are used to accommodate the fact that the gender wage differential is centered on 1985. Sample sizes vary with data availability for measures of working conditions and labor rights: weekly hours (50 country observations), annual hours of work (27), long work schedules (37), fatal accident rate (33), life expectancy (113), civil liberties index (108), child labor force participation rate (107), forced labor varieties (106), and gender wage difference (57).

The underlying cross-country regression model is:

$$(4.1A) \quad LC_i = a_0 + a_1 (GDPCAP)_i + a_2 OPEN_i + \Sigma \beta_j INSTITUTIONS_{ij} + \varepsilon_i$$

As in the analyses for chapter 3, the dependent variable for each regression, LC_i, is a measure of a working condition or labor right in country i. The independent variables respectively measure real per capita income, openness to international competition, and j measures of economic and political institutions and social diversity. (The vector of variables, $INSTITUTIONS_j$, includes the measures of rule of law, risk of expropriation, democracy and civil liberties, ethnic diversity, and religious diversity used in chapter 3.) All variables except the INSTITUTIONS vector are in natural logarithms, and all observations are weighted by the country's labor force. The random error term is ε_i. The analysis tests for a relationship between each labor condition and OPEN, measured alternately by exports plus imports as a fraction of GDP (TRADE SHARE), and a multi-hurdle, updated Sachs–Warner indicator of open trade policies (OPEN POLICY) (Wacziarg and Welch 2003).

The coefficient, a_2, provides the crucial test of whether the *direct* effect of openness is to improve or degrade labor conditions. Note that the *total* effect of openness on labor conditions includes the direct effect plus the indirect effect that occurs as a country's per capita income is affected. The a_2 coefficient tests only for the direct effect of openness because the regressions statistically control for the effects of per capita income on labor conditions. That is, the indirect effect of openness is included in the a_1 coefficient. Since higher per capita income is associated with superior labor conditions (chapter 3), and since, as discussed in chapter 4, there is a consensus that openness raises per capita GDP, the hypothesis that openness degrades labor conditions requires more than a negative direct effect, a_2. It requires that a_2 be sufficiently negative to overwhelm the positive indirect effect of openness. To degrade a country's labor conditions, greater economic openness would have to cause a *direct* deterioration in labor conditions that overwhelms its positive indirect influence.

If labor conditions and some measures of openness are jointly deter-mined (see discussion in main text of chapter 4), ordinary least squares (OLSQ) will produce biased estimates of the relationship between openness and labor conditions. As a result, table A4.1 reports both OLSQ and instru-mental variables (IV) estimates of the cross-country, labor-force-weighted relationships. "Gravity" models of international trade flows provide suitable instruments for the trade share of GDP—exogenous variables that are cor-related with trade but are unlikely to influence labor conditions except through their influence on trade. The gravity variables used to instrument TRADE SHARE and OPEN POLICY are the labor-to-land ratio, a dummy variable for small countries, and a dummy for island economies. (See appen-dix A for details.) The first-stage regressions account for 25 to 50 percent of the variance in TRADE SHARE and from 40 to more than 90 percent of the variance in OPEN POLICY, depending on the labor condition under analysis.

Given the scaling of the different measures of labor conditions, a finding that $a_2 > 0$ will indicate that openness directly improves wages and life ex-pectancy, and a finding that $a_2 < 0$ will indicate that openness directly improves hours of work, job safety, civil liberties, freedom of association, forced labor, and slavery. The opposite findings would be consistent with the hypothesis that poorer labor conditions accompany openness to international trade.

Table A4.1 reports OLSQ and IV estimates of the a_2 coefficients (with robust standard errors) for working conditions (pay, hours of work, job risks) from the regression model described in equation 4.1A. The OLSQ and IV estimates of a_2 often differ substantially in magnitude, supporting concerns that OLSQ may yield biased estimates. None of the IV estimates of TRADE SHARE and OPEN POLICY associations with working conditions are sta-tistically significant. These results imply that openness has only an indirect influence on these working conditions. Larger trade shares or open trade policies improve working conditions by raising per capita GDP (as shown in chapter 3) but have no further direct influence on working conditions. (Re-call that the a_2 estimates come from regressions that already control for per capita GDP.) In two cases, the statistical significance of the estimated openness coefficient changes with the estimation method. The OLSQ implications that countries with open trade policies have lower wages and a larger proportion of the labor force working more than 50 hours per week, ceteris paribus, disappear in the IV estimates. (The small sample of countries reporting annual hours data includes no closed economies, so a test for an association with open policy is not possible.)

In contrast, OLSQ, IV, and, for the measures of child labor and forced labor, tobit estimates indicate that openness has more direct associations with most measures of labor rights (table A4.2). (Tobit estimation follows from the fact that data on child labor force participation rates and the number of va-rieties of forced labor are censored at zero for many countries.) Countries with open trade policies have significantly more civil liberties (although not

Table A4.1
Openness and Working Conditions

Working condition	Cross-section		Panel
	OLSQ	IV	Fixed effects
Compensation			
Trade share	−.101	.007	.003
	(.111)	(.217)	(.114)
Open policy	−.323	−.500	−.062
	(.185)★★★	(0.356)	(0.062)
Weekly work hours			
Trade share	−.029	−.051	−.009
	(.023)	(.041)	(.008)
Open policy	−.008	−.040	.004
	(.046)	(.087)	(.005)
Annual work hours			
Trade share	−.072	−.099	−.011
	(.067)	(.131)	(.009)
Open policy	n.a.	n.a.	−.001
			(.004)
Long work hours			
Trade share	−.054	−.103	−.002
	(.143)	(.266)	(.027)
Open policy	.407	−2.862	−.005
	(.120)★	(5.049)	(.011)
Fatal accidents			
Trade share	.214	−1.483	−.234
	(.520)	(1.118)	(.169)
Open policy	1.357	−3.807	−.379
	(1.040)	(7.031)	(.156)★★
Life expectancy			
Trade share	.0001	.023	.093
	(.0115)	(.027)	(.009)★
Open policy	−0.012	−.0068	.048
	(.030)	(.0793)	(.007)★

Notes: Regression coefficients and robust standard errors (in parentheses) for OPEN variable in regression model (4.1A) described in the text of this appendix. Each coefficient is from a different regression.

★ p-value <.01

★★ p-value <.01

★★★ p-value <.01

Table A4.2
Openness and Labor Rights

Labor right	Cross-section		Panel
	OLSQ	IV	Fixed effects

Civil liberties

	OLSQ	IV	Fixed effects
Trade share	.204	.505	−.036
	(.147)	(.360)	(.040)
Open policy	−.613	−.834	−.115
	(.144)★	(.511)★★★	(.032)★

FACB index

	OLSQ	IV	Fixed effects
Trade share	−1.286	−1.024	n.a
	(.600)★★	(1.184)	
Open policy	−.197	.624	n.a.
	(.788)	(2.697)	

Discrimination

	OLSQ	IV	Fixed effects
Trade share	−.024	.177	n.a.
	(.058)	(.108)	
Open policy	.146	.428	n.a.
	(.075)★★	(.127)★	

Child labor#

	OLSQ	IV	Fixed effects
Trade share	−.435	n.a.	−1.254
	(1.410)		(.437)★
Open policy	−4.966	n.a.	−1.352
	(1.512)★		(.507)★

Forced labor#

	OLSQ	IV	Fixed effects
Trade share	−25.763	n.a.	n.a.
	(14.172)★★★		
Open policy	−36.547	n.a.	n.a.
	(16.393)★★		

Slavery

	OLSQ	IV	Fixed effects
Trade share	−2.885	−1.986	n.a.
	(.778)★	(1.89)	
Open policy	1.856	−4.069	n.a.
	(1.53)	(6.66)	

Note: See notes to table A4.1.
Tobit estimates

more freedom of association and collective bargaining rights), lower child labor participation rates, fewer varieties of forced labor, but a larger net gender wage differential than countries with closed trade policies, after controlling for the influences of level of development, economic and political institutions, and social diversity. Countries with relatively high trade shares have a superior FACB rating, less forced labor and fewer slaves, but the significant findings for trade shares do not survive in the IV estimates. Unfortunately, it was not possible to recover IV tobit estimates for the child labor and forced labor estimates.

Panel Analysis

Further biases may exist if unobserved country-specific influences on labor conditions are also correlated with openness. The (unobserved) domestic regulation of labor conditions by national governments or by labor unions might be correlated with a country's openness to international competition, for example. For all labor conditions except for the FACB index, discrimination, and the forced labor measures, the availability of panel data permits fixed-effects estimation, which uses within-country changes over time to estimate the coefficients of the regression model. The appendix to chapter 3 describes the country panel data used in the analysis. Tables A4.1 and A4.2 also report fixed-effects estimates of the relationship between openness and working conditions and between openness and labor rights, respectively. These estimates confirm the absence of a statistically significant relationship between openness and pay or any of the measures of hours of work. They also provide a more positive read on the relationship between openness and job safety; countries that change to more open trade policies experience a reduction in fatal job accidents and an increase in life expectancy, ceteris paribus. The fixed-effects estimates also confirm that openness is associated with more civil liberties and less child labor.

Appendix to Chapter 6

Chapter 6 includes a discussion of whether countries with poor labor conditions gain unusually large shares of foreign direct investment (FDI), other things equal. This appendix provides details of cross-country and panel regression analyses underlying that chapter's discussion of this issue. (Appendix A summarizes the definitions and data sources of all variables.)

The analysis describes why the share of FDI inflows varied among countries in the 1980s and 1990s. The approach is to estimate a baseline model of FDI inflows and then to test for whether the addition of measures of labor conditions and national labor regulations improves our understanding of the variation in FDI among countries. The dependent variable is the natural logarithm of a country's share of world FDI inflows. The baseline analysis assumes that decisions about the location of FDI consider the risks to investment, the scope of the market, the availability of complementary inputs, such as land and labor skills, and the openness of alternative host countries. These considerations govern the choice of independent variables. Expropriation, repudiation of contracts, corruption, and other failures of the rule of law all threaten investment returns. In practice, these factors are highly intercorrelated among countries, so an index of the risk of expropriation (EXPROP) serves as a measure of risk in the cross-country analysis. (EXPROP is scaled so that high values indicate a lower risk of expropriation.) The share of government consumption in GDP (GOVSHARE), often used as a proxy for the scope government intervention in markets, serves as a second measure of potential investment risks. Population (POP) and per capita GDP (GDPCAP) measure the scope of the market. A variable for the AREA of a country (measured in millions of square kilometers) is included to test whether FDI and land are complementary. Chapter 6 reviews the debate over the role of labor force skill in attracting FDI. The years of schooling (educational attainment) of people over 25 years of age (EDUC) serves as proxy for skill and provides an opportunity to test for whether FDI is complementary with high- or low-skill labor. This analysis tests for the relationship between FDI shares and two measures of openness: exports and imports as a fraction of GDP (TRADE SHARE) and the updated Sachs-Warner indicator of open trade policies (OPEN POLICY).

The regression model of FDI shares is estimated on cross-country data for the early 1990s and panel data for the 1980s and 1990s. The cross-country sample consists of a maximum of about 80 countries at various stages of economic development. (Limitations in data availability for some labor conditions and labor regulations reduce the sample size for some regressions.) Given the annual volatility in FDI inflows, the dependent variable in the cross-section analysis is the natural logarithm of a country's share of world FDI averaged over 1991–96. To mitigate concerns about causality, the values of independent variables are for 1990, the year preceding the beginning of the period over which the dependent variable is measured.

The random-effects panel estimates of the model take advantage of within-country variance over time as well as cross-country differences. (A Hausman specification test did not reject the hypothesis that the random-effects and fixed-effects coefficients are the same.) The panel consists of data for a country's share of world FDI inflows averaged over 1980–85, 1986–1991, and 1991–96 with corresponding values of independent variables for 1980, 1985, and 1990.

The regression results strongly support the baseline model of why FDI inflow shares vary among countries (table A6.1). Regressions (1) and (2) report cross-country, labor-force-weighted OLSQ estimates of the FDI model, while regression (3) reports the random-effects estimates. This discussion and the narrative in chapter 6 focus on these cross-country results, but notable differences between the two sets of estimates are discussed below.

Table A6.1
Baseline FDI Share Regressions, All Countries

	Cross-country		Random effects
	(1)	(2)	(3)
EXPROP	.805	1.073	.057
	(.233)★	(.254)★	(.051)
GOVSHARE	−5.784	−7.870	−3.882
	(2.367)★★	(2.349)★	(1.475)★
ln POP	.599	.196	.731
	(.149)★	(203)	(.095)★
ln GDPCAP	−0.096	−0.884	1.215
	(.320)	(.404)★★	(.194)★
AREA	.00025	.00026	.00020
	(.00006)★	(.00008)★	(.00006)★
EDUC	.102	.149	.002
	(071)	(.078)★★★	(0.068)
ln TRADE SHARE	1.360		0.916
	(.379)★		(0.224)★
OPEN POLICY		.727	
		(.326)★★	
Constant	−18.552	−5.089	−22.724
R^2	.906	.881	.850
Root MSE	.683	.776	
Countries	78	77	86

Notes: Dependent variable is natural logarithm of a country's share of world FDI inflows. All observations weighted by labor force. Robust standard errors in parentheses. Variables defined in text and in Appendix A.
★ p-value < .01
★★ p-value < .05
★★★ p-value < .10

In the cross-country estimates, both of the investment risk factors—the risk of expropriation and the proxy for government intervention into the economy, significantly influence a country's share of FDI inflows in the predicted direction. (Recall that high values of EXPROP indicate a lower risk of expropriation.) More populous countries receive larger FDI shares. Both the land size and (more weakly) education level of a country appear to complement FDI share. Countries with a relatively large trade sector (regression 1) or open trade policies (regression 2) receive larger FDI shares, other factors equal, but the open trade policy specification is weaker statistically. The overall regression fit is good, with the model accounting for more than ninety percent of the variance in FDI inflow shares among 78 countries. (A similar pattern emerges from unreported, unweighted estimates, although the effect of the risk factors is measured much less precisely.) Random-effects estimates parallel the cross-country findings, except that the risk of expropriation variable is no longer statistically significant.

As a check on the robustness of the findings, the cross-country model was also estimated on a sample of non-OECD countries. A similar pattern of findings emerges except that the positive correlation between education and FDI share is measured more precisely for these lower income countries (table A6.2). Both measures of openness remain significant, but the regression with trade volumes continues to have superior statistical properties.

The various measures of working conditions and labor rights were added one at a time to the baseline specification to test for an influence of labor conditions on a country's share of world FDI inflows. The left columns in table A6.3 report the coefficients and robust standard errors from those tests. Each coefficient is from a separate (labor-force-weighted) regression. With

Table A6.2
FDI Share Regression, Non-OECD Countries

	Cross-country		Random effects
	(1)	(2)	(3)
EXPROP	.679	.739	0.075
	(.236)**	(.257)*	(0.060)
GOVSHARE	−8.289	−8.351	−4.138
	(2.259)*	(3.338)**	(1.618)*
ln POP	.575	.372	0.618
	(.175)*	(.168)**	(.121)*
ln GDPOP	−0.239	−0.556	1.124
	(.423)	(.438)	(.246)*
AREA	.00021	.00024	0.00028
	(.00004)*	(.00007)*	(.00010)*
EDUC	.185	.241	0.007
	(.093)**	(.102)**	(0.087)
ln TRADE SHARE	.819		0.871
	(.227)*		(.264)*
OPEN POLICY		.806	
		(.408)***	
Constant	−13.999	−7.302	−20.95
R²	.94	.94	.99
Root MSE	.566	.574	
Countries	56	56	63

Note: See notes to table A6.1.
* p-value < .01
** p-value < .05
*** p-value < .10

Table A6.3

Effects of Labor Conditions and Labor Regulations on FDI Shares 1991–1996

Labor condition	Coefficient	n	Labor regulation	Coefficient	n
Work hours	−0.081 (.056)	39	Employment relations	2.424 (1.271)★★★	58
Fatal accidents	−0.04 (.015)★★	31	Firing cost	2.283 (1.261)★★★	58
Child labor	−0.013 .029	78	Hours cost	.958 (.560)★★★	58
Civil liberties	−.029 (.132)	79	Collective relations	−.971 (1.915)	58
FACB	−0.006 (0.058)	66	Civil rights	−1.224 (1.633)	58
Forced labor	−0.091 (.161)	76	Social security	1.556 (.943)	58
Slavery	.016 (.025)	54			
Gender differential	−1.621 (.983)	51			

Note: See notes to table A6.1. Each coefficient (with robust standard error) is from a different regression.

n = number of countries

★ p-value < .01

★★ p-value < .05

★★★ p-value < .10

the exception of the fatal industrial accident rate (which is *inversely* related to FDI), the measures of labor conditions are not significantly related to national FDI shares. The evidence from this relatively small sample of 31 countries for which on-the-job accident data are available indicates that FDI is attracted to safe, not unsafe, working conditions. (Unreported unweighted estimates parallel the weighted results with one exception. Marginally significant results for the Freedom House index of civil liberties indicate that countries with stronger civil liberties attract more FDI, a finding that again is not consistent with the hypothesis that weak labor rights attract foreign investment.) Similar conclusions emerged from an (unreported) analysis of FDI shares in non-OECD countries. Only the fatal industrial accident rate was significantly correlated with FDI share, with FDI again inversely related to the accident rate.

One of the concerns expressed by globalization skeptics is that governments may compete for FDI by limiting their labor regulations. The Lex Mundi project has developed and published indices of the strength of national labor regulations in several areas (Botero et al. 2004). The next chapter discusses this study in more detail, but the indices are used here to test for significant associations between the strength of national labor regulations and a country's ability to attract FDI. There are indices of the strength of national government regulations of the employment relationship (EMPLOYMENT), collective relations (COLLECTIVE), CIVIL RIGHTS, and SOCIAL SECURITY. There are also indices of the cost that employers incur if they dismiss a worker (FIRING COSTS) or lengthen employee work hours (HOURS COSTS). All indices range from zero (weak regulation) to one (strong regulation) and are available for 60 countries. These indices were added one at a time to the baseline FDI specification to test for an influence of national labor regulations on a country's share of world FDI inflows. The right columns in table A6.3 report the coefficients and robust standard errors from those tests in the weighted regressions.

These (labor-force-weighted) estimates indicate reasonably precisely measured positive relationships between international differences in FDI shares and differences in national regulation of employment, social security, hours, and dismissals after controlling for the influence of the baseline variables. (The p-values for the coefficients on the regulation measures range between .062 and .105.) No significant relationship emerges for regulation of collective relationships or civil rights in the cross-country regressions. (Interestingly, unreported, unweighted regressions reveal no statistically significant relationship between FDI shares and measures of labor regulation.) Two conclusions may be drawn about the relationship between FDI and labor regulations. First, the relationship is strongest in countries with the largest labor forces. The largest countries in the sample are China (641.5 million workers), India (366.5), the United States (123.5), Japan (62.5), Pakistan (60.5), and Bangladesh (52.5). Second, where a significant relationship exists, *stronger* national regulations are associated with *larger* FDI shares, ceteris paribus. (At worst, the unweighted estimates reveal no statistically significant relationship.) These estimates reveal no tendency for countries with weak labor regulations to attract larger shares of world FDI inflows, ceteris paribus. In unreported analyses for non-OECD countries, FDI shares were not significantly related to *any* of the measures of national labor regulations.

Appendix to Chapter 7

Chapter 7 refers to regression analyses of (1) the relationship between openness and the scope of national labor regulations and (2) the effects of national labor regulations on labor conditions. This appendix provides details on these analyses. (Appendix A summarizes the definitions and data sources of all variables.)

Openness and National Labor Regulations

The discussion in chapter 7 notes that the strength of national labor regulations is not significantly associated with measures of openness. That conclusion is based on an analysis of the following regression model estimated across i countries for each variety of national labor regulation:

$$(7.1A) \quad REGULATION_i = a_0 + a_1\ GDPCAP_i + a_2\ LEGAL_i + a_3\ LEFT_i + a_4\ OPEN_i + \varepsilon_i$$

The dependent variables are indices of the strength of national employment, collective relations, civil rights, and social security regulations and the costs of instituting longer work hours or of dismissing workers as of the late 1990s (Botero et al. 2004). (The availability of data for only one date ruled out a panel data analysis of the relationship between national labor regulations and openness.) As discussed in chapter 7, a country's "score" for each index is based on an analysis of relevant national statutes and normalized to fall between zero and 1, with higher scores denoting stronger protection of labor. The independent variables include the per capita GDP (GDPCAP), dummy variables indicating the origin of a country's legal system (LEGAL), a variable for the percentage of years between 1975 and 1995 in which the country's chief executive and largest party in congress have left or center political orientation (LEFT), and the two measures of openness introduced earlier in the book: TRADE SHARE (the share of exports and imports in GDP) and OPEN POLICY (the update of the multi-hurdle, Sachs–Warner open policy measure. Data for all variables but the openness measures are from Botero et al. (2004).

As discussed in the chapter, the direction of causality between labor regulations and openness is ambiguous, in principle. To address the direction of causality issue, we supplement OLSQ estimation with IV estimates, in which gravity variables instrument the trade variables. The gravity variables used are AREA, DISTANCE from the capital city of major trading partners, and a dummy variable for whether the country is an ISLAND. These variables are correlated with openness but should not influence the strength of labor regulations except through their effect on the openness measures. In the first-stage regressions, the gravity variables explain 27 (38) percent of the variance in TRADE SHARE (OPEN POLICY). Effectively, we ask whether the variation in openness measures attributable to gravity variables influences international differences in labor regulation.

For each type of labor regulation, four regressions were estimated, testing the two measures of openness with two estimation methods. Table A7.1 reports the openness coefficients (and robust standard errors) from these regressions. The two dozen coefficients are easily summarized: Neither the OLSQ nor the IV estimation finds significant relationships between the measures of openness and most varieties of labor regulation. The main exception to this summary is social security regulation. In the OLSQ estimation there is a marginally significant relationship between trade volumes and social security regulation: social security regulation tends to be weaker in countries with relative large trade volumes. In the instrumental variables estimation,

Table A7.1
Openness and Employment Regulations

	Trade share	Open policy
Employment relations		
OLSQ	.0001	.0003
	(.0003)	(.0628)
IV	.0003	−.1255
	(.0005)	(.1980)
Collective relations		
OLSQ	−.0001	.0116
	(.0003)	(.0429)
IV	.0003	−.1207
	(.0006)	(.1717)
Civil rights		
OLSQ	−.0011	−.0414
	(.0003)*	(.0445)
IV	−.0006	−.2093
	(.0006)	(.2293)
Social security		
OLSQ	−.0007	−.0619
	(.0004)***	(.0657)
IV	−.0012	−.3841
	(.0007)***	(.2087)***
Hours costs		
OLSQ	.0005	−.1277
	(.0007)	(.1626)
IV	.0013	−1.0024
	(.0011)	(.4742)**
Firing costs		
OLSQ	.0004	.1085
	(.0006)	(.1033)
IV	.0004	.3995
	(.0012)	(.3445)

Note: Robust standard errors in parentheses.
* p–value<.01
** p–value<.05
*** p–value<.10

both measures of openness are negatively related to social security regulation, although these relationships remain marginally significant statistically. A highly significant negative relationship between trade volumes and civil rights regulation emerges in the OLSQ estimation, but this relationship does not survive in instrumental variables estimation, and no significant association with open trade policy emerges from the data. Finally, the IV estimation indicates that the costs of expanding work hours are significantly lower in countries with open trade policies. The reported estimates are for unweighted data, which seemed appropriate since decisions over national regulations are made at the country level. A check of labor-force-weighted estimates mainly confirmed the inverse relationship between measures of openness and the social security and civil rights indices.

Labor Regulations and Labor Conditions

Chapter 7 also discusses the effectiveness of national labor regulations in improving domestic labor conditions. Part of that discussion is based on the following cross-country regression analysis, which tests for a link between the strength of national labor regulations and the measures of working conditions and labor rights. The underlying regression model is:

(7.2A) $LC_i = b_0 + b_1 \, GDPCAP_i + b_2 \, REGULATION_i$

That is, the measures of labor conditions used throughout this book are regressed on real per capita income (controlling for a country's level of development) and the indices of national labor regulations developed by Botero et al. (2004).

We are interested in whether the implementation of labor regulations alters labor conditions, but we must recognize that some countries may simply legislate regulations that codify existing workplace practice. The latter scenario, which has lower political costs, will introduce bias in ordinary least squares estimates of the relationship between national labor regulations and labor conditions. Therefore, both ordinary least squares and instrumental variables techniques were used to estimate the relationship. Following Botero et al. (2004), each country's legal tradition instruments the level of national labor regulation.

Neither estimation method produced significant estimates for the national labor regulations variables. International differences in labor conditions continued to reflect the influence of differences in the level of development (real per capita GDP) but did not reflect the strength of national labor regulations.

NOTES

Chapter 1

1. Accessed at http://www.baobabconnections.org.
2. Accessed at http://www.globalexchange.org/campaigns/sweatshops.

Chapter 2

1. The two sets of studies differ in many other ways. Deaton (2004) reviews the difficulties in reconciling the two sets of estimates of world poverty.
2. The authors use parameters from the value of life literature discussed in chapter 3 to place monetary values on longevity gains between 1965 and 1995.
3. See Ehrenberg (1994, chap. 2) for a compilation of holiday, vacation, and leave policies in industrialized countries.
4. The index, which is based on actual practice rather than constitutional guarantees, also evaluates the freedom of the press, religious freedom, independence of the judiciary, and so on.
5. The 37 criteria pertain to national restrictions on rights to establish and join worker organizations, on civil liberties related to collective bargaining, on rights to collective bargaining, on the right to strike, and on rights in export processing zones. Appendix A has details on the construction of this index.
6. For this smaller sample of countries, the correlation between the two freedom of association indices is .76.
7. Net gender wage differentials may be estimated from a decomposition technique or the coefficient on a dummy variable for gender. The meta-analysis by Weichselbaumer and Winter-Ebner includes estimates by either method.
8. Debates about the interpretation of this measure continue. Unobserved gender differences in productivity favoring males may account for an unknown proportion of the net differential.
9. These estimates, from the LABORSTA database of the International Labor

Organization, underestimate worldwide child labor. When the minimum legal working age is 15 years or older, a country may not collect labor force information on younger children, raising the question of whether increases in the number of countries reporting a child participation rate of zero reflect labor market developments or changes in labor law. Where child labor prohibitions exist, work by children may be underreported, even when there is some effort to collect the data. Following international statistical conventions, the data also exclude unpaid household work. For an illustration of possible consequences, see Basu 1999, p. 1085. Other analysts raise concerns about the consistency of the data over time. Edmonds and Pavcnik write: "Much of the intertemporal variation in child labor in the LABORSTA data is thus driven by the imputations and adjustments done for LABORSTA rather than independent observations on child labor. As a result, we do not view the LABORSTA data useful for analyzing changes in child labor over time" (p. 201).

10. http://www.unicor.gov/about/index.htm.

11. Federal Prison Industries claims that the productivity of inmates is low and that "the average Federal inmate has an 8th-grade education, is 37 years old, is serving a 10-year sentence for a drug related offense, and has never held a steady job." It does not provide information on the characteristics of inmate employees specifically. See http://www.unicor.gov/history/foreword.htm.

12. http://www.unicor.gov/history/overview_of_fpi.htm.

13. For several countries, including developed countries such as New Zealand and Norway, no data are provided because he was unable to determine an appropriate estimate. (These countries have been recorded here as "missing data" rather than zero.)

14. In the double-sampling or capture-recapture method of estimation, two teams of researchers worked independently to produce two independent lists of validated reports of forced labor cases using a variety of ILO and non-ILO sources. "A validated reported case of forced labour was defined as a piece of information on a page or a screen of an original source containing the following four elements: an activity recognized as a form of forced labour . . . ; a numerical figure indicating the number of identified or identifiable persons involved; a geographical area where the activity is reported to have taken place; and a corresponding date or time interval falling within the period 1995–2004." The ILO cautions that "this methodology leads to a strict minimum estimate of forced labour for a number of reasons, in particular because of the restriction to credible sources and validated data items. The seven languages known by the researchers have also set limits on their search for geographically dispersed sources" (2005, p. 11).

15. Simple country averages would understate the influence of labor conditions in the most populous countries (e.g., China, India, and the United States) and overstate the influence of conditions in the least populous countries. National labor force weights are applied to all data. Weighting does not alter the qualitative conclusions drawn from the data. Table 2.1 presents the facts for the largest number of countries reporting data at the beginning and end of the period, a choice that reduces the sample size for some labor conditions.

16. Recall that lower values of the civil liberties indices indicate superior civil liberties.

17. The other industrialized countries experiencing hours increases include Israel, Italy, New Zealand, and the United States.
18. In 1972, Burundi, Central African Republic, Chad, China, Guinea, Iraq, Syria, and Uganda had the weakest civil liberties in our sample of countries. In 2000, the worst civil liberties were found in Afghanistan, Iraq, Saudi Arabia, Somalia, Sudan, and Syria.
19. The highest fatal accident rates in 2000 were in Togo (65.2) and Burkina Faso (35.9). Since neither country reported data in 1970, we cannot say whether this represents an improvement.
20. The same average tariff rate can emerge from different tariff structures. Simple averages of tariff rates ignore the relative importance of different commodities, but trade-weighted average tariffs give too little weight to high-tariff items whose trade is most discouraged by tariffs. An excellent survey by Berg and Krueger (2003) addresses this point and many other measurement difficulties.
21. The black market or parallel exchange rate premium captures the effects of discriminatory exchange rate policies that offer exporters a more appreciated exchange rate than importers. Such policies are equivalent to a tariff.
22. A country is considered open if it has (1) an average tariff rate below 40 percent, (2) nontariff barriers covering less than 40 percent of trade, (3) a black market exchange rate premium below 20 percent on average during the 1970s and 1980s, (4) a nonsocialist economic system, and (5) no state monopoly on major exports. The binary classification cannot address degrees of trade restriction beyond "open" and "closed."
23. Sachs and Warner also developed trade policy liberalization dates over the period 1950–1994 for their sample countries. The liberalization dates are not tightly bound to the five criteria used to construct the openness dummy variable, because data on all five criteria frequently were unavailable for the entire period. Instead, the liberalization dates are developed from case studies of trade policy. Based on these liberalization dates, Wacziarg and Welch (2003) developed openness dummy variables for each decade since 1970, enabling a panel estimation of open trade policies' effects on growth and labor conditions.
24. An absence of data prevents including sub-Saharan Africa in the regional breakdown of the data.
25. Using World Bank data, Schneider and Enste (2002, chap. 5) provide estimates of the informal labor force for 76 countries. Their regional patterns parallel the ILO estimates in the text.
26. The ILO sometimes uses data on worldwide self-employment "as a proxy for informal self-employment, which is the major component of informal employment" (ILO 2002, p. 17).

Chapter 3

1. Golub (1997) and Rodrik (1996, 1999) obtain similar results from smaller samples of countries and different time periods.
2. Such wage differentials provide a basis for estimating the value of a (statistical) life (Thaler and Rosen 1975; Viscusi and Aldy 2003).
3. An alternative hypothesis holds that families may value work by their children, since it raises overall family income. If this were the dominant motivation, one would observe a positive correlation between child labor and family income.

Introducing additional motivations, such as transfers from children to parents, may introduce a nonmonotonic relationship between income and child labor (Rogers and Swinnerton 2004).

4. The main qualification on the effect of income growth concerns work for a family business, where higher incomes may contribute to an expansion of the business and greater demand for labor.

5. Fixed-effects estimation also removes time-invariant measurement error that may be introduced by differences in national statistical systems.

6. Although the elasticity (proportionate sensitivity) of long hours to per capita income is not statistically significant, the semi-elasticity (absolute sensitivity) is substantively and statistically significant. See the appendix to this chapter.

7. The table reports the ratio of each country's residual (actual value of the labor condition minus the value predicted on the basis of the country's real per capita GDP) to the root mean square error of the regression. The latter number expresses an average residual for the sample against which each country's residual can be compared.

8. Alesina et al. (2003) argue that "much of Africa's growth failure is due to ethnic conflict, partly as a result of absurd borders left by former colonizers" (p. 1). Also see Easterly and Levine 1997, which makes the same point.

9. The ethnolinguistic and religious diversity variables used in this study equal one minus the Herfindahl index of ethnolinguistic or religious group shares in the early to mid-1990s (Alesina et al. 2003).

10. The appendix to this chapter describes the regression analyses that produce these results.

Chapter 4

1. One illustration of how these results emerge concerns management resistance to union organizing in the United States, a country with decentralized bargaining, which might allow union wage pressure to significantly jeopardize a company's competitive prospects. Unfair labor practice charges against employers (and related indicators of management resistance) are highest in industries with significant exposure to international markets (Flanagan 2005).

2. The study updates many aspects of the famous Sachs–Warner (1995) study. It finds that by the 1990s, so many countries had adopted open trade policies that the Sachs-Warner openness dummy no longer discriminated between fast-growing and slow-growing economies as it had in the 1970s and 1980s. Fixed-effects estimates reveal that the positive growth effects of adopting open trade policies increased during every decade and peaked during the 1990s. The analysis shows that trade liberalization is followed by increases in foreign investment and trade volumes *within* countries during the postwar period.

3. In the words of a recent article on the clothing industry in El Salvador: "In a country with a 42 percent unemployment rate, these workers are considered lucky to have a job, even if it does pay the lowest of the country's three minimum wages" (Becker 2004, p. 15).

4. This development cannot be attributed to sharp declines in union representation during the economic and political transitions in Soviet bloc countries in the early 1990s. The Soviet bloc countries are not included in the computations for Table 4.2 because the experience in those countries is not comparable to that in other countries.

5. Trade theories reviewed earlier in the chapter offer an alternative mechanism, which rationalizes a positive correlation between labor conditions and trade. Free trade leads a country to specialize in sectors of comparative efficiency, a process that induces labor and other resources to move into sectors in which they are relatively productive internationally. Moving into relatively productive (higher wage) sectors should improve labor conditions.

Chapter 5

1. In early 1997, the cheapest airfares between Europe (an average of fares from the major cities in France, Germany, and the United Kingdom) and the United States were roughly 60 percent of the airfares between the United States and Egypt, India, or Taiwan, for example (Conley and Ligon 2002, table 1). Regional fare differences notwithstanding, the growing importance of air transport greatly reduced postwar migration costs in all countries.

2. See Brucker et al. (2002) for a well-documented discussion of postwar migration in Europe.

3. An ILO survey of member states reports some revival of bilateral agreements in the 1990s and early 2000s. Many of the new agreements involved central or eastern European countries or former U.S.S.R. countries and focused on recruitment in European Union countries (2004b).

4. A recent OECD study summarizes the fiscal incentives provided by industrialized nations for highly skilled immigrants (Dumont and Lemaître 2005, table 6).

5. The difficulty of obtaining migration data by level of education restricts the computations to OECD destination countries. This is probably not a serious limitation for brain drain studies. Developed countries received 50 percent of world migration in 2000 (United Nations 2002), and with pro-skill immigration policies in such major receiving countries as Australia, Canada, and the United States, the proportion of highly skilled migrants settling specifically in OECD countries was surely much higher. Note that the age cutoff removes most foreign students in OECD countries from the high-skill emigration count.

6. Respondents are asked (1) to indicate how much they agree with the view that their country "should limit the import of foreign products in order to protect its national economy" and (2) how much the number of immigrants to their economy should be increased.

7. These topics were also the focus of a later ILO report on international migration (2004b).

8. A recent example: with encouragement and even training from their home government, about 600,000 Sri Lankan women worked abroad, as housemaids, by 2005. Most found jobs in Middle Eastern countries, where they lacked legal status to challenge employers and consequently were often subjected to sexual harassment and physical abuse. One report notes, "While attention has focused on the failure of countries like Saudi Arabia to prevent or prosecute abuses, the de facto complicity of the countries that send their women abroad has largely escaped scrutiny" (Waldman 2005).

9. Chapter 7 contains a discussion of the process of formulating ILO labor standards (technically known as conventions). ILO Conventions 97 (ratified by 42 countries) and 143 (ratified by 18 countries) address the treatment of migrant workers.

10. One reason that the offshore outsourcing example is not definitive is that it represents a small proportion of trade and has small employment effect in countries at both ends of the trading relationship. Reviewing evidence from India and the Philippines in the early twenty-first century, Bhagwati, Panagariya and Srinivasan (2004, p. 99) conclude, "It is unlikely that the number of workers engaged in providing offshore services to the U.S. companies could have averaged more than 90,000 to 100,000 per year." Moreover, complementarities between the offshore services and skills in client countries can raise employment in the latter.

Chapter 6

1. Large multinationals have a somewhat fragile hold on their relative position. Only half of the 10 largest multinationals in 1980 remained on that list in 2000; only 60 percent of the top 50 multinationals in 1980 remained in that position 20 years later (De Grauwe and Camerman 2003).
2. According to the United Nations, foreign direct investment involves lasting interest and control of companies in one country by a parent company in another country; it "implies that the investor exerts a significant degree of influence on the management of" the foreign affiliate (UNCTAD 2003, p. 231).
3. Aitken, Harrison, and Lipsey (1996) analyze data for Mexico, Venezuela, and the United States; Te Velde and Morrissey (2001) analyze data from surveys of manufacturing enterprises in Cameroon, Ghana, Kenya, Zambia, and Zimbabwe.
4. The Bureau of Economic Analysis in the U.S. Department of Commerce publishes data on the compensation and productivity of foreign affiliates of U.S. multinational companies. See http://www.bea.gov/bea/di/di1usdop .htm.
5. Other countries with high government shares include Bangladesh (44 percent), Rwanda (35 percent), and Zimbabwe (33 percent).
6. The exact definitions and sources of these variables appear in the appendix to this chapter along with the full regression results.
7. The discussion of labor standards in chapter 7 includes a fuller discussion of these data.
8. http://www.un.org/Overview/rights.html.
9. The core labor standards are freedom of association, nondiscrimination, abolition of forced labor, and reduction of child labor.
10. http://www.ilo.org/public/english/employment/multi/download/english .pdf.
11. Survivors of the Nazi Holocaust have brought actions under ATCA against foreign companies and banks that rejected their efforts to recover money or insurance claims after World War II. Though none of these ever came to trial, they helped to induce significant settlements. Other cases were filed against foreign dictators, but these proved to be largely symbolic given the limited assets that the defendants had in the United States.
12. Though the Supreme Court has not weighed in on human rights issues, it did endorse the continued use of the act itself in an unrelated decision, stating "for the purposes of civil liability, the torturer has become—like the pirate and the

slave trader before him—*hostis humani generis*, an enemy of all mankind" (*Sosa v. Alvarez-Machain et al.,* 542 U.S. (2004). Decided June 29, 2004).

Chapter 7

1. Botero et al. (2004) provide extensive detail on the definition, construction, and sources for each index.
2. The common law doctrine of employment at will provides an example. In the words of one judge, the doctrine permits employers to fire employees "for good reason, bad reason, or no reason at all."
3. The classification is based on the Sachs–Warner criteria discussed in earlier chapters as updated for the 1990s by Wacziarg and Welch (2003).
4. For a review of the large literature on the effects of domestic labor regulations on labor conditions in industrialized countries, see Layard and Nickell (1999).
5. http://www.ilo.org/public/english/about/mandate.htm.
6. For insightful perspectives on the conceptual issues, see Bhagwati and Hudec (1996), Brown (2000), Fields (1995), Maskus (2000), OECD (1996), Srinivasan (1996), and Stern (1996).
7. For a more complete description of the standards-setting process, see http://www.ilo.org/public/english/standards/norm/comefrom/legsys/index.htm.
8. Recommendations are intended to guide national action, but they are not open to ratification and are not legally binding.
9. In the former category are conventions on hours of work, workers' compensation, forced labor, and so on. Other conventions focus more narrowly on conditions in particular occupations, such as seafarers, dockworkers, and fishermen.
10. Article 33 was invoked only once—against Burma in March 2000 regarding the use of forced labor. Six months after final approval of the action, no member countries had taken action against Burma. See Elliot 2001 and http://www.ilo.org/public/english/sitemap.htm (the ILO website) for more details on compliance issues.
11. The other countries in this category are Armenia, China, and Myanmar.
12. Gaps between international law and domestic labor legislation persist in some countries for several reasons, including political hubris and the technical difficulties of reconciling the legal variation that can emerge in a federalist system with a single international standard. Lee Swepston (2003) and Edward E. Potter (2003) provide informative discussions of factors behind the low ratification rate of the United States.
13. Lists of similar length are proposed for assessing compliance with labor standards for nondiscrimination (a total of 31 indicators), child labor (29 indicators) and forced labor (16 indicators) (National Academy of Sciences 2004).
14. Costa Rica, El Salvador, Guatemala, Honduras, and Nicaragua signed a Central American Free Trade Agreement with the United States in August 2004.
15. All quotes in this paragraph were taken from the free trade agreement between Chile and the United States, but the labor provisions of the free trade agreements with Singapore and five Central American countries includes identical language.

REFERENCES

Acemoglu, Daron. Simon Johnson, and James Robinson. 2004. Institutions as the fundamental cause of long-run growth. National Bureau of Economic Research working paper no. 10481 (May). Cambridge, Mass.

Acemoglu, Daron, Simon Johnson, James Robinson, and Pierre Yared. 2005. Income and democracy. National Bureau of Economic Research working paper no. 11205 (March). Cambridge, Mass.

Adams, Richard H., Jr. 2004. Remittances and poverty in Guatemala. World Bank Policy Research working paper 3418 (September). Washington, D.C.

Adams, Richard H., Jr., and J. Page. 2003. The impact of international migration and remittances on poverty. Paper prepared for the DFID/World Bank Conference on Migrant Remittances, London, Oct. 9–10.

Aitken, Brian J., and Ann E. Harrison. 1999. Do domestic firms benefit from direct foreign investment? Evidence from Venezuela. *American Economic Review* 89 (June): 605–618.

Aitken, Brian J., Ann E. Harrison, and Robert E. Lipsey. 1996. Wages and foreign ownership: A comparative study of Mexico, Venezuela, and the United States. *Journal of International Economics* 40 (May): 345–371.

Alatas, Vivi, and Lisa Cameron. 2004. Should Nike and Reebok pay higher wages? The impact of minimum wages on employment in a low income country. Working paper, Department of Economics, Melbourne University.

Alesina, Alberto, Arnaud Devleeschauwer, William Easterly, Sergio Kurlat, and Romain Wacziarg. 2003. Fractionalization. *Journal of Economic Growth* 8: 155–194.

Almeida, Rita. 2003. The effects of foreign owned firms on the labor market. IZA (Institute for the Study of Labor), discussion paper no. 785 (May). Bonn, Germany.

Alsen, Marsella, David E. Bloom, and David Canning. 2004. The effect of population health on foreign direct investment. National Bureau of Economic Research working paper no. 10596 (June). Cambridge, Mass.

Anderson, James E., and Eric van Wincoop. 2004. Trade Costs. *Journal of Economic Literature* 42 (September): 691–751.

Anti-Slavery International/ICFTU. 2001. *Forced labor in the twenty-first century*. London.

Arbache, Jorge Saba, Andy Dickerson, and Francis Green. 2004. Trade liberalization and wages in developing countries. *Economic Journal* 114 (February): F73–96.

Arnold, Wayne. 2004. Unions face pressure in Indonesia. *International Herald Tribune*, May 22–23: 13.

Aw, B. Y., and G. Batra. 1998. Technology, exports, and firm efficiency in Taiwanese manufacturing. Department of Economics Working Paper, Pennsylvania State University. University Park, Pa.

Bales, Kevin. 2000. Slavery and the shadow economy. *Journal of International Affairs* 53 (2): 461–484.

———. 2004a. *Disposable People: New Slavery in the Global Economy*. Rev. ed. Berkeley: University of California Press.

———. 2004b. International labor standards: Quality of information and measures of progress in combating forced labor. *Comparative Labor Law and Policy Journal* 24: 321–363.

Bannister, Judith. 2005. Manufacturing earnings and compensation in China. *Monthly Labor Review* 128 (August): 22–40.

Barro, Robert, and Xavier Sala-i-Martin. 1995. *Economic growth*. New York: McGraw-Hill.

Barro, Robert J., and Rachel McLeary. 2002. Religion and political economy in an international panel. National Bureau of Economic Research working paper no. 8931 (May). Cambridge, Mass.

Basu, Kaushik. 1999. The economics of child labor. *Journal of Economic Literature* 37 (3): 1083–1120.

———. 2000. The intriguing relation between the adult minimum wage and child labor. *Economic Journal* 110 (462): C50–61.

Becker, Elizabeth. 2004. Trade deal: What's in it for the workers? *International Herald Tribune*, April 7, p. 15.

Becker, Gary S. 1957. *The economics of discrimination*. Chicago: University of Chicago Press.

Becker, Gary S., Tomas J. Philipson, and Rodrigo R. Soares. 2005. The quantity and quality of life and the evolution of world inequality. *American Economic Review* 95 (1): 277–291.

Beegle, Kathleen, Rajeev Dehejia, and Roberta Gatti. 2003. Child labor, income shocks, and access to credit. World Bank Policy Research working paper no. 3075 (June). Washington, D.C.

Belot, Michele, and Sjef Ederveen. 2005. Cultural and institutional barriers in migration between OECD countries. Working paper, Department of Economics, University of Essex. Essex, England.

Berg, Andrew, and Anne Krueger. 2003. Trade, growth, and poverty: A selective survey. In *New Reform Strategies,* ed. B. Pleskovic and N. Stern. Annual Bank Development Conference. Washington, D.C.

Berik, Günseli, Yana van der Meulen Rodgers, and Joseph E. Zveglich, Jr. 2004.

International trade and gender wage discrimination: Evidence from East Asia. *Review of Development Economics* 8 (2): 237–254.

Bernard, A. B., and J. B. Jensen. 1995. Exporters, jobs, and wages in U.S. manufacturing, 1976–1987. *Brookings Papers on Economic Activity: Microeconomics*: 67–119.

———. 1999. Exceptional exporter performance: Cause, effect, or both? *Journal of International Economics* 47 (1): 1–25.

———. 2001. Why some firms export. Tuck School of Business, Dartmouth College, Hanover, April. Mimeographed. (Version 4.0; first version April 1997.)

Bernard, Andrew B., and Joachim Wagner. 1997. Exports and success in German manufacturing. *Weltwirtschaftliches Archiv/Review of World Economics* 133 (1): 134–157.

Besley, Timothy, and Robin Burgess. 2004. Can labor regulation hinder economic performance? Evidence from India. *Quarterly Journal of Economics* 119 (February): 91–134.

Bhagwati, Jagdish. 2004. *In defense of globalization.* New York: Oxford University Press.

Bhagwati, Jagdish, and Robert E. Hudec, eds. 1996. *Fair trade and harmonization: Prerequisites for free trade?* Cambridge: MIT Press.

Bhagwati, Jagdish, Arvind Panagariya, and T. N. Srinivasan. 2004. The muddles over outsourcing. *Journal of Economic Perspectives* 18 (fall): 93–114.

Bhalotra, Sonia. 2003. Child labor in Africa. OECD Social, Employment, and Migration, working paper no. 4. Paris.

Black, Sandra, and Elizabeth Brainerd. 2004. Importing equality? The impact of globalization on gender discrimination. *Industrial and Labor Relations Review* 57 (4): 540–559.

Bognanno, Mario, Michael P. Keane, and Donghoo Yang. 2005. The influence of wages and industrial relations environments on the production location decisions of U.S. multinational corporations. *Industrial and Labor Relations Review* 58 (January): 171–200.

Bordo, Michael D., Alan M. Taylor, and Jeffrey G. Williamson, eds. 2003. *Globalization in historical perspective.* Chicago: University of Chicago Press.

Borjas, George, and Valerie Ramey. 1995. Foreign competition, market power, and wage inequality. *Quarterly Journal of Economics* 110 (November): 1075–1112.

Botero, Juan, Simeon Djankov, Rafael La Porta, Florencio Lopez-de-Silanes, and Andrei Shliefer. 2004. The regulation of labor. *Quarterly Journal of Economics* 119 (November): 1339–1382. (Data on each sub-index will be posted at: http://iicg.som.yale.edu//.)

Bourguignon, Francois, and Christian Morrisson. 2002. Inequality among world citizens: 1820–1992. *American Economic Review* 92 (September): 727–744.

Brown, Drusilla K. 2000. International trade and core labor standards: A survey of the recent literature. OECD Labor Market and Social Policy Occasional, working paper no. 43, DEELSA/ELSA/WD (2000) 4, October. Paris.

Brown, Drusilla K., Alan V. Deardorff, and Robert M. Stern. 2004. The effects of multinational production on wages and working conditions in developing countries. In *Challenges to Globalization: Analyzing the Economics,* ed. Robert E. Baldwin and L. Alan Winters, 279–326. Chicago: University of Chicago Press.

Brucker, Herbert, Gil S. Epstein, Barry McCormick, Gilles Saint-Paul, Alessandra Venturini, and Klaus Zimmermann. 2002. Managing migration in the European welfare state. In *Immigration Policy and the Welfare System*, ed. T. Boeri et al. New York: Oxford University Press.

Busse, Matthias, and Sebastian Braun. 2003a. Export structure, FDI, and child labor. Hamburg Institute of International Economics, discussion paper 216 (January).

———. 2003b. Trade and investment effects of forced labor: An empirical assessment. *International Labor Review* 142 (1): 49–71.

Carrington, William J., and Enrica Detragiache. 1998. How big is the brain drain? International Monetary Fund working paper no. 201. Washington, D.C.

Caves, Richard E. 1996. *Multinational enterprise and economic analysis*, 2nd ed. Cambridge: Cambridge University Press.

Chang, Leslie T. 2005. A migrant worker sees rural home in a new light. *Wall Street Journal*, June 8: A1, A12.

Chiswick, Barry R., and Timothy J. Hatton. 2003. International migration and the integration of labor markets. In *Globalization in Historical Perspective*, ed. M. D. Bordo, A. M. Taylor, and J. G. Williamson, 65–117. Chicago: University of Chicago Press.

Clerides, S. K., S. Lach, and J. R. Tybout. 1998. Is learning by exporting important? micro-dynamic evidence from Colombia, Mexico, and Morocco. *Quarterly Journal of Economics* 113 (3): 903–947.

Cline, William R. 1997. *Trade and income distribution*. Institute for International Economics, Washington, D.C.

———. 2004. *Trade policy and global poverty*. Institute for International Economics, Washington, D.C.

Conley, T., and E. Ligon. 2002. Economic distance and cross-country spillovers. *Journal of Economic Growth* 7: 157–187.

Conyon, Martin, Sourafel Girma, Steve Thompson, and Peter Wright. 1999. The impact of foreign acquisition on wages and productivity in the UK. Center for Research on Globalization and Labor Markets research paper 99/8. Nottingham, England.

Costa, Dora L., and Matthew E. Kahn. 2002. Changes in the value of life, 1940–1980. National Bureau of Economic Research working paper 9396 (December). Cambridge, Mass.

Criscuolo, Chiara, Jonathan Haskel, and Matthew J. Slaughter. 2005. Global engagement and the innovation activities of firms. National Bureau of Economic Research working paper no. 11479 (July). Cambridge, Mass.

Dean, Jason, and Pui-Wing Tam. 2005. The laptop trail. *Wall Street Journal*, June 9: B1, B8.

Deaton, Angus. 2004. Measuring poverty in a growing world (or measuring growth in a poor world). Research Program in Development Studies, Woodrow Wilson School, Princeton University, February.

De Grauwe, Paul, and Filip Camerman. 2003. How big are the big multinational companies? *World Economics* 4 (2): 23–37.

Dehejia, Rajeev H., and Roberta Gatti. 2002. Child labor: The role of income variability and access to credit across countries. National Bureau of Economic Research working paper 9018 (June). Cambridge, Mass.

Docquier, Frederic, Olivier Lohest, and Abdeslam Marfouk. 2005. Brain drain in developing regions (1990–2000). IZA discussion paper no. 1668 (July).

Docquier, Frederic, and Abdeslam Marfouk. 2004. Measuring the international mobility of skilled workers (1990–2000)—Release 1.0. World Bank Policy Research working paper 3382. Washington, D.C.

Docquier, Frederic, and Hillel Rappaport. 2004. Skilled migration: The perspective of developing countries. World Bank Policy Research working paper 3381. Washington, D.C.

Doms, Mark E., and J. Bradford Jensen. 1998. Comparing wages, skills, and productivity between domestically and foreign-owned manufacturing establishments in the United States. In *Geography and Ownership as Bases for Economic Accounting,* ed. R. E. Baldwin, R. E. Lipsey, and J. D. Richardson. Chicago: University of Chicago Press.

Dumont, J. C., and Lemaître G. 2005. Counting immigrants and expatriates: A new perspective. OECD Social, Employment, and Migration working paper. Directorate for Employment Labor and Social Affairs. Paris.

Easterly, William. 2002. *The elusive quest for growth.* Cambridge: MIT Press.

Easterly W., and R. Levine. 1997. Africa's growth tragedy: Policies and ethnic divisions. *Quarterly Journal of Economics* 111 (4): 1203–1250.

Edmonds, Eric V. 2003a. Child labor in South Asia. OECD Social, Employment, and Migration, working paper no. 5. Paris.

———. 2003b. Does child labor decline with improving economic status? National Bureau of Economic Research working paper 10134. Cambridge, Mass.

Edmonds, Eric, and Nina Pavcnik. 2002. Does globalization increase child labor? Evidence from Vietnam. National Bureau of Economic Research working paper No. 8760 (February). Cambridge, Mass.

———. 2005. Child labor in the global economy. *Journal of Economic Perspectives* 19 (1): 199–220.

Edwards, Sebastian. 1998. Openness, productivity, and growth: What do we really know? *Economic Journal* 108 (March): 383–398.

Ehrenberg, Ronald. 1994. *Labor markets and integrating national economies.* Washington, D.C.: Brookings Institution Press.

Elliot, Kimberly Ann. 2001. Fin(d)ing our way on trade and labor standards? Policy brief no. PB01–5. Institute for International Economics, Washington, D.C.

Elliott, Kimberly Ann, and Richard B. Freeman. 2003. *Can labor standards improve under globalization?* Institute for International Economics, Washington, D.C.

Faini, Riccardo. 2003. Is the brain drain an unmitigated blessing? WIDER discussion paper no. 2003/64 (September).

Feenstra, Robert C., and Gordon H. Hanson. 2001. Global production sharing and rising inequality: A survey of trade and wages. National Bureau of Economic Research working paper no. 8372 (July). Cambridge, Mass.

Feliciano, Zadia, and Robert E. Lipsey. 1999. Foreign ownership and wages in the United States, 1987–1992. National Bureau of Economic Research working paper no. 6923. Cambridge, Mass.

Fields, Gary S. 1995. Trade and labor standards: A review of the issues. OECD, Paris.

Fireman, Paul. 2005. What we can do about Burma. *Wall Street Journal,* June 7: C2.

Flanagan, Robert J. 1993. European wage equalization since the treaty of Rome. In *Labor and an Integrated Europe,* ed. Lloyd Ulman, Barry Eichengreen, and William T. Dickens, 167–187. Washington, D.C.: Brookings Institution Press.

————. 1999. Macroeconomic performance and collective bargaining: An international perspective. *Journal of Economic Literature* 37 (September): 1150–1175.

————. 2001. HR practices in global organizations. Working paper, Graduate School of Business, Stanford University.

————. 2003a. Labor standards and international competitive advantage. In *International Labor Standards: Globalization, Trade and Public Policy,* ed. Robert J. Flanagan and William B. Gould IV, 15–59. Stanford, Calif.: Stanford University Press.

————. 2003b. Macroeconomic performance and labor unions. In *International handbook of trade unions,* ed. John Addison and Claus Schnabel, 172–196. London: Edward Elgar.

————. 2005. Has management strangled U.S. unions? *Journal of Labor Research* 26 (winter): 33–63.

Freedom House. 2005. Online. Available: http://www.freedomhouse.org/.

Galli, Rossana, and David Kucera. 2003. Informal employment in Latin America: Movements over business cycles and the effects of worker rights. Institute for Labor Studies discussion paper 145. Geneva.

Girma, Sourafel, and Holger Görg. 2003. Evaluating the causal effects of foreign acquisition on domestic skilled and unskilled wages. IZA, discussion paper no. 903 (October.)

Glewwe, Paul. 2000. Are foreign-owned businesses in Vietnam really sweatshops? *Minnesota Agricultural Economist* 701 (summer): 1–4.

Goldberg, Pinelopi Koujianou, and Nina Pavcnik. 2003. The response of the informal sector to trade liberalization. *Journal of Development Economics* 72 (December): 463–496.

————. 2004. Trade, inequality, and poverty: What do we know? Evidence from recent trade liberalization episodes in developing countries. National Bureau of Economic Research working paper 10593 (June). Cambridge, Mass.

Golub, Stephen. 1997. Are international labor standards needed to prevent social dumping? *Finance and Development* (December): 20–23.

Görg, Holger, and Eric Strobl. 2001. Multinational corporations and productivity spillovers: A meta analysis. *Economic Journal* 111 (November): F723–739.

————. 2005. Spillovers from foreign firms through worker mobility: An empirical investigation. *Scandinavian Journal of Economics* 107 (4): 693–709.

Görg, Holger, Eric Strobl, and Frank Walsh. 2002. Why do foreign-owned firms pay more? The role of on-the-job training. IZA, discussion paper No. 590 (October.)

Gross, James A., ed. 2003. Workers' rights as human rights. Ithaca, N.Y.: ILR Press.

Guest, Robert. 2004. How to make Africa smile: A survey of sub-Saharan Africa. *Economist* (January): 3–16.

Hahn, Chin Hee. 2004. Exporting and performance of plants: Evidence from Korean manufacturing. National Bureau of Research working paper no. 10208 (January). Cambridge, Mass.

Hamermesh, Daniel S. 1993. *Labor demand.* Princeton, N.J.: Princeton University Press.

Hamilton, B., and J. Whalley. 1984. Efficiency and distributional implications of global restrictions on labor mobility. Calculations and policy implications. *Journal of Development Economics* 14: 61–75.

Hammitt, James, Jin-Tan Liu, and Jin-Long Liu. 2000. Survival is a luxury good:

The increasing value of a statistical life. Unpublished manuscript. School of Public Health, Harvard University.

Hanson, Gordon H. 2005. Emigration, labor supply, and earnings in Mexico. National Bureau of Research working paper no. 11412 (June). Cambridge, Mass.

Harms, Philipp, and Heinrich W. Ursprung. 2002. Do civil and political repression really boost foreign direct investments? *Economic Inquiry* 40 (4): 651–663.

Harvard Business School. 1999. The Han Young labor dispute (A). Case no. 9–799–084. Harvard Business School, Cambridge, Mass.

———. 2000. The Han Young labor dispute (B). Case no. 9–700–018. Harvard Business School, Cambridge, Mass.

Haskel, Jonathan E., Sonia C. Pereira, and Matthew J. Slaughter. 2000. Does inward foreign direct investment boost the productivity of domestic firms? National Bureau of Economic Research working paper no. 8724. Cambridge, Mass.

Hassel, Anke. 1999. The erosion of the German system of industrial relations. *British Journal of Industrial Relations* 37 (September): 483–505.

Hatton, T. J., and J. G. Williamson. 1998. *The age of mass migration: An economic analysis.* New York: Oxford University Press.

———. 2001. Demographic and economic pressure on migration out of Africa. National Bureau of Economic Research working paper no. 8124 (February). Cambridge, Mass.

———. 2004. International migration in the long run: Positive selection, negative selection, and policy. Paper delivered to Kiel Institute, Kiel, Germany, May 2004.

———. 2006. *World mass migration: Two centuries of policy and performance.* Cambridge: MIT Press.

Hauk, Jr., William R., and Romain Wacziarg. 2003. A Monte Carlo study of growth regressions. Working paper, Graduate School of Business, Stanford University (October).

Heckman, James J., and Carmen Pages (Eds). 2004. *Law and employment: Lessons from Latin America and the Caribbean.* Chicago: University of Chicago Press.

Heckscher, Eli F., and Bertil Ohlin. 1991. *Heckscher-Ohlin trade theory.* Trans. Harry Flam and June Flanders. Cambridge: MIT Press.

Hellman, Joel S., Geraint Jones, and Daniel Kaufmann. 2002. Far from home: Do foreign investors import higher standards of governance in transition economies? Working paper, World Bank (August). Washington, D.C.

Heston, Alan, Robert Summers, and Bettina Aten. 2002. Penn world table version 6.1. Center for International Comparisons at the University of Pennsylvania (CICUP) (October).

Human Rights Center. 2004. *Hidden slaves: Forced labor in the United States.* Berkeley, Calif.

Hymer, S. H. 1960. The international operations of national firms: A study of direct foreign investment. Ph.D. diss., MIT Economics Department.

International Country Risk Guide. 2005. Available at http://www.prsgroup.com/icrg/icrg.html.

International Labor Organization (ILO) website. Available at http://www.ilo.org/.

International Institute for Management Development (IMD). 1992. *The world competitiveness report, 1992.* World Economic Forum. Geneva.

————. 2003. *The world competitiveness yearbook, 2003.* Institute for Management Development. Lausanne.

International Labor Office (ILO). 1999. *Export Processing Zones.* Geneva.

————. 2001. *Yearbook of labor statistics.* Geneva.

————. 2002. *Women and men in the informal economy: A statistical picture.* Geneva.

————. 2003a. *Employment and social policy in respect of export processing zones (EPZs).* Committee on Employment and Social Policy. Document No. GB.286/ESP/3 (March). Geneva.

————. 2003b. *Key indicators in the labor market.* Geneva.

————. 2004a. *A fair globalization: Creating opportunities for all.* Report of the World Commission on the Social Dimension of Globalization. Geneva.

————. 2004b. *Towards a fair deal for migrant workers in the global economy.* Geneva.

————. 2005. *A global alliance against forced labor.* Geneva.

Iregui, Ana María. 2003. Efficiency gains from the elimination of global restrictions on labor mobility: An analysis using a multiregional CGE model. World Institute for Development Economics Research discussion paper no. 2003/27 (March). Helsinki, Finland.

Jacobson, Louis. 1998. Compensation programs. In *Imports, Exports, and the American Worker,* ed. S. M. Collins, 473–537. Washington, D.C.: Brookings Institution Press.

Jacoby, Hanan. 1994. Borrowing constraints and progress through school: Evidence from Peru. *Review of Economics and Statistics* 76 (1): 151–160.

Kletzer, Lori G. 2004. Trade-related job loss and wage insurance: A synthetic review. *Review of International Economics* 12 (5): 724–748.

Kucera, David. 2002. Core labor standards and foreign direct investment. *International Labor Review* 141 (1–2): 31–70.

Kurdelbusch, Antje. 2002. Multinationals and the rise of variable pay in Germany. *European Journal of Industrial Relations* 8 (3): 325–349.

Krugman, Paul R., and Maurice Obstfeld. 2003. *International economics: Theory and policy,* 6th ed. New York: Addison-Wesley.

LaFraniere, Sharon. 2005. Nightmare for African women: Birthing injury and little help. *New York Times,* Sept. 28, p. A3.

Landes, David. 1998. *The wealth and poverty of nations.* New York: W. W. Norton.

La Porta, R., F. Lopez-de-Silanes, A. Shleifer, and R. W. Vishny. 1999. The quality of government. *Journal of Law, Economics, and Organization* 12: 1074–1078.

Layard, Richard, and Stephen Nickell. 1999. Labor market institutions and economic performance. In *Handbook of Labor Economics,* Vol. 3C, ed. Orley Ashenfelter, and David Card. Amsterdam: North Holland.

Lewis, W. Arthur. 1955. *Theory of economic growth.* London: George Allen and Unwin.

Lim, L. C. 2001. *The globalization debate.* ILO, Geneva.

Lindert, Peter H. and Jeffrey G. Williamson. 2003. Does globalization make the world more unequal? *In Globalization in Historical Perspective,* ed. M.D. Bordo, A. M. Taylor, and J. G. Williamson, 227–271. Chicago: University of Chicago Press.

Lipsey, Robert E. 2002. Home and host country effects of FDI. National Bureau of Economic Research working paper no. 9293. Cambridge, Mass.

Lipsey Robert E., and Fredrik Sjoholm. 2001. Foreign direct investment and wages in Indonesian manufacturing. National Bureau of Economic Research working paper no. 8299. Cambridge, Mass.

———. 2002. Foreign firms and Indonesian manufacturing wages: An analysis with panel data. National Bureau of Economic Research working paper 9417 (December). Cambridge, Mass.

Liu, Minquan, Luodan Xu, and Liu Liu. 2003. Labor standards and FDI in China: Some survey findings. In *The Impact of Trade on Labor,* ed. Rana Hasan and Devashish Mitra, 189–243. Amsterdam: North Holland.

Longhi, Simonetta, Peter Nijkamp, Jacques Poot. 2004. A meta–analytic assessment of the effect of immigration on wages. Tinbergen Institute, discussion paper no. 2004–134/3.

Lorentzen, Peter, John McMillan, and Romain Wacziarg. 2004. Death and development. Graduate School of Business, Stanford University, working paper (October).

MacIsaac, D., and M. Rama. 1997. Determinants of hourly earnings in Ecuador: The role of labor market regulations. *Journal of Labor Economics* 15 (3-Part Two).

Maloney, William F., and Jairo Nunez Mendez. 2004. Measuring the impact of minimum wages: Evidence from Latin America. In *Law and employment: Lessons from Latin America and the Caribbean,* ed. James J. Heckman and Carmen Pages. Chicago: University of Chicago Press. pp. 109–130.

Markel, D. 1994. Finally, a national labor law. *China Business Review* 21: 46–49.

Markusen, James R. 2002. *Multinational firms and the theory of international trade.* Cambridge: MIT Press.

Martin, Philip. 2005. *Globalization and guest workers: Migration for employment in the twenty-first century.* New Haven, Conn.: Yale University Press.

Martin, Philip, and Jonas Widgren. 2002. International migration: Facing the challenge. *Population Bulletin* 57 (1): 3–40.

Maskus, Keith E. 2000. Should core labor standards be imposed through international trade policy? World Bank working paper. Washington, D.C.

Milanovic, Branko. 2005. *Worlds apart: Measuring international and global inequality.* Princeton, N.J.: Princeton University Press.

Milanovic, Branko, and Lyn Squire. 2005. Does tariff liberalization increase wage inequality? Some empirical evidence. National Bureau of Economic Research working paper 11046 (January). Cambridge, Mass.

Mishra, Prashi. 2003. Emigration and wages in source countries: Evidence from Mexico. Manuscript, Department of Economics, Columbia University (Oct. 1).

Montenegro, Claudio E., and Carmen Pages. 2004. Who benefits from labor market regulations? Chile, 1960–1998. In *Law and employment: Lessons from Latin America and the Caribbean,* ed. James J. Heckman and Carmen Pages, pp. 401–434. Chicago: University of Chicago Press.

Moran, Theodore H. 2004. Trade agreements and labor standards. Policy brief #133. Washington, D.C.: Brookings Institution Press.

National Academy of Sciences. 2004. *Monitoring international labor standards: Techniques and sources of information.* National Academy of Sciences, Washington, D.C.

Nicoletti, Giuseppe, Andrea Bassanini, Ekkehard Ernst, Sébastien Jean, Paulo Santiago, and Paul Swaim. 2001. Product and labor markets interactions in OECD countries. OECD Economics Department working paper no. 312 (December). Paris.

North, Douglass. 1991. *Institutions, institutional change, and economic performance.* Cambridge: Cambridge University Press.

Obstfeld, Maurice, and Alan M. Taylor. 2003. Globalization and capital markets. In *Globalization in Historical Perspective,* ed. Michael D. Bordo, Alan M. Taylor, and Jeffrey G. Williamson, 122–183. Chicago: University of Chicago Press.

O'Leary, Christopher J., Paul Decker, and Stephen A. Wandner. 1998. Reemployment bonuses and profiling. Staff working paper no. 98–51. Upjohn Institute, Kalamazoo, Mich.

Oostendorp, Remco. 2004. Globalization and the gender wage gap. Working paper, Amsterdam Institute for International Development, Free University of Amsterdam (January).

Organization for Economic Cooperation and Development (OECD). 1996. *Trade, employment, and labor standards: A study of core worker's rights and international trade.* Paris.

———. 1998. *Employment outlook.* Paris.

———. 1999a. *Employment outlook.* Paris.

———. 1999b. *Open markets matter.* Paris.

———. 2000. *The guidelines for multinational enterprises, revision 2000.* Paris.

———. 2002. *Measuring globalization: The role of multinationals in OECD economies, 2001.* Paris.

———. 2003. *Employment outlook.* Paris.

———. 2005. *Employment outlook.* Paris.

O'Rourke, Kevin H. 2003. Heckscher-Ohlin theory, and individual attitudes towards globalization. National Bureau of Economic Research working paper 9872 (July). Cambridge, Mass.

O'Rourke, Kevin, and Jeffrey Williamson. 1999. *Globalization and history: The evolution of a nineteenth-century Atlantic economy.* Cambridge: MIT Press.

Pierre, Gaëlle, and Stefano Scarpetta. 2004. Employment regulations through the eyes of employers. Do they matter and how do firms respond to them? World Bank Policy Research working paper no. 3463 (December). Washington, D.C.

Posner, Michael, and Justine Nolan. 2003. Can codes of conduct play a role in promoting workers' rights? In *International Labor Standards: Globalization, Trade, and Public Policy,* ed. Robert J. Flanagan and William B. Gould IV, 207–226. Stanford, Calif.: Stanford University Press.

Potter, Edward E. 2003. A pragmatic assessment from the employers' perspective. In *Workers' Rights as Human Rights,* ed. James A. Gross, 118–135. Ithaca, N.Y.: ILR Press.

Psacharopoulos, George. 1985. Returns to education: A further international update and implications. *Journal of Human Resources* 20: 583–604.

Psacharopoulos, George, and Harry A. Patrinos. 2002. Returns to investment in education: A further update. World Bank Policy Research working paper 2881 (September). Washington, D.C.

Ravallon, Martin, and Quentin Wodon. 1999. Does child labor displace schooling? World Bank Policy Research working paper No. 2116 (May). Washington, D.C.

Rodrik, Dani. 1996. Labor standards in international trade: Do they matter and what do we do about them? In *Emerging Agenda for Global Trade: High Stakes for Developing Countries,* ed. R. Z. Lawrence, D. Rodrik, and J. Whalley. Policy essay no. 20. Overseas Development Council, Washington, D.C.

———. 1999. Democracies pay higher wages. *Quarterly Journal of Economics* 114 (3): 707–738.

Rogers, Carol Ann, and Kenneth A. Swinnerton. 2004. Does child labor decrease when parental incomes rise? *Journal of Political Economy* 112 (4): 939–946.

Roy, A. D. 1951. Some thoughts on the distribution of earnings. *Oxford Economic Papers* 3: 135–146.

Sachs, Jeffrey D., and Andrew Warner. 1995. Economic reform and the process of global integration. *Brookings Papers on Economic Activity* 1: 1–95.

Sala-i-Martin, Xavier. 2002. The world distribution of income (estimated from individual country distributions). National Bureau of Economic Research working paper 8933 (May). Cambridge, Mass.

Sala-i-Martin, Xavier, Gernot Doppelhofer, and Ronald I. Miller. 2004. Determinants of long-term growth: A Bayesian averaging of classical estimates (BACE) approach. *American Economic Review* 94 (4): 813–835.

Samuelson, Paul A. 1948. International trade and the equalization of factor prices. *Economic Journal* 58: 163–184.

Schank, Thorsten, Claus Schnabel, and Joachim Wagner. 2004. Exporting firms do not pay higher wages, ceteris paribus. First evidence from linked employer-employee data. IZA, discussion paper no. 1185 (June).

Scheve, Kenneth F., and Matthew J. Slaughter. 2001. Labor market competition and individual preferences over immigration policy. *Review of Economics and Statistics* 83: 133–145.

Schneider, Friedrich, and Dominik Enste. 2002. *The shadow economy: An international survey.* Cambridge: Cambridge University Press.

Smith, A. [1776] 1976. *The wealth of nations.* Chicago: University of Chicago Press.

Spero, Sterling D., and Abram L. Harris. 1931. *The black worker.* New York: Columbia University Press.

Srinivasan, T. N. 1996. Trade and human rights. Economic Growth Center, discussion paper no. 765. Yale University, New Haven, Conn.

Stern, Robert M. 1996. Issues of trade and international labor standards in the WTO system. School of Public Policy discussion paper no. 387. University of Michigan, Ann Arbor.

Stolper, Wolfgang, and Paul A. Samuelson. 1941. Protection and real wages. *Review of Economic Studies* (November): 51–68.

Swepston, Lee. 2003. Closing the gap between international law and U.S. labor law. In *Workers' Rights as Human Rights,* ed. James Gross, 53–77. Ithaca, N.Y.: ILR Press.

Te Velde, Dirk Willem, and Oliver Morrissey. 2001. Foreign ownership and wages: Evidence from five African countries. Center for Research in Economic Development and International Trade working paper no. 01/19. University of Nottingham, England.

Thaler, Richard, and Sherwin Rosen. 1975. The value of saving a life: Evidence from the labor market. In *Household Production and Consumption,* ed. N. E. Terleckyj, 265–300. New York: Columbia University Press.

Thurow, Roger. 2005. Married at 11, a teen in Niger returns to school. *Wall Street Journal,* June 13: A1.

Timmer, Ashley S., and Jeffrey G. Williamson. 1998. Immigration policy prior to the 1930s: Labor markets, policy interactions, and globalization backlash. *Population and Development Review* 24 (4): 739–771.

Tsou, Meng-Wen, Jin-Tan Liu, and James K. Hammitt. 2002. Exporting and productivity. Mimeographed. Harvard School of Public Health, Boston, December.

United Nations Conference on Trade and Development (UNCTAD). 1993. *World investment report, 1992.* New York.

———. 2000. *World investment report, 1999.* New York.

———. 2002a. Are transnationals bigger than countries? Press release TAD/INF/PR/47, Dec. 8.

———. 2002b. *World investment report, 2002.* New York.

———. 2003. *World investment report.* New York.

United Nations Industrial Development Organization (UNIDO). 2001. *International yearbook of industrial statistics.* New York.

United Nations (UN). 1948. Universal declaration of human rights.

United Nations Department of Economic and Social Affairs. 2004. *World economic and social survey 2004: International migration.* New York.

United Nations Population Division. 2000. Replacement migration: Is it a solution to declining and ageing populations? Doc. ESA/P/WP.160. New York.

———. 2002. *International migration report 2002.* New York.

United States Commission for the Study of International Migration and Cooperative Economic Development. 1990. *Unauthorized migration: An economic development response.* Washington, D.C.: Government Printing Office.

Van Biesebroeck, Johannes. 2003. Exporting raises productivity in Sub-Saharan African manufacturing plants. National Bureau of Economic Research working paper no. 10020 (October). Cambridge, Mass.

Van Liemt, Gijsbert. 2004. Human trafficking in Europe: An economic perspective. Available at http://www.ilo.org/dyn/declaris/DECLARATIONWEB.DOWN LOAD_BLOB?Var_DocumentID=3501

Viscusi, W. Kip, and Joseph E. Aldy. 2003. The value of a statistical life: A critical review of market estimates throughout the world. National Bureau of Economic Research working paper no. 9487 (February). Cambridge, Mass.

Visser, Jelle. 2003. Unions and unionism around the world. In *International handbook of trade unionism,* ed. John Addison and Claus Schnabel, pp. 68–99. London: Edward Elgar.

Wacziarg, Romain, and Jessica Seddon Wallack. 2004. Trade liberalization and intersectoral labor movements. *Journal of International Economics* (December): 411–439.

Wacziarg, Romain, and Karen Horn Welch. 2003. Trade liberalization and growth: New evidence. National Bureau of Economic Research working paper no. 10152 (December). Cambridge, Mass.

Waldman, Amy. 2005. Sri Lankan maids' high prize for foreign jobs. *New York Times,* May 8: 1.

Weber, Max. 1959. *The Protestant ethic and the spirit of capitalism.* New York: Charles Scribner's Sons.

Weichselbaumer, Doris, and Rudolf Winter-Ebner. 2003. A meta-analysis of the international gender wage gap. IZA, discussion paper no. 906 (October).

Williamson, Jeffrey G. 1995. The evolution of global labor markets since 1830:

Background evidence and hypotheses. *Explorations in Economic History* 32: 141–196.

———. 2002. Land, labor, and globalization in the Third World, 1870–1940. *Journal of Economic History* 62 (March): 55–86.

Winters, L. Alan, Terrie L. Walmsley, Zhen Kun Wang, and Roman Grynberg. 2003. Liberalizing temporary movement of natural persons. *World Economy* 26 (8): 1137–1161.

Wolf, Martin. 2004. *Why globalization works.* New Haven, Conn.: Yale University Press.

World Bank. 2001a. *World development indicators.* Washington, D.C.

———. 2001b. *World development report 2000/2001.* Washington, D.C.

———. 2003. *Global development finance 2003.* Washington, D.C.

———. 2004. *World development indicators.* Online database. Available at http://devdata.worldbank.org/dataonline/.

Yardley, Jim, and David Barboza. 2005. Help wanted: China finds itself with a labor shortage. *New York Times,* April 3, pp. A1, A10.

Zhou, Li. 2003. Why do exporting firms pay higher wages? Mimeographed. Emory University, Atlanta.

INDEX

Italicized page numbers refer to figures and tables.

and labor regulations, 156
and labor unions, 78
and multinational corporations, 119,
    122, 125
and protectionist policies, 59
and wages, 88
European Monetary Union, 31
European Union (EU), 68, 94–96, 98–
    99, 113, 115, 156, 227n3
exchange rate, 26–27, 225nn21,22
    and compensation data, 191, 202
    and multinational corporations, 119
exporting, 26, 66–72, 177–78, 209,
    226n3
    and discrimination, 63
    and freedom of association, 64
    and international trade theories, 55–
        59, 84–85
    and labor standards, 160, 169
    and productivity, 69–70
    and race-to-the-bottom, 80–81,
        227n5
export processing zones (EPZs), 56, 68,
    71–72, 151, 177, 193
export wage premium, 68–69
expropriation, risk of, 195
    and foreign direct investment, 133–35,
        137, 214–16, 215, 216
    and institutions/social diversity, 49,
        52, 205
    and open economies, 208, 209
Exxon Mobil, 119

FACB index, 17, 193–94, 195
    and foreign direct investment, 217
    and income elasticities, 45, 205
    and institutions/social diversity, 207
    and open economies, 29, 29, 212, 213
    and outlier countries, 47, 48
factor price equalization theorems, 112–
    15
family reunification, 98–99, 100, 108–9
fatal industrial accidents, 15, 175, 195,
    225n19
    changes in, 23, 24, 25
    and foreign direct investment, 135,
        217, 217
    and income elasticities, 46, 204, 205,
        206
    and institutions/social diversity, 52–53,
        52
    and labor standards, 165, 166

and open economies, 28, 28, 74, 208,
    209, 211, 213
    in outlier countries, 47, 48
FDI. See foreign direct investment
Federal Prison Industries, Inc., 21–22,
    224n11
Finland, 125–26, 197
firing costs, 41, 136, 156, 159, 195, 217,
    218–19, 220
fixed effects
    and child labor data, 194
    and civil liberties data, 77
    and compensation data, 38–39, 192,
        202
    and economic growth, 226n2
    and foreign direct investment, 137,
        214
    and hours of work data, 192–93
    and income elasticities, 45, 204, 205,
        206, 226n5
    and labor regulations, 168
    and open economies, 74, 211, 212,
        213
    and workplace health and safety data,
        193
footwear industry, 38–39, 39, 192, 202,
    203
forced labor, 5, 13, 16, 20–23, 24, 174,
    194, 195, 224nn11,13,14
    and codes of conduct, 228n9
    and economic development, 44
    and foreign direct investment, 134,
        136, 217
    and income elasticities, 45, 46, 203,
        204, 205, 206
    and institutions/social diversity, 52–53,
        52, 207
    and international migration, 89, 179
    and international trade, 56, 64
    and labor standards, 162–65, 166, 168,
        229n13, 229nn9,10
    and legal action over labor practices,
        141–42
    and open economies, 79–80, 208, 209–
        10, 212, 213
    in outlier countries, 47
    and targeted incentive policies, 186–88
foreign direct investment (FDI), 132–37,
    213–18, 215, 216, 217
    and corruption, 144–45
    and economic growth, 226n2
    and exporting, 66

and reallocation of resources, 57
and unemployment insurance, 82–83
Iran, 16–17, *48*, *198*
Iraq, 16, 25, 49, *198*, 225n18
Iregui, Ana María, 109
Ireland, 17, 88, 91, *92*, 120, *125–26*, *197*
Israel, *48*, 102, 139, 225n17
Italy, 16, 91, *92*, 94, *94*, 95, *197*,
    225n17

Jamaica, *48*, 53, *122*
Japan
    and foreign direct investment, 134,
        218
    and hours of work, 24
    and international migration, 110, 117
    and international trade, 57
    and multinational corporations, 120,
        122, *125–26*
    as open economy, *197*
job safety. *See* workplace health and
        safety
Jordan, *48*, 106, 170, *197*

Kenya, 21, 37–38, *48*, *198*, 228n3
knowledge capital, 70, 83, 124, 128,
        130
Korea, 23–24, *48*, 68, *97*, *122*, 134, *197*
Krueger, Anne, 225n20

labeling policies, 185–86
labor force weights, 23, *24*, 224n15
labor regulations, 146–73, 176–79
    and economic development, 36, 41,
        202
    and exporting, 68
    EPZs, 72, 80
    and foreign direct investment, 135–37,
        144, 217–18, *217*
    international, 160–71, 183–84
        current system of, 161–64, 229nn8–
            10
        monitoring compliance of, 169–70,
            229n13
        political economy of, 164–68, *165*,
            166, 229nn11,12
        and race-to-the-bottom, 168–69,
            170
        reasons for, 160–61
        and regional trade agreements, 170–
            71, 229n15

and international migration, 97
and international trade, 56, 74
and multinational corporations, 127
national, 147–59, 229n1
    and globalization, 150–53, *152*
    and labor conditions, 153–58
    and labor unions, 158–59
    reasons for, 148–50
and self-employment, 33
labor rights. *See* child labor; forced labor;
        nondiscrimination
labor standards, 7, 13, 160–73, 183–84
    current system of, 161–64, 229nn8–10
    and economic development, 38
    and ILO, 4, 111, 138–39, 160–70,
        183, 227n9, 228n9, 229nn8–10
    and international migration, 111, 117,
        227n9
    and international trade, 56
    monitoring compliance of, 169–70,
        229n13
    and multinational corporations, 120,
        138–40, 144
    political economy of, 164–68, *165*,
        166, 229nn11,12
    and race-to-the-bottom, 80, 168–69,
        170
    reasons for, 160–61
    and regional trade agreements, 170–
        71, 229n15
labor supply
    and international migration, 88–89,
        102
    and labor regulations, 155, 159, 163
    and multinational corporations, 122–
        23
labor unions, 16–17, 176, 193, 223n6
    and foreign direct investment, 134–37
    and international migration, 89, 101
    and labor regulations, 147–49, 157,
        157, 158–59, 162–63, 165, 168,
        171
    and multinational corporations, 124,
        127, 141
    and open economies, 74, 77–79, *79*,
        213, 226n4
    and outsourcing, 64
Laos, 17
Latin America
    and employment distribution, *31*, 32–
        33

Organization for Economic Cooperation
and Development (OECD)
and export processing zones, 177
and foreign direct investment, 134
Guidelines for Multinational Enterprises,
138–39
and income distribution, 10–11
and institutions/social diversity, 49
and international migration, 101, 104–
6, 109–10, 115, 227n6, 227nn4,5
and labor regulations, 154–56, 182
and multinational corporations, 125
organizing rights. *See* unionization
O'Rourke, Kevin, 91, 93, 113–14
outliers, 47, *48*, 120, 205, 226n7
outsourcing, 60–61, 64, 113

Pages, Carmen, 156–57
Pakistan
and bonded labor, 21–22
and child labor, 75
as closed economy, 84, *198*
and foreign direct investment, 218
and multinational corporations, 119
Pakistan School Nutrition Program, 75
Panama, *48*, 120, *122*, *198*
panel studies
and compensation, 38
and economic growth, 65, 176
and foreign direct investment, 137,
213–14
and income elasticities, 44–45, 202–5,
204, *206*
and institutions/social diversity, 51–52,
52, 207
and international trade, 56, 70, 74, 85,
211, *212*, 213
and labor regulations, 168, 219
and multinational corporations, 128,
130
Pavcnik, Nina, 223–24n9
pay. *See* compensation; social benefits;
wages
pay differentials
gender (*see* gender)
international, 95–97, *97*
pay spillovers, 130–31
per capita GDP. *See* per capita income
per capita income, 10–12, 52–53, *52*,
175–77, 188
and child labor, 62
and discrimination, 76

and economic development, 35–36,
54
and forced labor, 44, 64, 187
and foreign direct investment, 134–35,
214, *215*
and hours of work, 40–41
and income elasticities, 44–46, 202–5,
204, 226nn5,6
and institutions/social diversity, 49–50,
207
and international migration, 107
and international trade, 56, 64–66, 85,
207
and international trade theories, 58, 84
and labor regulations, 148, 152, 167,
219, 221
and open economies, 73–74, *208*, 209–
10
in outlier countries, 47, 226n7
and workplace health and safety, 15,
42–43
Peru, 53, 75, 119, 148, *198*
Philippines, 106, 110, *198*
Poland, 159, *198*
political economy, 146, 164–68, *165*,
166, 221
political institutions, 52–53, *52*, 176
and economic development, 49–50,
54, 205–7
and international trade, 55, 58
and open economies, 65, 209, 213
political theories, 150–52, 219
Portugal, 17, *97*, *125*, 128, *198*
Potter, Edward E., 229n12
poverty, 11, 175, 223n1(ch2)
and child labor, 20, 43, 62, 76
and economic development, 35
and ethnic/religious diversity, 51
and international migration, 89, 106,
179
and international trade, 55–56
and labor regulations, 156–57
prison factories, 20–23, 163, 224n11
productivity, 177–78, 182, 192, *196*
and democracy, 49
and economic development, 36–40,
37, *39*, 201–2, *203*, 225n1
and employment distribution, 30
and exporting, 69–71, 80–81, 84
and foreign direct investment, 133–34,
137
and freedom of association, 64